Handbook for
ENVIRONMENTAL PLANNING

Handbook for ENVIRONMENTAL PLANNING

The Social Consequences of Environmental Change

Edited by

The Late James McEvoy III

and

Thomas Dietz
University of California, Davis

A WILEY-INTERSCIENCE PUBLICATION

JOHN WILEY & SONS, New York • London • Sydney • Toronto

Copyright © 1977 by John Wiley & Sons, Inc.

All rights reserved. Published simultaneously in Canada.

No part of this book may be reproduced by any means,
nor transmitted, nor translated into a machine language
without the written permission of the publisher.

Library of Congress Cataloging in Publication Data:

Main entry under title:

Handbook for environmental planning.

"A Wiley-Interscience publication."
Includes bibliographical references and index.
1. Environmental policy. 2. Man—Influence of
environment. 3. Environmental impact statements.
4. Social policy. I. McEvoy, James E., 1920–1976

HC79.E5H328   301.31   76-57239
ISBN 0-471-58389-8
Printed in the United States of America

10 9 8 7 6 5 4 3 2 1

The changeable sky
Of the northern districts
Prevented me from seeing
The full moon of autumn

MATSUO BASHŌ
(Translated by
Nobuyuki Yuasa)

The future is made, not
predicted.
The only question is,
who among us
will share in its making?

RICHARD APPELBAUM
J. Plous Memorial
Lecture, 1976

This volume is dedicated to the memory of its editor, James McEvoy. At a point when the draft manuscript was essentially complete, Jim McEvoy died. The loss was and is severe. As an editor, mentor, and colleague he maintained a balance between the practical and the grandiose and argued that the production of this volume was neither simple nor impossible. As a friend he offered continued stimulation, warmth, energy, and support. He often referred to this project as an effort in "social science fiction," which is a telling description, for the worth of a social impact analysis is like that of a science fiction story. It speaks not of what will happen, but of what might happen, and what those events will mean to people.

A number of people have helped me to complete this volume. In addition to those acknowledged in the editor's preface, I would like to thank the contributors for their patience, cooperation, and perseverance; Elizabeth McEvoy and Phillip Terry for their support; and Bob Johnston, Dan Ray, John Barone, Jim Cramer, Tom Love, Craig Johnson, and Bernadette Tarallo for their comments and encouragement.

THOMAS M. DIETZ

Davis, California
January 1977

Notes on the Contributors

CAROLE A. COOP is a graduate of Ripon College and holds an M.S. in Zoology and a Juris Doctor degree from the University of California, Davis. She is the author or coauthor of several papers on environmental matters and is currently employed as an attorney for the California State Water Quality Control Board.

THOMAS M. DIETZ is a doctoral candidate in Ecology at the University of California, Davis and a lecturer in the Sociology Department there. An undergraduate at Kent State University, he is a Danforth Fellow and has served as a consultant on population and demographic research to the federal Department of Health Education and Welfare and to the California Department of Water Resources.

THEODORE D. BERNS received his undergraduate degree at the University of Iowa and his Juris Doctor from the University of California, Davis. He has served as a consultant in environmental matters to the Tahoe Regional Planning Agency and is currently with the Municipal Attorney's office in Anchorage, Alaska.

THOMAS E. DICKINSON is presently Associate Professor of Economics at Chico State University in Chico, California. Formerly a member of the faculty at the University of California, Davis, Division of Environmental Studies, he received his A.B. from Berkeley and his doctoral degree from Michigan State University. He has done extensive research on the economic effects of residential development on governmental bodies.

JAMES R. BLACKMARR, a Ph.D. candidate in Ecology at the University of California, Davis, holds a B.S. in biological sciences from Stanford University. His primary research interests now concern land use control and land use policy analysis.

R. DANIEL SCHOTT is currently with the California State Department of Rehabilitation and is a doctoral candidate in Ecology at the University of California, Davis. His training is in psychology, and he has previously served as a transportation planner with the California Department of Transportation.

RABEL J. BURDGE is Associate Professor of Environmental Sociology at the Institute for Environmental Studies, University of Illinois at Urbana-Champaign. The author of two books, *Social Change and Rural Society* and *Leisure and Recreation Places* (with Neal Cheek and Donald Field), he is also the editor of the *Journal of Leisure Research*.

SUE JOHNSON attended the University of New Mexico and the University of Texas at Austin where she received a Ph.D. in Sociology. She is the author of numerous articles on social aspects of environmental change and is the former director of the Center for Developmental Change at the University of Kentucky.

ROBERT A. JOHNSTON is Assistant Professor of Environmental Studies at the University of California, Davis. He holds a B.A. in Art and Architecture from Dartmouth College, an M.S. in Resource Management from the University of Nevada, Reno, and a Master of City Planning degree from the University of Southern California. He has authored several publications concerning the consequences of environmental legislation and policies at both the state and federal levels and was closely involved in the first efforts at regional planning in the Lake Tahoe basin of California-Nevada.

JAMES McEVOY III was Associate Professor of Sociology and Environmental Studies and Associate Dean for Research at the University of California, Davis. He was the author or editor of four books and a number of other publications, many of which concern environmental issues.

. . . It is, indeed, obvious that our view can never reach far enough for us to be certain that any action will produce the best possible effects. We must be content, if the greatest possible balance of goods seems to be produced within a limited period.

. . . The commonest rules of conduct involve such considerations as the balancing of future bad health against immediate gains; and even if we can never settle with any certainty how we shall secure the greatest possible total of good, we try at least to assure ourselves that probable future evils will not be greater than the immediate good."

G. E. Moore
Principia Ethica

Preface and Acknowledgments

The conception and eventual execution of this book has, at least to the editor, a rather interesting history. Briefly, the issues it addresses—measuring the social consequences of environmental change in American society—were for 2 years the focus of a seminar of graduate and undergraduate students on the Davis campus of the University of California. As the instructor of these classes I was delighted at the high level of intelligence and commitment of many of the participants. Many of their ideas have found their way into my other teaching and research activities and into this book as well. In particular, Ted Berns, Tom Dietz, Janet Ward, Mark Feigen, Gary Simon, Rich Blackmarr, Dan Schott, Jane Nyberg, Mark Working, Larry Fahn, and Steve Sharp helped make these classes the most stimulating experiences I have had as a teacher. Four chapters of this book were written in whole or in part by members of this group.

In addition, my colleague Sy Schwartz, an economic-engineer systems and policy analyst taught with me for one quarter and added much to our field work and discussions. Other colleagues including Leonard O. Myrup, Kenneth E. F. Watt, Robert A. Johnston, Thomas Cahill, and Peter J. Richerson also aided the classes with instruction and data analysis.

What was perhaps most unusual in all this was the extraordinary range of disciplinary orientations represented in the students and in the effective interdisciplinary interactions that took place in the field and the classroom. The range can be illustrated by noting that we employed methodological strategies from qualitative-social science (ethnography), survey research, mathematical modelling and simulation, heavy metal analysis using the cyclotron, aerial photograph interpretation, econometrics, census analysis and reduction, and aggregation of city revenue data—to name but a few. The students' majors ranged from mathematics, to sociology, to bacteriology.

In the first year we studied an "imaginary" project—a dam planned but not yet constructed. We went about trying to discover what would happen if it were built. In reality we were less interested in the accuracy of our forecasts than in learning how it might be possible to use existing methods of research or develop new ones that would put the assessment of environmental impacts on a sounder scientific basis than it was (and remains) at that time. Our second year took us into the city of Sacramento, California where we studied in considerable detail the effects of a newly constructed (but not yet open) and a newly opened section of freeway. This was a setting in great contrast to that examined the previous year. However, our work on methodological issues proved transferable and we completed an ambitious series of "real" studies of "real" effects caused by the two highways.

The focus of our studies from the very beginning was on social or human factors that were affected by the two public works projects we examined. The disciplinary breadth of the group permitted us to carry out some research that was somewhat peripheral to this focus, but we found or anticipated very few changes which did not in some way have a potential social effect. Thus an ecologist conducting an animal species survey or inventory might find the results of his "environmental" research closely scrutinized by hunters and fishermen because of their interest in maintaining both sites and game to support these forms of recreation.

A truism worth repeating, because it so often confronted us in our studies, is that man is part of the environment and cannot be neatly separated from it, and that the knowledge gained from a biological study may often be essential in anticipating a change in a person, a social group, or a culture.

Our experiences, then, suggest that in undertaking the preparation of a complex environmental impact statement an agency or firm will benefit from the formation of a cohesive multidisciplinary team of researchers. This approach avoids the segmental and compartmentalized examination of issues that are, in fact, closely connected, maximizes the sharing of information between investigators, and in my opinion will lead to more comprehensive knowledge of the overall effects of a given project.

I would like to acknowledge the assistance of the Bureau of Reclamation, the California State Department of Water Resources, and Mrs. Thelma Johnson, formerly of that department, in particular for her extensive contributions of time and thoughtful evaluation of our early work. The California Department of Transportation (particularly the District III Office of the Division of Highways), the U.S. Army Corps of Engineers, Sacramento Office, and the Census Service Facility at the University of California, Berkeley all contributed to our research in significant ways. Gloria Seborg and Delphine Jacobson provided essential editorial and typing service for which all the authors are most grateful, and Professor William Burch of Yale and my colleague John F. Scott persuaded me to abandon an impossible version of my introductory chapter. I am grateful to all these persons for their help.

Funds for field work were provided by the Division of Environmental Studies, the Department of Sociology, and the Rockefeller Foundation.

Finally, a note of caution to our readers is in order. Rapid legal and methodological change is occurring in the area of environmental impact assessment. For this reason we have tried to concentrate on principles and general strategies, but no one should, for example, assume that the last word on EIRs has been heard from the courts or that new and better methods of assessment will not be developed in the future.

JAMES McEVOY III

Davis, California
June 1975

How to Use This Book

There are seven thematic chapters in this volume, each dealing with one broad category of social impacts. They include law, demography, land use, economics, transportation, sociocultural, and the display and integration of information. As editor, I have attempted to directly cross-reference areas of overlap or similarity in the chapters by incorporating textual references to the location of this material in the book. These references are of greatest assistance to those readers who read only segments of the book, but I believe they also help provide continuity to the text which it would not otherwise have.

Second, the following pages contain a series of chapter outlines and topical indices that should be of considerable assistance to those readers looking for an overview of the contents of each chapter and specific locations of such things as impact checklists or data sources. These topical indices were constructed from all the chapters and are listed both by page number and chapter. Taken together, these two sets of indices should make the book of greater utility as a "handbook" than would a simple, highly disaggregated index. For example, if a reader is attempting to decide if an EIR is required and if it is, what "social" variables are necessary for inclusion, an examination of the outline of Ms. Coop's chapter on legal issues will direct him or her to the proper location.

The Environmental Analysis and the Project Planning Process

When in the Planning Process Must the Environmental Analysis Be Completed?
Does the Discovery of Serious Environmental Consequences Require Mitigation or Abandonment?

NEPA and Social Impacts

CHAPTER III   DEMOGRAPHY   DIETZ

Impact Identification and the Qualitative Approach to Assessment

Predevelopment Period
The "No-Project" Option
Impact Identification

Construction phase effects
Changes in carrying capacity
Economic and employment effects
Housing and site characteristics

Sources of Information

U.S. Census Data
State Agencies
Other Sources

Population Estimation and Projection Techniques

Direct Trend Extrapolation
Prorating (Area Ratios)
The Vital Rates and Composite Methods
Composite Methods of Estimation
Multiple Regression Techniques
Housing Unit and Related Methods
The Component Method

State and Federal Agency Reports
Archive Information
Data from Personal Interviews

Summary and Conclusion

CHAPTER VIII   SOCIAL IMPACT INFORMATION   JOHNSTON

Issues in Social Impact Portrayal

Political Relevance
Data Accuracy
Mitigation

Politically Relevant Impact Categories

Mutual Exclusivity of Impact Categories
Calculation of Incidence of Impacts; Examples from Planning in Impact Analysis
Issue Orientation

Accurate Data Representation

Inaccurate Data Representation through Pseudoquantification
Weaknesses of Benefit-Cost Analysis
Accurate Data Portrayal by Lichfield

Linking Adverse Impacts to Mitigative Actions

Conclusions

Broader Planning Concern Needed
The Role of the Planner

IMPACT CHECKLIST

Chapter   Page

DATA SOURCES

METHODS OF ANALYSIS

CASE STUDIES

EVALUATION OF IMPACTS

Contents

ONE

An Introduction to the
Identification and Measurement of
the Social Consequences of
Environmental Change

The true scope of this chapter is so great that it is difficult to imagine that even a thirty-volume scholarly treatise could do more than sketch a brief outline of human knowledge on the issue. Because social change is often responsible for environmental change and vice versa, consideration of the development of technology and culture becomes essential to an adequate treatment of the topic in its broadest formulation. Thus the history of the Old and New Kingdoms of Egypt, with particular attention to the development of irrigation systems below the first cataract and their effects on Egypt's social structure, population size, division of labor, and the like, would make up a single case study of the effects of environmental alterations on social structures. A thousand others, ancient and modern, would be equally interesting to explore. This is impossible, although not in some larger sense totally undesirable.

To proceed it becomes necessary to place boundaries on one's objectives and to be selective in the choice of issues to be discussed. Nevertheless, the ubiquity of man-induced changes on the environment and the history of the effects of those changes on man are worth noting, because they emphasize that the analysis of social impacts is necessarily the analysis of a dynamic system with complicated feedback networks. Artificial disjunction or segmentation of that system into, say, environmental and social variables may be useful and even necessary to conceptualize a given problem and to meet the practical requirements of natural science, social science, and planning. But the less segmented and the more systematic planning and research for planning are, the closer the resulting knowledge will be to objective reality.

At the same time I am not arguing that either current systems theory or systems analysis is adequate to the task of environmental impact assessment, because neither is. The problems the planner faces in preparing studies of projected environmental impacts of various projects are not likely to be solved solely by the traditional methods of science. Indeed, the experimental methods of natural science are ruled out altogether because of the particularistic character of projects, and the experimental methods of social science have little if any utility.

An equally serious limitation placed on the study of the consequences of environmental change is the absence of any general theory combining the laws and theories of natural science with the far more tenuous intellectual constructs of the social sciences. Although general systems theory's proponents assert the isomorphism of knowledge and forecast eventual integration of currently incommensurate data and metrics, these events have not as yet taken place. At this time perhaps the best that can be hoped for in planning research is the construction of a set of probability statements concerning the effect (future time) of a given project and accurate descriptions (present time) of the phenomena that are to be affected. The boundaries in space and time that are placed on the project by the planner will have a decisive effect on the range of variables or phenomena that are considered in the analysis. Obviously, the difficulty of preparing accurate descriptions or forecasting effects varies, among other things, with the distance in time and space of the anticipated effect. Temporal categories such as primary, secondary, and tertiary are, again, useful means of segmenting reality into analytical units, but there are severe limitations on the degree to which it is possible to estimate the magnitude of impacts that are expected to occur in the most distant time horizons or "frames" used by planners in their work.

In a recent interview, Edmund G. Brown, Jr., governor of California, said "All there is to planning is thinking ahead intelligently . . . ," and went on to comment that "[planners] speak in alphabet soup . . . [planning] proliferates options at the highest level of abstraction such that no one can perceive that very little is being said."[1] Obviously, if planning and impact description and forecasting are to be anything but empty abstraction, they will have to be based on intelligent thinking. At the same time if that thinking goes on in a fact-free environment—as it often has in environmental impact assessments now required by law—the temptations of obscurantism and excessive abstraction are hard to avoid.

The principal role of science and the social sciences in the planning and impact analysis process is the generation of relevant data through the application of a large repertoire of scientifically respectable methods to a given problem. By inclusion of the methods of social sciences in the development of data bases for environmental impact assessments, a better factual or empirical picture of the impact of a given project will be available. At the same time the generation of scientific knowledge, especially knowledge gained from social science, should not be equated with either the planning or political processes. As Johnston argues in the final chapter of this book, public participation in an open planning process may permit data to be interpreted differently, reveal false or incomplete assumptions underlying a plan or data-set, and permit more democratic decisions to be taken in a given case.

Regardless of how objective the data collection for a given project may be and despite efforts at expanding citizen participation by agencies, it is still true that the decisions as to which data are to be collected often constitute important political actions by themselves. By setting the agenda for a research program, public officials are at least partially controlling the range of possible outcomes from that program. Beyond this, as Bish points out in a recent article,[2] there is a paradox created by the potentially infinite range of choices that are created by expanding knowledge. Eventually, choices become impossible, so they become arbitrary. In addition, Bish stresses the well-known fact that phenomena that are easily studied are very often those that are studied. In social impact analysis the most immediate consequences of this pattern are seen in neglect of research on factors such as the intangibles—aesthetics, quality of life, happiness, and security.

SOCIAL SCIENCE AND THE MEASUREMENT AND IDENTIFICATION OF SOCIAL VARIABLES

In 1961 Earnest Nagel, the philosopher of science, pointed out that ". . . the social sciences today possess no wide-ranging system of explanations judged as adequate by a majority of professionally competent students, and they are characterized by serious disagreements on methodological as well as substantive questions."[3] In the years since this was written there has been substantial improvement in the methodological capabilities of the social sciences where technical and mathematical methods, such as survey research and simulation, are accepted and utilized by researchers. In large part these improvements have been made possible by the availability of computing machines with the capability to manipulate quantities of data that were previously unmanageable. Associated with this has been an advancement of statistical methods per se and the application of other methods (such as path analysis, taken from genetics) developed in other sciences to social science data. There has, however, been relatively little change with respect to Nagel's other criticisms of social science generally.

Fortunately, for the purposes of planning, methodological developments in the social sciences have the potential of pushing planning more in the direction of a science, from its present location as an applied art. The majority of the material in this volume concerns these methods (not all of which are new) and describes how they may be used in planning and the preparation of environmental impact statements (EIS).

Despite their disagreements, social scientists have defined certain domains of inquiry for their disciplines and, within these domains, have (as I suggested earlier) valuable descriptive potential in addition to their improved capability in methodology.

With the exception of Coop's chapter on legal requirements for EISs, each of the chapters in this book is drawn from two primary areas of social science—economics and sociology. Since I assume that many of our readers are relatively familiar with economics but may know little or nothing of sociology, a brief comment on the domain of sociology's interest may prove useful. The sociologically oriented chapters (Chapters 3, 6, and 7), I hope, put flesh on what is obviously a skeletal definition of a complex and extensive body of knowledge.

Societies can be thought of as one level of organization within a set of such levels ranging, on the one hand, from galaxies, through ecological communities, to subatomic particles.[4] The study of societies is typically undertaken by historians and sociologists—often using comparative methods. Sociology is concerned primarily with macrolevel phenomena such as the institutions, norms, beliefs, traditions, laws, stratification systems, mechanisms of socialization of the young, and political subsystems that make up social structures and that maintain their existence independently of the existence of any single person. An increasing number of sociologists conceive of societies in evolutionary terms, reflecting the fundamental theory of biological sciences.

Sociology is a discipline from which much can be drawn by the planner in preparing an estimate of the social consequences of a given environmental change. Demography, a discipline which is rooted in sociology, is perhaps foremost among the list of possible borrowings. Dietz, in Chapter 3, describes in detail the impacts of environmental change that can be measured by the study of a population's movement (migration), age, and reproductive characteristics. In addition, sociology is a field in which a good deal of attention has been given to the role that beliefs and values play in directing human behavior. The recent concern with the measurement of "intangible" phenomena—such as aesthetics,[5] emvironmental, or wilderness values—reflected in the work of the National Water Commission and the Water Resources Council's Principles and Standards for Planning Water and Related Land Resources, is an enterprise that will have to rely heavily on sociological research. However, other social science fields, particularly social psychology, psychology, and landscape architecture, have made extensive contributions in this area as well.[6]

Community studies are often a highly relevant portion of an impact analysis (discussed by Burdge and Johnson in Chapter 7). The methods and goals of these studies have been well developed within sociology, and they offer a model for social research on the effects of relatively circumscribed projects. Burdge and Johnson also employ numerous other concepts and data (including, again, demography) in their recommendations for the conduct of research on sociocultural impacts. In his discussion of the impacts of transportation systems, Schott (Chapter 6) similarly employs numerous variables of interest to the sociologist, including the displacement and disruption of populations.

Schott's paper also incorporates a brief discussion of events that may impinge with differential consequences on individual persons—in this case his concern is with the health-related consequences of air pollution, noise, and safety. This orientation is fundamentally psychological, and although there is a substantial literature developing in the field of environmental psychology, I regret that there is relatively little beyond Schott's discussion that concerns, directly, purely psychological phenomena in this book. Of course, when an impact is identified, such as the disruption of a neighborhood, one can anticipate a range of psychological responses on the part of the individuals affected. Surveys offer one means of accessing these responses—Johnston's arguments (Chapter 8) for open planning and intelligible display of information will, if implemented, also serve that goal.

Economic geography and economics form the disciplinary background of the two other substantive chapters concerned with social research. Dickinson and Blackmarr's discussion of the costs and benefits of community growth shows in detail how the methods of economics can be used to assist planners in identifying social changes that may occur in growing communities. As the attention of resource economists has turned from an almost complete focus on the economic benefits thought to accompany growth to the tangible, economic costs that also are incurred,[7] economic analysis has become far more balanced and circumspect. Economics has always been a useful tool in the analysis of social affairs. Recent advances have enhanced rather than detracted from its scientific value in the analysis of the social consequences of environmental change. As Berns asserts, (Chapter 4) land use and particularly, changes in the use of land in themselves constitute at least a major and/or (in his view) the major focus of analyzing environmental impacts. Most of the other chapters have (as is the case with demography) frequent references to or cite examples of land use change as indicators of social and behavioral change generally.

At the conclusion of the preface to this book I noted the rapid change that is occurring in the field of environmental assessment and the implications of those changes for the expected utility of this book. At the same time, of course, it should be readily apparent to our readers that we have hardly provided a comprehensive guide to the measurement and assessment of all possible social impacts. For reasons of space or lost contributors, chapters I had hoped to include on the psychological consequences of altered physical environments and on outdoor recreation—to name only two areas of deficiency—were not included in the book. However, if information of the sort described in the substantive chapters of this volume is gathered by planners and incorporated in the process of "thinking ahead intelligently," I believe that a substantial improvement in the discovery and display of the impacts that changing of the environment have on human behavior, groups, and institutions will be clarified to a far greater degree than is now the case in most environmental planning. Beyond that, it will improve the data base available to social science generally and, hopefully, assist in eventual correction of the theoretical problems noted by Professor Nagel.

NOTES

1. *San Francisco Sunday Examiner and Chronicle*, Section A, p. 2, June 15, 1975.
2. Bish, Robert L., The Assumption of Knowledge in Policy Analysis *Policy Stud. J.*, 3 pp. 256–262, Spring, 1975.
3. Nagel, Ernest, *The Structure of Science*, Harcourt, Brace, and World, New York, p. 449, 1961.

4. Lenski, Gerhard, *Human Societies, A Macro Level Introduction to Sociology*, McGraw Hill, New York, pp. 5–22, 1970.

5. See my discussion of this in The Measurement of Environmental Quality in *Environmental Quality and Water Development*. C. R. Goldman, J. McEvoy, and P. J. Richardson, Eds., W. H. Freeman, San Francisco, pp. 122–129, 1973.

6. See Kenneth Craik, Assessing the Objectivity of Landscape Dimensions, Resources for the Future Conference on Research on Wildlands, Wildlife and Scenic Resources, 1971.

7. See K. William Kapps' now famous study, *The Social Costs of Private Enterprise* published in 1950 for an extensive catalogue of social damage incurred by profit-oriented firms. Much of his discussion is relevant to the economic behavior of governmental bodies. Recently, Robert Haveman's studies of the Corps of Engineers and studies by the San Francisco-based firm of Livingston and Blaney have provided substantial evidence that profit or benefits are, at best, uncertain to accompany growth or project development. See Robert H. Haveman, *The Economic Performance of Public Investments, An Ex Post Evaluation of Water Resource Investments*, Johns Hopkins Press, Baltimore, 1972. The studies by Livingston and Blaney are available from the Palo Alto, California Planning Department and the City of Santa Rosa, California Planning Department.

TWO
Legal Requirements for Environmental Impact Reporting

CAROLE COOP ATHERTON

M ost of the material in this book concerns the methodologies and technology for accurate assessment and analysis of the impacts, particularly social impacts, of governmental choices concerning environmental change. The emphasis of this chapter, however, is on the legal requirements that constrain the process of deciding whether to undertake a particular project which may have environmental, including social, consequences. This process includes the decision as to whether to undertake an impact analysis, the decision as to the depth and breadth of material that analysis will include, and the decision as to who will prepare the analysis. In short, this chapter deals with the specific requirements of state and federal laws that mandate preparation of written impact analyses as these requirements have been interpreted by the courts.[1]

The history of impact analysis law is short. The National Environmental Policy Act (NEPA) was passed in 1969 and went into effect on January 1, 1970. After the adoption of NEPA, a number of states followed suit by adopting environmental policy/protection requirements of state-wide applicability. At this writing, eighteen states and Puerto Rico have such requirements. However, not all these states have the same requirements for analysis of environmental impacts as the national act, and not all these requirements have their origin in legislation. Some have merely been administratively adopted. Fourteen states and Puerto Rico have legislatively enacted environmental policies and/or protection requirements. Those enactments are as follows:

State	Statute
California	Public Resources Code Section 21000, et seq.
Connecticut	Public Act No. 73-562, June 22, 1973
Delaware	7 Delaware Code Section 7001 et seq.
Indiana	Indiana Statutes Section 35-5301, et seq.
Maryland	Chapter 702, Maryland Laws of 1973
Massachusetts	Chapter 781, Acts of 1972
Minnesota	Chapter 412, Laws of 1973
Montana	Resources Code Section 69-6501,et seq.
Nevada	Section 704.820, et seq., Nevada Revised Statutes
New Mexico	New Mexico Statutes Section 12-20-1, et seq.
North Carolina	N. C. General Statutes Section 113A, et seq.
Puerto Rico	Title 12 Laws of Puerto Rico Section 1121, et seq.
Virginia	Chapter 384, Va. Laws of 1973
Washington	Chapter 43.21C, et seq. Resources Code of Washington
Wisconsin	Wisc. Statutes Section 1.11, et seq., and Section 23.11(5)

In addition, the remaining four states have, in effect, the equivalent of a state environmental policy act as a result of adoption of a statewide administrative policy.

These states and the relevant administrative orders are as follows:

State	Order
Arizona	Game and Fish Commission Policy of July 2, 1971
Hawaii	Governor's Executive Order (August 23, 1971)
Michigan	Executive Directive 1971-10 issued by the Governor
Texas	Policy for the Environment, January 1, 1973

Even though, as the preceding discussion indicates, the history of acts requiring the protection of environmental quality as opposed to the protection of limited aspects of the environment (such as water quality, fish, and wildlife) is short, litigation under the broad acts has been considerable. The Council on Environmental Quality (CEQ), which was created by Title II of NEPA to study and advise the President and federal agencies about the quality of the environment and methods of improving it, reported in 1973 that by the middle of the year over 400 lawsuits concerning various aspects of NEPA had been filed. Challenges to state and local government actions based on state NEPA-like statutes do not appear to be proportionately as large in number as federal suits based on NEPA. However, in a certain sense litigation concerning state legislation is at a more advanced stage than federal litigation in that a number of state supreme courts have ruled on the meaning of various portions of their state acts, rendering their proper interpretation more certain, whereas as of this writing the U.S. Supreme Court has not interpreted the national act.[2]

For example, the California Supreme Court handed down an opinion in September, 1972 concerning CEQA, the California Environmental Quality Act. In that decision, Friends of Mammoth v. Board of Supervisors of Mono County,[3] the California court ruled that certain ambiguous language in the statute, enacted by the California legislature in 1970, was intended to make the legislation applicable to actions of private parties which required governmental approval. And the Washington Supreme Court has ruled that Washington's act, referred to as SEPA, the State Environmental Policy Act, permits the Washington courts to consider not only whether governmental decision makers followed the proper procedures in making a decision that may adversely affect environmental quality, but also whether they have reached the proper decision.[4]

CONTENTS OF IMPACT ANALYSIS LAWS

Because of the large number of state environmental policy acts, it is not possible to discuss the requirements of each state's act individually here. Therefore, this chapter centers around the contents of NEPA and discusses its similarities to and differences with state laws where they are of particular interest.

The national act consists of a declaration of Congressional purpose plus two titles. Title I is discussed in detail later in this section. Title II requires the President to transmit an annual report to Congress that discusses, among other things, the current status of the major aspects of the environment, both natural and man-made, major trends in the quality, management, and utilization of the environment, and the effects of those trends on the social, economic, and other requirements of the nation. The second title also creates the CEQ to aid the President in preparation of this report, to supervise research concerning environmental quality, to provide advice to the President concerning improvement of environmental quality, and to aid federal agencies in modifying their activities to conform to national environmental policy as expressed in Title I of the act. This council consists of three members appointed by the President as well as such staff as is necessary to carry out the requirements of the title.

The CEQ has provided a number of valuable services during its short life, including the production of comprehensive annual reports and the origination of guidelines to aid federal agencies in preparing the impact statements required by Title I of the act.[5] However, it has become clear that by far the most significant portion of the act is Title I, the "Declaration of National Environmental Policy."

Title I actually contains much more than its name suggests; it is not merely a declaration of abstract policy but rather a series of commands to federal agencies to conduct themselves in a specified fashion. To those unfamiliar with the history of implementation of the act, this distinction might seem academic. But as a look at early judicial decisions under the act shows, it was not entirely clear during NEPA's early development whether the act would be anything more than an unenforceable declaration of worthy goals. For example, in one of the first judicial decisions involving NEPA, the Federal District Court for the Northern District of California ruled that the act "would not seem to create any rights or impose any duties of which a court can take cognizance."[6]

However, a long series of decisions by the federal courts have now made it unquestionable that Title I does create new responsibilities for federal agencies, the fulfillment of which may be judicially compelled. However, the breadth of judicial enforceability has still not been fully resolved. Based on numerous Court of Appeal decisions, it is clear that the federal courts can compel production of an impact statement by an agency that has failed to comply with the requirements of NEPA, and, presumably, a state court interpreting one of the many state statutes with similar language would reach a similar result. It is also clear that revision of an inadequate impact statement can be compelled. However, whether, a court may compel an agency to take (or not to take) a certain course of action based on the agency's findings contained in an impact statement is still unclear. This question is discussed more fully in the subsection of this chapter that deals with environmental analysis and the planning process.

What are the provisions of NEPA's Title I? Title I contains four major parts, only one of which is the requirement for production of an EIS. However, the impact statement provision [Section 102(2)(C) of the act] has received the most attention by the public, the courts, and the federal agencies affected. Most of the remainder of this chapter deals with the requirements of Section 102(2)(C).

The three other major provisions of Title I are discussed in the following paragraphs. First, the title contains a broad statement of the need for environmental quality and a policy of protection of the environment by the federal government [Sections 101(a) and 101(b)]. These sections place a general responsibility on federal agencies to consider the effects of programs or projects they intend to undertake on the whole environment.

For agencies with major statutory responsibilities in an area other than protection of the environment, for example, resource management (such as the Bureau of Land Management, the Forest Service, and the Bureau of Mines), development (such as the Federal Highway Administration and the Corps of Engineers), or research and/or regulation (such as the Federal Power Commission, and the Atomic Energy Commission), passage of NEPA created a new mandate to consider the overall effect of their actions on the quality of the environment and, presumably, to abandon a particular course of action when the social and economic benefits do not outweigh the environmental costs.[7] To say that an agency must undertake this balancing process, however, is not to say that the agency must reach any particular conclusion about the proper balance of social, economic, and environmental costs and benefits. As mentioned previously, the section of this chapter concerning environmental analysis and the planning process deals further with this issue.

For agencies whose responsibilities included protection of specific aspects of the environment prior to enactment of NEPA, the act broadened those responsibilities. These agencies must now consider the effects their programs to protect one portion of the environment have on other aspects of environmental quality. This responsibility has been limited somewhat, however, at least in the case of the Environmental Protection Agency's (EPA) water pollution control responsibilities, by another federal law passed subsequent to NEPA. Section 511(c)(1) of the Federal Water Pollution Control Act Amendments of 1972, P. L. 92-500, exempts the agency, from any responsibility to prepare an EIS in connection with the issuance of a permit to discharge pollutants to waters of the United States, unless the permit is for a discharge from a "new source" as defined in the act. Further, the federal courts have, on a number of occasions, ruled that the EPA need not prepare Environmental Impact Reports (EIRs) for its environmentally protective activities where the act under which EPA is proceeding requires the preparation of a record that is essentially the equivalent of an impact statement.[8]

The second important provision of NEPA's Title I is the requirement in section 102(1) that "the policies, regulations, and public laws of the United States shall be interpreted and administered in accordance with the policies set forth in this Act. . . ." The basic thrust of this provision was to make environmental quality control a part of the mandate of every federal agency that had responsibilities which might result in adverse effects on the environment. Rather than amending each agency's statutory authority individually, Congress simply included a provision that each agency was to interpret and administer its existing authority in a manner consistent with the act.

To my knowledge, this section of the act has never been used alone by an opponent of a federal project to compel a change in or abandonment of the project. It has been used by a federal agency, however, to support its decision not to grant a permit for a project that the agency found would have severe environmental consequences. In the lawsuit styled Zabel v. Tabb,[9] the Fifth Circuit Court of Appeal upheld the Corps of Engineers' decision to refuse permission to the developer of a trailer park to place a fill in Boca Ciega Bay, Florida. In handing down its decision the court ruled that the corps had properly reinterpreted its authority to grant permits for construction in navigable waters under Title 33 U.S. Code Section 403 such that after passage of NEPA, the corps had authority to consider the effect of proposed construction not only on navigation but also on environmental quality. It is significant that the court made this ruling in spite of an admission on the part of the Corps that the particular project would have no adverse effect on navigation.

The third major provision of Title I of NEPA is the requirement for the use of certain research techniques by federal agencies. Sections 102(2)(A) and 102(2)(B), respectively, require federal agencies to "(A) utilize a systematic, interdisciplinary approach which will insure the integrated use of the natural and social sciences and the environmental design arts in planning and decision-making which may have an impact on man's environment" and "(B) identify methods and procedures . . . which will insure that presently unquantified environmental amenities and values may be given appropriate consideration in decisionmaking along with economic and technical consideration."

The relationship between these sections and the Section 102(2)(C) EIR requirements is still hazy. The act gives no time schedule for the accomplishment of the tasks required by these sections and does not appear to tie them to an evaluation of each individual action or project proposed by the government in the way that Section 102(2)(C) requires EIRs prior to each major action. Neither is it clear whether an EIR is acceptable if the agency preparing it can be shown to have failed to develop procedures for the integrated use of the natural and social sciences and the "environmental design arts," or if it can be shown that the agency failed to develop methods for giving unquantified values proper consideration.

In a late 1972 decision, Akers v. Resor,[10] the U.S. District Court for the

Western District of Tennessee deals with the question of whether the requirements for an "interdisciplinary approach" and development of methods for taking into account "unquantifiable values" are judicially enforceable mandates.

In that decision the court ruled that it was within the power of the court to
consider which parties and organizations had been consulted by an agency in
reaching a challenged decision to determine whether the proper interdisciplinary approach had been used. In that court's opinion an agency's decision
failed to meet the requirements of NEPA when it could be shown that another
agency or agencies with expertise bearing on the decision in question was not
consulted. The Soil Conservation Service was not consulted in this case, even
though the project in question was a river channel enlargement, a type of
project on which the Soil Conservation Service is eminently qualified to comment, nor did the corps consult with the Tennessee Planning Commission, a
group generally opposed to building in river flood plains, which building the
project would have facilitated.

The Akers decision also suggests that, even if all relevant agencies are asked
to review a proposed action, the agency's EIS may not be in compliance with
NEPA, if the request for review was general and did not point out to reviewing
agencies specific areas where the expertise of given agencies was critical to an
accurate determination of the environmental effects of the project.

As the court said:

It is true that the Corps sent a copy of its Environmental Impact Statement . . . . ,
together with its proposed Fish and Wildlife Mitigation Plan . . . to the Highway
Department (which would have responsibility for maintenance of the project) for comment, and it is true that the Corps' estimate of maintenance cost is embedded in these
documents, and it is true that the Highway Department did not comment, but we do not
believe this satisfies the requirement that the Corps exercise an inter-disciplinary
approach. Certainly the Corps could and should have made specific inquiry with respect
to projected maintenance cost.[11]

The Akers v. Resor decision also dealt with the question of whether a court
could halt a project because the action-taking agency had failed to develop
procedures for giving appropriate consideration to "unquantified environmental values" [NEPA Section 102(2)(B)]. In the opinion of the Akers court
such procedures are necessary; however, whether the court would halt a project
based on the failure to develop such procedures alone is not clear. The thrust of
the court's decision on this topic is contained in the following passage:

In acknowledging that it had been urged by others, including the Tennessee Game and
Fish Commission, that much more than the proposed acquisition of 14,400 acres of mitigation land should be acquired to reduce the loss of these unquantified values, the Corps
replied that acquisition of more land "involves the exercise of judgment." The point is

that the EIS and Mitigation Plan must affirmatively show that the Corps has made an in depth study of these unquantified values that are to be lost and has made an objective judgment as to the effect such loss should have on the decision to drain these wetlands and on the decision, if the project is to proceed, as to how much mitigation land should be purchased and developed.[12]

The District Court for the Eastern District of Arkansas viewed the requirements of Sections 102(2)(A) and (B) with similar strictness in the Gillham Dam case,[13] and the District Court for the Northern District of Mississippi in a case challenging the Corps of Engineers' Tennessee-Tombigbee Waterway ascribed similar importance to these sections but ruled that the corps had complied with them.[14]

The fact that these courts put considerable emphasis on Sections 102(2)(A) and (B) of NEPA and implied that compliance with them is judicially enforceable and the question of whether other courts will do likewise is of especial significance to those concerned with the social impacts of governmental decision making. These sections, more directly than any others in the act, mandate that the effects of projects on social as well as natural systems should be explored. Section 102(2)(A) specifically mentions that the "social sciences" are to be employed in planning and decision-making, and 102(2)(B) requires that procedures for giving "unquantified environmental amenities and values" proper consideration be developed. These values are frequently social in nature, for example, and impacts on community cohesiveness, mental and physical health and safety, and are discussed later in this book by several authors.

PREPARATION OF IMPACT ANALYSIS DOCUMENTS: WHEN IS THEIR PREPARATION REQUIRED?

Where to Go for Guidance

As previously mentioned, Section 102(2)(C) of NEPA has enjoyed the most attention from citizens' groups, industry, agencies, and the courts. The requirement for preparation of impact statements has turned out to be the single most powerful tool available to citizens' groups concerned with minimizing the environmental consequences of governmental proposals, and it has also been used successfully by industry to challenge decisions regulating their operations that were made without benefit of an impact statement.[15]

Through the mechanism of courtroom challenge and judicial interpretation, the rather sketchy framework of the act, particularly Section 102(2)(C), is gradually being filled in. This chapter makes frequent reference to judicial decisions that have interpreted the act. In addition, almost every federal agency, ranging from the Law Enforcement Assistance Administration to the Corps of Engineers has published regulations giving guidance to its personnel concerning compliance with the act. Additionally, the CEQ, discussed previously, has prepared guidelines for preparation of EISs.[16] These guidelines are intended for use by every federal agency in preparing its own, more detailed regulations concerning environmental impact analysis and to serve as direct guidance to federal agencies concerning the proper procedures for such analysis.

Most states that have their own environmental analysis legislation also have a tiered guidance and regulatory framework. In California, for example, the Resources Agency, which has overall responsibility for natural resource development and protection, has prepared guidelines for implementation of the California Environmental Quality Act.[17] In addition, each California state agency that undertakes or approves projects which may have a significant effect on the environment has its own regulations describing the procedures for determining when a full-scale environmental analysis must be done and for undertaking the analysis when it is required.

In California there is a third set of regulations and guidance to be considered when a project is to be undertaken by a local government entity such as a city, county, or services district or when a project is being undertaken by a private party but requires local government approval. In these instances the party undertaking the project must consider the environmental analysis regulations of the local entity or entities involved as well as the Resources Agency guidelines mentioned previously. This means, then, that a project being done at the local level in California requiring permits or funding from state and federal sources would be subject to the environmental analysis regulations of any local agencies involved, each specific state agency involved, the statewide Resources Agency guidelines, the regulations of each specific federal agency involved, and the overall Federal Council on Environmental Quality guidelines.

As this listing illustrates, project proponents should carefully determine the types of permits and funding that they will require for a particular project prior to beginning the planning process. In the great majority of cases the requirements of federal, state, and local impact analysis laws and regulations are similar, and a single analysis document will serve for all jurisdictions. However, the laws and regulations of each jurisdiction involved must be carefully checked for possible differences. When there are differences they are likely to be in areas such as scheduling, requirements for public notice and public input, and requirements for consultation with agencies having expertise bearing on the project. When the requirements are similar but those of one jurisdiction are more stringent, the project proponent must follow the most stringent of the requirements. When the requirements are additive, that is, when a local ordinance requires consultation with certain local entities but state approval is required and the state regulations require consultation with certain state agencies, the cumulative requirements of both the local and state governments must be followed.

In some states the topics that must be covered in an impact statement are broader than those required by NEPA. An impact analysis for a project requiring both state and federal approval in a state having such additional topical requirements must, of course, cover the extra topics. In California, for example, growth-inducing impacts and mitigation measures proposed to minimize the impact of the project must be discussed in addition to the five topics required by NEPA.[18] (NEPA's five topical requirements are discussed in detail later in this chapter.)

Under What Circumstances Must a Full-Scale Analysis be Prepared?

In the language of NEPA's Section 102(2)(C), all agencies of the federal government must: "include in every recommendation or report on proposals for legislation and other major Federal actions significantly affecting the quality of the human environment, a detailed statement by the responsible official on . . . " (five topical requirements are then listed). Standing alone, however, the previously quoted language raises a number of questions among them: (1) what type of activity constitutes an "action" within the meaning of the act, (2) how much federal involvement is necessary for an action to be a "federal action," (3) what is a "major" action, and (4) what is a "significant effect?"

WHAT IS AN ACTION?

Numerous judicial decisions have made it clear that the type of action regulated by the NEPA requirements is not merely construction. As was stated by the U.S. Court of Appeals in the decision entitled Scientists' Institute v. The Atomic Energy Commission:

The statutory phrase "actions significantly affecting the quality of the environment" is intentially (sic) broad, reflecting the Act's attempt to promote an across-the-board adjustment in federal agency decision making so as to make the quality of the environment a concern of every federal agency. The legislative history of the Act indicates that the term "actions" refers not only to construction of particular facilities, but includes "project proposals, proposals for new legislation, regulations, policy statements or expansion or revision of ongoing programs."[19]

In the Scientists' Institute decision the court added another item to the list of kinds of actions requiring preparation of an impact statement: the major federal research program. Specifically, in this case the court found that the Atomic Energy Commission (AEC) must do an impact statement on its liquid-metal fastbreeder-reactor research program and indicated that NEPA would apply to any research program aimed at development of new technology that, when applied, would significantly affect the quality of the human environment.

Other actions that have been determined to be within the impact statement provisions of the act include: a program to control fire ants,[20] construction of a federally assisted college high-rise housing project,[21] an Interstate Commerce Commission decision approving abandonment of a railroad line,[22] and a decision to terminate federal purchases of helium under a contract with private producers.[23] (Note that this list of actions requiring impact statements includes decisions to terminate or allow the termination of existing projects in addition to decisions to undertake or allow the undertaking of new projects.) Finally, according to the CEQ guidelines[24] and the language of NEPA itself,[25] actions covered by the act also include proposals for legislation.

HOW MUCH FEDERAL INVOLVEMENT IS NECESSARY?

NEPA applies by its terms to major federal actions. The degree of federal government involvement necessary to render an activity a "federal action" within the meaning of the law has been the subject of considerable litigation.

No particular test has yet been developed for the requisite degree of federal involvement. In Metropolitan Washington Coalition v. Department of Economic Development[26] the District of Columbia District Court ruled that an activity was federal when a private or local government entity could not proceed without federal approval. However, in Kings County Association v. Hardin[27] the Ninth Circuit Court of Appeals ruled that no federal action existed where farm subsidies were used by recipients to purchase pesticides and fertilizers use of which could have an adverse effect on the environment. According to the court: "Payment of the subsidies is mandatory under the Agriculture Act of 1970, 84 Stats. 1358. The recipient is free to use the money in any way he sees fit. The fact that it (or other money of the recipient) was put to a use affecting the environment cannot convert that private use into a federal action."[28]

On the other hand, a federal block grant under the Law Enforcement Assistance Act (LEAA) has been ruled to require impact statment preparation. In Ely v. Velde[29] it was held that an impact statement was required prior to construction of a prison reception and medical center in a scenic and historical area. Twenty percent of the prison facilities was to be paid for by a grant from the LEAA. This case is, of course, distinguishable from Kings County on the basis that the LEAA grant was to be used for limited purposes with potential environmental consequences. A more difficult question, the answer to which may be foreshadowed by the Kings County case, is whether the requirements of

NEPA would apply to a grant of federal funds under a revenue-sharing program when those funds were not earmarked for limited purposes. The CEQ guidelines are consistent with Kings County. They exclude from the types of actions covered by NEPA "general revenue sharing funds distributed under the state and local Fiscal Assistance Act of 1972, 31 U.S.C. 1221, et seq., with no Federal agency control over the subsequent use of such funds."[30]

Cases involving federal-state highway construction have resulted in a series of opinions concerning the scheduling and budgeting of the federal government's participation in relation to the impact statement requirement. The tenor of the cases is that it is impermissible for a state highway department to commit itself to a certain course of action prior to accepting federal funds and in this way to avoid the federal impact analysis requirements or at least delay consideration of environmental impacts until critical time and dollar commitments have already been made.[31]

The federal courts have also dealt with the question of whether states may discontinue federal funding for a project previously slated for such funding and thus avoid the requirements of NEPA by claiming that no federal action is involved. In San Antonio Conservation Society v. Texas Highway Department[32] the court ruled that the state's action in returning funds already granted by the federal government for a particular stretch of highway did not relieve the state of its obligation to comply with NEPA. The court's decision, however, appeared to be influenced by the admission of the state that other state projects would be substituted to take up the federal funding relinquished for the particular project in controversy. Ultimately, the U.S. Congress, with the concurrence of the Texas and federal highway agencies, withdrew all federal funding attributable to this project, and the project was permitted to go forward without NEPA compliance.[33]

In Ely v. Velde[34] the U.S. District Court for the Eastern District of Virginia refused to hold NEPA applicable to the planning and construction of a prison reception and medical center that earlier was held to be subject to NEPA[35] but which the state subsequently decided to fund solely with state monies. The court based its ruling on the fact that the plaintiffs could not prove that the federal funds originally allocated to the prison project in question were reallocated to other projects where they were used to free state money for the project in controversy.

If this decision were followed, the difficulty of presenting the necessary proof would make it possible for agencies in states that do not have their own impact analysis laws to judiciously allocate federal funds in such a way as to avoid the strictures of NEPA in selected controversial cases. However, the Fourth Circuit Court of Appeals reversed this decision on appeal, ruling that Virginia was required to reimburse the federal government for all federal funds originally allocated to the construction of the project in question. To do otherwise, the court found, would permit Virginia to frustrate Congress' intent to preserve the nation's environmental quality.[36]

WHAT IS A MAJOR ACTION?

Most judicial decisions that have considered the question of whether a particular proposed action constituted a "major action significantly affecting the quality of the human environment" have not addressed the question as having two component parts: (1) Is the action major and (2) will it significantly affect the environment? They have simply ruled that the activities in question were or were not "major actions significantly affecting the quality of the human environment."

The CEQ guidelines for preparation of EISs[37] indicate that an action that will have a significant effect on the environment is necessarily major. As stated in Section 1500.6(a) of the guidelines: " . . . such actions may be localized in their impact but if there is a potential that the environment may be significantly affected, the statement is to be prepared."

The converse, however, need not always be true. That is, an action could be major and yet not have a significant effect on the environment. This point was recognized by the Second Circuit Court of Appeals in Hanly v. Mitchell,[38] a case involving a challenge to the construction of a $20,000,000 combination office building and correctional center in Manhattan. In that case the court said:

> Plaintiffs argue that if an action is "major" as defendants now concede this one is, it must have a "significant" effect on the environment and call for an impact statement. Defendants claim that the term "major federal action" refers to the cost of a project, the amount of planning that preceded it, and the time required to complete it, but does not refer to the impact of the project on the environment. We agree with the defendants that the two concepts are different. . . . [39]

In Citizens Organized to Defend the Environment v. Volpe,[40] the U.S. District Court for the Southern District of Ohio, Eastern Division, stated: "A 'major Federal action' is one that requires substantial planning, time, resources or expenditures." Similar standards were used in National Resources Defense Council v. Grant,[41] and Julis v. Cedar Rapids.[42]

Application of this descriptive standard in combination with a knowledge of actions that have been defined as major or not major by the courts should be of some help in analyzing the applicability of the 102(2)(C) provisions in any given case. The following table gives examples of actions that have been placed in one or the other of these categories by a Federal court.

Major Actions

Citation	Description of Action Involved
Natural Resources Defense Council v. Grant, 3 ERC 1883	Channelization of 66 miles of creek, expenditure of $706,684 of federal funds, several years of planning.
Businessmen v. Washington D.C., City Council, 3 ERC 1906	A five-block urban renewal project in downtown Washington, D.C.
Hanly v. Mitchell, 4 ERC 1152	Construction of two 9-story buildings in Manhattan (one to be used as a correctional facility) at a cost of $20,000,000.
Scherr v. Volpe 3 ERC 1586 and 1588 upheld by Court of Appeal, 4 ERC 1435	Conversion of 12 miles of two-lane highway to four-lane freeway in rural Wisconsin.
Billings v. Camp, 4 ERC 1744	Approval by Comptroller of Currency of bank's application to construct a branch in Woodstock, Vermont.
Silva v. Romney, 4 ERC 1948	Provision of a mortgage guarantee of $4,000,000 and interest grant of $156,000 by the Department of Housing and Urban Development to a private developer for construction of low-income housing.
Monroe County Conservation Council v. Volpe, 4 ERC 1886	Construction of 4.25 miles of six-lane divided expressway requiring condemnation of 11 acres of urban park.
Sierra Club v. Morton, 4 ERC 1686	Dredging of 720,000 cubic yards of material from New Haven harbor and redepositing in Long Island Sound.
Wyoming Council v. Butz, 5 ERC 1844	Sale of 15 million board feet of timber on Forest Service land.
Tierrasanta Community Council v. Richardson, 6 ERC 1065	Construction of a youth facility, planning required: 2 years, cost: $4.5 million, for 250 inmates and staff of 140.

Probably more definitive of the term major action, however, are those projects the courts have ruled do not fit into the category. Some of those projects are described in the following table:

Nonmajor Actions

Citation	Description of Action Involved
Virginians for Dulles v. Volpe, 4 ERC 1232	Introduction of 727-200 jets into Washington National Airport to replace 727-100 jets previously in use.
Maddox v. Bradley, 4 ERC 1258	The fencing of 6800 acres of land around a reservoir by the Department of Interior.
Julis v. Cedar Rapids, 4 ERC 1863	Fourteen-block city street widening project, total cost: $651,515, federal contribution: $313,000, required no land acquisition.
Citizens v. Volpe, 4 ERC 1952	Secretary of Transportation's approval of specifications for moving mining equipment across federal-aid highway 10 times in 40 years.
Kisner v. Butz, 4 ERC 1693	Construction of 4.3 miles of one-lane gravel road in a national forest.
Duke City Lumber v. Butz, 7 ERC 1104	Change in Forest Service timber set-aside program which would permit higher percentage of timber to be harvested by small businesses but would not change total amount of timber harvested.
Gifford-Hill v. Federal Trade Commission, 7 ERC 1335	Decision of Federal Trade Commission to initiate antitrust enforcement proceedings against construction materials company.

The preceding lists of cases by no means cover the complete range of types and sizes of projects that might be so major as to require an impact statement. As was said by the Third Circuit Court of Appeal: "Whether a project is a 'major federal action' is, of course, a question which can only be resolved through a careful case-by-case analysis."[43]

WHAT IS A SIGNIFICANT EFFECT ON THE QUALITY OF THE
HUMAN ENVIRONMENT?

The definition of "significant effect," like the definition of major action is not static. It is affected by the factual situation surrounding the activity in question. An action that may in one context be devastating may be virtually harmless in another. Construction of an asphalt bicycle path in an urban area, for instance, would have relatively minor effects, whereas in a pristine wilderness the effects of such an action would be gross. On the other hand, the cutting of fifty trees in a heavily forested area would have a relatively minor effect, whereas the effects of cutting fifty trees in the central city would be significant.

The CEQ gives considerable attention to the discussion of what constitutes a significant effect in its guidelines. (In this same portion of the guidelines the council also offers its assistance to agencies unable to determine whether a particular project they anticipate undertaking will significantly affect environmental quality.) According to CEQ:

The Act (NEPA) indicates the broad range of aspects of the environment to be surveyed in any assessment of significant effect. The Act also indicates that adverse significant effects include those that degrade the quality of the environment, curtail the range of beneficial uses of the environment, and serve short-term to the disadvantage of long-term, environmental goals. Significant effects can also include actions which may have both beneficial and detrimental effects, even if on balance the agency believes that the effects will be beneficial. Significant effects also include secondary effects. . . . The significance of a proposed action may also vary with the setting with the result that an action that would have little impact in an urban area may be significant in a rural setting or vice versa.[44]

Some further definition of the phrase "significantly affecting the quality of the human environment" is provided by the judicial decisions that have considered its meaning.

Probably the best discussion is contained in the Second Circuit Court of Appeals decision in the case titled Hanly v. Kleindienst. The court's opinion in that case included the following discussion of the meaning of "significantly":

In the absence of any Congressional or administrative interpretation of the term, we are persuaded that in deciding whether a major federal action will "significantly" affect the quality of the human environment the agency in charge, although vested with broad discretion, should normally be required to review the proposed action in the light of at least two relevant factors: (1) the extent to which the action will cause adverse environmental effects in excess of those created by existing uses in the area affected by it, and (2) the absolute quantitative adverse environmental effects of the action itself, including the cumulative harm that results from its contribution to existing adverse conditions or uses in the affected area. Where conduct conforms to existing uses, its adverse consequences will usually be less significant than when it represents a radical change.[45]

The court goes on to point out that the latter statement is not always true. For example, a small additional use in an area may cause significant harm because the incremental addition of, say, air or water pollution is enough to overtop the assimilative capacity of the natural systems of the area. The court refers to this last increment as "the straw that breaks the back of the environmental camel."[46]

The importance of cumulation of effects occurring as the result of separate federal actions and the importance of considering indirect as well as direct effects of federal actions in determining whether an action will significantly affect the environment are discussed in Citizens v. Volpe. As the court in that case stated:

A federal action "significantly affecting the quality of the human environment is one that has an important or meaningful effect, directly or indirectly, upon any of the many facets of man's environment." (citation omitted) The phrase must be broadly construed to give effect to the purposes of NEPA. A ripple begun in one small corner of an environment may become a wave threatening the quality of the total environment. Although the thread may appear fragile, if the actual environmental impact is significant, it must be considered. See, e.g.,*Port of New York Authority* v. *U.S.*, 451 F.2d 783 (3 ERC 1691) (2d. Cir. 1971). (Recognizing tertiary environmental effects are included within the NEPA's ambit). . . ."[47]

Projects Undertaken Prior to NEPA and Continuing Projects or Programs

Even when a governmental action fits within the definition of a "major federal action significantly affecting the quality of the human environment," as discussed previously, it may not be subject to the impact statement requirement of NEPA if it was begun prior to the effective date of the act. Of course, when a federal action was clearly completed prior to adoption of NEPA, the act does not apply. Numerous lawsuits have arisen, however, over the applicability of NEPA to what might be called (1) "ongoing" and (2) "continuing" projects. An ongoing project may be defined as one that has a distinct termination point which had not been reached as of the effective date of NEPA, such as construction of a freeway or a dam. A continuing project or program is one that has an indefinite life involving periodic decisions by federal officials to undertake or continue activities which may adversely affect the environment, such as maintenance and operation of a dam or a program of periodic dredging of a harbor. The number of lawsuits involving ongoing projects has been decreasing and can be expected to continue to drop off as the effective date of NEPA recedes further into the past. The number of challenges involving continuing projects may be expected to increase, however, as critics of federal projects which adversely affect the environment because of the way they are operated begin to recognize the applicability of NEPA to continuing operation.

In general, federal courts have ruled NEPA applicable to ongoing projects unless (1) the project is of the type requiring only one-time federal approval and that approval was granted prior to January 1, 1970 (see Pennsylvania Environmental Council v. Bartlett[48]) or (2) the project is so far advanced that the cost of alteration or termination clearly outweighs the benefits to be gained. This second exception of the applicability of NEPA has been sparingly applied. For example, federal courts have ruled that NEPA applied to a dam construction project for which two-thirds of the funds alloted had already been expended. However, no work on the dam itself had actually begun. The court characterized the work remaining as a "further major federal act" (see Environmental Defense Fund v. Corps of Engineers[49]).

Federal courts have also liberally applied NEPA to continuing projects, as defined previously. In Lee v. Resor,[50] for example, the court ruled that the Corps of Engineers must do an impact statement on its program of spraying to control water hyacinths in the St. Johns River which was begun over 20 years prior to NEPA's effective date. And in Minnesota PIRG v. Butz[51] the court ruled that timber sales contracts entered into by the Forest Service after January 1, 1970 amounted to a major federal action, even though the sales were done in conformance with a timber management plan adopted prior to that date.

In contrast to these cases, the court in Morris v. TVA[52] refused to apply NEPA to the TVA's continued operation of a dam completed in 1933. However, the court's decision seems to be predicated on an incorrect application of the ongoing project standard found in Pennsylvania Environmental Council v. Bartlett[53] to a continuing project. This case involved a challenge by an owner of property adjoining a TVA-operated reservoir. Fluctuations in the lake level as operated by the TVA caused debris to accumulate in sloughs near the plaintiff's property. However, contrary to the Morris case is Sierra Club v. Mason[54] in which the court rejects the Corps of Engineers' argument that maintenance of an existing public works project is not subject to NEPA.

REQUIRED CONTENTS OF IMPACT STATEMENTS

The NEPA (Section 102(2)(C)) requires that each impact statement prepared must deal with five specific subject areas. These are:

1. The environmental impact of the proposed action;
2. Any adverse environmental effects that cannot be avoided;

3. Alternatives to the proposed action;

4. The relationship between short-term uses of the environment and the maintenance and enhancement of long-term productivity; and

5. Any irreversible commitments of resources.

Some state acts (such as Washington's SEPA, discussed previously) include the same topical requirements as NEPA. Other states have expanded the list of requirements. California's act, as mentioned previously, includes additional requirements that impact reports contain: (1) a discussion of mitigation measures proposed to minimize the effects of the project and (2) the growth-inducing impacts of the project.[55] The Wisconsin and Connecticut acts require discussion of the economic effects of the proposed action.[56]

Each of the topics required to be discussed by the federal act is considered in more detail on the following pages.

The Environmental Impacts of the Proposed Action

Implicit within the requirement that the report contain a discussion of the environmental impact of the proposed action, the CEQ and the courts have found a number of other requirements.

According to CEQ, for example, agencies dealing properly with this subject should discuss: (1) the environment of the area affected as it exists prior to the proposed action,[57] (2) the interrelationship of the project in question with other federal projects in the area,[58] (3) population and growth characteristics of the affected area,[59] and projected effects of the project on population,[60] (4) the relationship of the project to local plans for the area,[61] and the secondary, or indirect, effects as well as primary, or direct, effects of the proposed action.[62] These secondary effects, according to CEQ, include "associated investments and changed patterns of social and economic activities."[63] Presumably, such physical impacts as development of second-home subdivisions near federal reservoirs, development of commercial zones along highways, and increases in traffic as a result of government-assisted construction of a building are included within these secondary effects as well as such potential social impacts as loss of neighborhood solidarity due to construction of a freeway through a residential area or increases in crime rates due to location of a rehabilitation facility in a residential neighborhood.[64]

The courts have dealt extensively with the adequacy of impact statements' discussions of the impacts to be anticipated from federal projects. The general standard which has evolved for adequacy is that the statement must result in "full disclosure." The standard was first enunciated in the Gillham Dam case, Environmental Defense Fund v. Corps of Engineers.[65] Full disclosure meant to the court in that case that all known possible environmental consequences of the proposed action should be set forth, including those possible consequences brought to the government's attention by members of the general public, other agencies, outside experts, and so on, even if the agency disagreed that these were possible consequences or that their effect would be significant.

The expansive view taken by the Gillham Dam court to require inclusion of outside input was not taken in a later District of Columbia Court of Appeals decision, Committee for Nuclear Responsibility v. Seaborg.[66] In that case the court ruled that an agency must include in its statement only a discussion of "responsible opposing views." The court qualified this limitation, however, by pointing out that merely because a view differed from the view of the project proponent did not mean the view was irresponsible.

Some courts also have differed with the Gillham Dam decision on the matter of the likelihood of the impacts that must be discussed. In that case the court required a discussion of all possible impacts, whereas in another case involving the same two principal parties but dealing with a waterway linking the Tennessee and Tomlingbee rivers,[67] the court indicated that only probable impacts need be discussed.[68] The court goes on to explain that this eliminates the need to discuss "remote effects, such as mere possibilities unlikely to occur as a result of the proposed activity."[69] When this qualifying language is considered, the possible and probable standards seem less divergent.

ARE STUDIES NECESSARY?

When questions remain as to the possible impacts of a project at the time the impact statement is prepared, some courts have required the project proponent to merely point out the lack of knowledge in a particular area, whereas others have required that studies to gain the necessary knowledge be completed prior to the proposed action. A case of the former type is Environmental Defense Fund v. Corps of Engineers (involving the Gillham Dam). In that case, in dealing with the EDF's claim that a study should be undertaken to determine which species were present in the Cassatot River, the court said the following:

The Court is not here stating that such a collection or study would be required in order to comply with NEPA. But the opinions of such qualified professionals (who claim that studies should be done) . . . should be made a part of the impact statement. The decisionmakers can then determine whether to proceed without such a study or to postpone the project while such a study is being undertaken.[70]

On the other hand, in Environmental Defense Fund v. Hardin[71] the District of Columbia District Court felt that NEPA required the completion of research necessary to the analysis of the environmental effects of the project *prior* to the undertaking of the proposed action, particularly when Sections 102(2)(A) and

102(2)(C) are read together. The facts of this case, however, may be distin-guished from the EDF v. Corps of Engineers case in that the degree of uncertainty facing the decision maker was greater in the Hardin case. The type of insect control being proposed was relatively untested and its consequences virtually unknown, whereas in the Corps of Engineers case the decision makers could rely on their knowledge of previous dam construction projects for the basic outline of the impacts to be anticipated.

CITATION OF AUTHORITY AND THE USE OF RESEARCH FOR STATEMENTS OF FACT OR OPINION IN IMPACT STATEMENTS

Technical literature is usually not very convincing if its contents are not substantiated with citations to recognized authority. The same is true of an EIS. The CEQ has emphasized this point in its guidelines[72] and in supple-mentary guidance given to federal agencies by way of memoranda. A memo-randum issued May 16, 1972 by the general counsel for CEQ, for example, concerns a number of methods for improving agency NEPA procedures in response to judicial decisions which had interpreted NEPA up to that time. The memorandum, under the heading "Reference to Underlying Documents," states the following: ". . . The requirement that agencies consider and respond to opposing views suggests that the 102 statement must consist of more than simple assertions about expected environmental impacts; the statement must also reflect the underlying information on which those assertions are based." The memorandum goes on to recommend:

Draft statements should indicate the underlying studies, reports, and other information obtained and considered by the agency in preparing the statement. The agency should also indicate how such documents may be obtained. If the documents are attached to the statement, care should be taken to ensure that the statement remains an essentially self-contained instrument. . . .

The current CEQ guidelines also contain an admonition that "Draft state-ments should indicate at appropriate points in the text any underlying studies, reports and other information obtained and considered by the agency in prepar-ing the statement"[73] and that "the sources of data used to identify, quantify, or evaluate any and all environmental consequences (should) be expressly noted."[74]

The CEQ guidelines also point out, however, that highly technical data should not be set forth in the body of the impact statement: "Highly technical and specialized analyses and data should be avoided in the body of the draft impact statement. Such materials should be attached as appendices or footnoted with adequate bibliographic references."

A decision of the U.S. District Court for the Eastern District of North

Carolina contains a specific example of the type of discussion that is inadequately supported. The court in that opinion, which deals with the Soil Conservation Service's EIR concerning channelization of Chicod Creek, stated as follows:

While disclosing the fact of this increase in sediment load, the statement contains no discussion of its downstream effects. The statement merely concludes, without supportive scientific data and opinion, that no significant reduction in quality of the waters of the Tar River, Pamlico River and Pamlico Sound is expected." Credible evidence suggests the opposite conclusion. Having conceded a massive increase in sedimentation, the statement disposes of its environmental effects in one conclusory statement unsupported by empirical or experimental data, scientific authorities; or explanatory information of any kind. Where there is no reference to scientific or objective data to support conclusory statements, NEPA's full disclosure requirements have not been honored.[75]

Another court has ruled that when an understanding of technical data is necessary to adequately comprehend the impacts of a proposed action, the technical material must be adequately explained so that all who read the impact analysis may understand it.[76]

In summary, the body of the impact statement should contain material understandable to the layman and should have an integrity of its own such that it can be understood with minimal reference to technical materials. In addition, the basis for its statements of fact and conclusions should be referenced so that those readers who do have the expertise to understand the underlying material may easily obtain and evaluate it.

The matter of adequate substantiation for assertions of fact brings up a related question. That is, when factual information that bears on the environmental impacts of a project is available, must it be discussed in the EIR? Obviously, an impact statement would not be deficient merely because it failed to mention one piece of literature with some minor bearing on the accurate revelation of environmental impacts. But when existing data or literature is of significant value in the prediction of impacts, it should be used to comply with the full disclosure requirements of the act. For example, the court in the Gillham Dam case[77] ruled that the Corps of Engineers' impact statement was defective in that, among other things, the corps did not include any discussion of data regarding the actual effects of existing dams on the river in question as a method of predicting the effects of the Gillham Dam.

Any Adverse Environmental Effects which Cannot be Avoided

Inasmuch as NEPA's Section 102(2)(C)(i) requires a discussion of "the environmental impact of the proposed action," it seems somewhat redundant that Section 102(2)(C)(ii) requires a discussion of "any adverse environmental effects which cannot be avoided." However, the language does reemphasize that impact statements must point up adverse effects and not merely conclude that the beneficial aspects will outweigh adverse aspects with no individual discussion of adverse impacts.

The CEQ guidelines advise federal agencies that Section 102(2)(C)(ii) may be complied with by preparation of "a brief section summarizing in one place those effects discussed in (the portion of the impact statement dealing with the environmental impact of the proposed action) that are adverse and unavoidable . . . ."[78]

Several judicial decisions discuss failure by agencies to discuss adequately "adverse effects which cannot be avoided."[80] But these decisions provide little additional insight into the meaning of Section 102(2)(C)(ii), except that Daly v. Volpe does seem to indicate that Section 102(2)(C)(ii), by implication, creates a requirement for discussion of measures that can be taken to minimize the harmful effects of the project.[80]

Alternatives to the Proposed Action

Consideration of alternatives to their proposed actions is probably the most important, but difficult, task given agencies by environmental impact analysis laws. It is important because, as pointed out by the first appellate court to interpret NEPA, the District of Columbia Court of Appeal in the Calvert Cliffs case, it should, if done properly, lead to the most "optimally beneficial" course of action, taking into account both environmental and economic costs and benefits.[81] It is difficult because agencies are naturally drawn to those methods of solving problems which are familiar to them and which they are able to implement. The federal courts have recognized this institutional bias on the part of federal agencies and have ruled that although those responsible for preparation of an impact statement need not cleanse themselves of their particular biases for the impact statement to be legally adequate, the impact statement itself must reflect "good faith objectively."[82]

The requirement that an agency consider alternatives stems from two sections of NEPA, Section 102(2)(C)(iii), which requires that one of the topics covered by an impact statement be "alternatives to the proposed action" and Section 102(2)(D), which requires all agencies of the federal government to "study, develop and describe appropriate alternatives to recommended courses of action in any proposal which involves unresolved conflicts concerning alternative uses of available resources." Note that the latter requirement is not restricted to proposals for "major federal actions significantly affecting the human environment."

These provisions have given rise to numerous lawsuits involving, among others, the following issues:

1. How broad must the range of alternatives considered be?
2. Must an agency consider alternatives that are not within its power to implement?
3. How detailed must the discussion of each alternative and its impacts be?
4. Does the requirement to consider alternatives give rise to a responsibility to consider methods to minimize or mitigate adverse impacts of the alternative chosen?

HOW BROAD MUST THE RANGE OF ALTERNATIVES BE?

It is now clear that under NEPA one of the alternatives an agency must consider is the complete abandonment of the project it proposes. For example, the District of Columbia Court of Appeals in its Calvert Cliffs decision ruled that the requirement to discuss alternatives "like the 'detailed statement requirement' seeks to ensure that each agency decision maker has before him and takes into proper account all possible approaches to a particular project (including total abandonment of the project) which would alter the environmental impact and the cost-benefit balance."[83] The requirement for discussion of the abandonment alternative appears in various judicial decisions, for example, the District Court's opinion in EDF v. Corps of Engineers (the Gillham Dam case)[84] and Keith v. Volpe,[85] and in the CEQ guidelines.[86]

For an agency interested in undertaking a proposed project, discussion of the abandonment alternative would obviously be difficult. Nevertheless, it is required. The situation is exacerbated when the project is to be undertaken by a private entity that requires governmental approval as, for example, when a private party needs a permit from the Corps of Engineers to construct a marina. In these cases the private applicant is frequently required to prepare a draft impact statement for consideration by all agencies that must grant approval for the project. This means that a private enterprise must expend resources to prepare a discussion of alternatives to its proposed project, including the alternative of not undertaking it at all as well as any reasonable methods of accomplishing the same goal, even though these methods may not be within the enterprises' own power to accomplish.

When profits as well as institutional biases are a factor, it can readily be anticipated that the task of exploring alternatives to the chosen course of action, including abandonment, would be approached with less than enthusiasm. Although the courts have made it clear that an agency may not merely adopt as its own, without independent evaluation, a private party's draft impact statement for a project that the agency must approve, the private project proponent can greatly influence the contents of the final agency statement by submission of a draft statement for the agency's use in preparing the agency statement.[87]

What alternatives other than abandonment must be considered? The following brief résumé of the standards developed by the courts up to the time of the decision (1973) was presented by the U.S. District Court for the Western District of Washington in Farwell v. Brinegar:

The courts have had difficulty in deciding when the omission of an alternative renders an EIS inadequate, and, when alternatives are set forth, in determining the required minimal scope of the discussion of the environmental advantages and disadvantages of the alternatives. Nonetheless, certain principles have emerged. Agencies must consider alternatives to "the fullest extent possible." Only alternatives which are "reasonably available" need be considered, not those which are "speculative and remote." The search for alternatives need not be "exhaustive." "It is not necessary that a particular alternative offer a complete solution to all technical, economic and environmental considerations, if a portion of the original purpose of the project, or its reasonably logical subcomponent, may be accomplished by other means" (citing Sierra Club v. Froehlke.)[88]

The CEQ guidelines also provide some indication of the range of alternatives that must be considered. They require "a rigorous exploration and objective evaluation of the environmental impacts of all reasonable alternative actions, particularly those that might enhance environmental quality or avoid some or all of the adverse environmental effects,"[89] and go on to say:

Examples of such alternatives include: The alternative of taking no action or of postponing action pending further study; alternatives requiring actions of a significantly different nature which would provide similar benefits with different environmental impacts (e.g., nonstructural alternatives to flood control programs, or mass transit alternatives to highway construction); alternatives related to different designs or details of the proposed action which would present different environmental impacts (e.g., cooling ponds v. cooling towers for a power plant or alternatives that will significantly conserve energy); alternative measures to provide for compensation of fish and wildlife losses including the acquisition of land, waters and interests therein.[90]

A recent District Court decision, EDF v. TVA, involving the Tellico Dam in Tennessee, held that nonstructural alternatives for flood control need not be considered when they would not provide complete flood protection.[91] However, this opinion appears clearly erroneous in light of the weight of judicial authority.

MUST AN AGENCY CONSIDER ALTERNATIVES NOT WITHIN
ITS POWER TO IMPLEMENT?

The U.S. Court of Appeals for the District of Columbia in Natural Resources Defense Council v. Morton,[92] a case challenging the adequacy of the Department of Interior's impact statement concerning the sale of oil and gas leases for certain submerged lands off Louisiana, ruled that the department must consider alternatives to the proposed sale, even though implementation of the alternatives would not be within its power.

The requirement to consider alternatives to the proposed action that are not accomplishable by the agency undertaking the impact analysis, if applied without limitation, might present an insurmountable task were it not for the boundaries placed on this requirement in the same decision which imposed it.

For example, the Court of Appeals went on to point out that in the situation under consideration when sale of the leases was proposed as a short-term solution to an immediate energy need, extensive discussion of alternatives that had a different time frame for completion was not necessary. In the court's view this included such alternatives as development of oil shale, desulphurization of coal, coal liquifaction and gasification, and development of tar sands and geothermal resources. The court pointed out that none of these alternatives would result in significant additions to the total energy supply until after 1980.

The court also pointed out that discussion of alternatives that would require the "overhaul of basic legislation"[93] need not be extensive, although the court in doing so made it clear that "the mere fact that an alternative requires legislative implementation does not automatically establish it as beyond the domain of what is required for discussion."[94]

Of course, this leaves the decision maker with the responsibility of determining which legislation is basic. Ultimately, however, the court pointed out that it is not possible to set down a general rule that will make clear which alternatives must be discussed in any particular case or in what depth the environmental effects of each of the alternatives must be discussed. The court concluded that agencies must apply a "rule of reason"[95] in making both of these determinations.

TO WHAT DEGREE MUST THE ENVIRONMENTAL EFFECTS OF EACH ALTERNATIVE BE EXPLORED?

As pointed out previously, the rule of reason laid down by the Louisiana oil-lease case applies not only to the determination of which alternatives must be discussed in an impact statement but also to the thoroughness with which the impacts of each alternative must be discussed. Various courts have laid down parts of what may eventually become a standard for making this decision. From several judicial decisions one can synthesize a rough standard for depth of consideration of alternatives. Basically, the depth of exploration of the impacts of any given alternative should be commensurate with the likelihood that the alternative could be accomplished,[96] the degree to which the alternative could solve the problem at hand, and the degree to which it avoids some or all of the adverse environmental effects of the project proposed.[97]

The Relationship Between Short-Term Uses of the Environment and the Maintenance and Enhancement of Long-Term Productivity [Section 102(2)(C)(iv)]—Irretrievable Commitments of Resources [Section 102(2)(C)(v)]

These required contents of NEPA impact statements have been given little attention by plaintiffs in environmental lawsuits and hence have received little discussion by the federal courts.

One possible explanation is that these latter two requirements are really matters of emphasis. Assuming that an impact statement accurately and adequately sets forth the environmental impacts of the proposed action and alternatives to the proposed action as required by other subsections of Section 102(2)(C), the reader should be able to develop a fairly good picture of the relationship between long-term productivity and short-term use without a separate discussion in the impact statement. However, separate attention to this topic (and the topic of irreversible commitments of resources) serves to point up and summarize these issues for the reader.

When the courts have mentioned the requirements of subsections (iv) and (v), the mention generally consists of little more than a statement that one or both of the two sections has been violated.

The trial court in the Gillham Dam case indicated that subsection (v) is a requirement for pointing up information that may also be contained in less explicit form elsewhere in the EIR by stating:

The statements do not adequately bring to the reader's attention all "irreversible and irretrievable commitments of resources which would be involved in the proposed action should it be implemented."[98]

Subsection (iv) requires a statement of "the relationship between local short-term uses of man's environment and the maintenance and enhancement of long-term productivity." Some aid in the interpretation of this subsection is provided by the CEQ guidelines that state: "Agencies should avoid construing the term 'resources' to mean only the labor and materials devoted to an action. 'Resources' also means the natural and cultural resources committed to loss or destruction by an action."[99]

Other Elements That Must be Analyzed

Under various state statutes certain other aspects of a project must be analyzed prior to its approval. Among these aspects are mitigation measures, growth induction, and economics. For example, the CEQA, California's act, requires agencies to consider "mitigation measures" proposed to minimize the adverse impacts of a project and the "growth inducing" impact of the project[100] in addition to the five topics required to be discussed by NEPA. Wisconsin[101] and Connecticut[102] require a consideration of economic factors. Minnesota also mentions economics, but rather than merely requiring a discussion of economics in relation to environmental impacts, the Minnesota act places the burden on state agencies that wish to undertake or permit activities that are likely to impair the quality of the state's environment to show that factors in addition to economics justify such activities.[103]

The CEQA also deals with economic factors but only in the context of requiring that techniques be devised by the Secretary of the state Resources Agency for the use of local governments in analyzing the economic effect of proposed projects.[104] These analytical methods were required to be developed and published in the form of an "economic practices manual" on January 1, 1975.

Although NEPA does not explicitly require discussion of growth induction, mitigation, or economic effects as part of an impact report, the requirements are certainly implicit in the language of the act. Both the CEQ guidelines and judicial interpretation of the statutes have made the need for discussion of these topics in NEPA impact analyses clear.

The CEQ guidelines include a requirement for discussion of mitigation measures which the agency will undertake as a correlary of the NEPA-required discussion of "any adverse environmental effects which cannot be avoided should the proposal be implemented." According to the guidelines: "Included in this section (concerning unavoidable impacts) for purposes of contrast should be a clear statement of how other avoidable effects . . . will be mitigated."[105]

Apparently, CEQ sees mitigation measures as the last step toward reduction of the adverse environmental impacts of a particular project. That is, even though an agency has chosen the alternative that will best achieve its goal with the least adverse environmental impact, it is nevertheless required to consider minimization of any remaining adverse effects of the alternative chosen.

As we have seen, the courts have required agencies to consider project alternatives not within their power to accomplish. Logically, the discussion of mitigation measures should also include measures beyond the power of the project proponent to accomplish. However, there does not appear to be a requirement to discuss mitigation measures which the agency does not actually intend to undertake itself or have some other entity undertake. This is consistent with the language of the guidelines which require a "statement of how other adverse effects . . . *will be* mitigated."

This brings up the question of the enforceability of an agency's statement that certain effects will be mitigated in a certain manner. NEPA does not explicitly provide for enforceability of these commitments, and it remains to be seen whether, if they are not kept, the courts will fashion a remedy for those who have relied on such promises.

Those who are concerned that mitigation measures discussed in an impact report may be forgotten as a project progresses should insist on firm commitments outside the environmental impact analysis documents. These may be in the form of contractual commitments or conditions contained in a permit. For example, when an agency intends to give a permit to develop a particular area and states in its impact statement that one of the mitigation measures will be the planting of a certain number of trees, the planting of those trees should be made a condition of the permit to the developers.

A recent case has dealt with the possibility of having a court order an administrative agency to fulfill promises made in an EIS. In Sierra Club v. Mason[106] the U.S. District Court for the District of Connecticut was asked by the Corps of Engineers to lift its injunction against the dredging of New Haven Harbor after the corps had completed preparation of its EIS. The plaintiff in turn asked that the injunction be modified to allow the dredging to go on but that the Corps be required to abide by certain assurances given in the EIS, including a promise to undertake research to monitor the effects of the dredging. The court refused to grant the plaintiff's request on the grounds that it had no reason to expect the Corps not to carry out its promises. However, the court did indicate that failure to live up to assurances made in an EIS might "give rise to a judicially cognizable cause of action."[107] The court also pointed out that the Corps itself had acknowledged during oral arguments that a substantial change in the scope and major aspects of the project as described in the original EIS would, in effect, constitute a new project requiring a new EIS.

In addition to the requirement for a consideration of mitigation measures, Section 1500.8(a)(3)(ii) of the federal guidelines discusses the need for coverage of growth inducing effects as follows:

Secondary or indirect, as well as primary, or direct, consequences for the environment should be included in the analysis. Many major Federal actions, in particular those that involve the construction or licensing of infrastructure investments (e.g., highways, airports, sewer systems, water resource projects, etc.) stimulate or induce secondary effects in the form of associated investments and changed patterns of social and economic activities. Such secondary effects, through their impacts on existing community facilities and activities, through inducing new facilities and activities, or through changes in natural conditions, may often be even more substantial than the primary effects of the original action itself. For example, the effects of the proposed action on population growth may be among the more significant secondary effects. Such population and growth impacts should be estimated if expected to be significant . . . and an assessment made of the effect of any possible change in population patterns or growth upon the resource base, including land use, water and public services of the area in question.

Thus CEQ directs agencies not only to consider growth inducing impacts, that is, the effect of a proposed project on population in the area, but to follow this analysis through to a discussion of what effects the increased population will in turn have on public services and the environment.

What about analysis of the economic effects of a proposed federal project? The portion of the federal guidelines quoted previously indicates that the economic effects of a project are among those which should be explored. Further, language contained in Section 1500.8(a)(8) of the guidelines indicates that agencies which prepare cost-benefit analyses for their projects should attach the analysis or a summary thereof to their EIS. These matters are given extensive consideration in the chapters by Berns and Dickinson and Blackmarr.

WHO PREPARES THE EIS?

NEPA states that every proposal for major federal actions must include a detailed environmental impact statement "by the responsible official." The meaning of this last phrase is still not resolved. There are two kinds of disputes surrounding its interpretation. First, when several federal agencies have jurisdiction over a given project, who is the responsible official? Second, may a federal agency delegate its responsibility to prepare an impact statement to a state agency or private party?

Several Agencies with Jurisdiction

The language of NEPA appears to assume either that each project covered by NEPA will involve only one federal agency or that each federal agency with jurisdiction over a given project will prepare its own individual impact statement.

Many projects involve a cooperative effort between several federal agencies or funding by one federal agency and implementation or licensing by another. NEPA itself does not indicate what approach is to be taken in preparation of environmental studies in these situations. To avoid repetitious work by each of the agencies with jurisdiction over a given project, the CEQ has included a "lead agency" concept in its guidelines. Section 1500.7(b) of the guidelines describes the lead agency as the agency with "supervisory responsibility for preparation of the EIR." According to this same section, factors to be considered by the federal agencies involved in determining who is the lead agency include: (1) the time sequence in which the agencies become involved in the project (2) the magnitude of each agency's involvement and (3) the agencies' relative expertise with respect to the project's environmental effects.

The guidelines go on to point out that CEQ will assist in resolving any dispute among federal agencies as to which is the appropriate lead agency.

In addition, the CEQ attempts to avoid the temptation of abrogation of their NEPA responsibilities by nonlead agencies. In this regard the guidelines[108] state that:

> . . . Where a lead agency prepares the statement, the other agencies involved should provide assistance with respect to their areas of jurisdiction and expertise . . . the statement should contain an environmental assessment of the full range of Federal actions involved, should reflect the views of all participating agencies, and should be prepared before major or irreversible actions have been taken by any of the participating agencies.

The CEQ guidelines recognize an alternative method for preparation of EIRs when several federal agencies have jurisdiction. The guidelines[109] suggest that the agencies involved use a cooperative (joint preparation) approach as an alternative to the lead agency approach. Presumably, under this approach each agency would have equal responsibility for preparation of the EIR. Although the guidelines provide little detail, they do make it clear that the joint preparation approach, like the lead agency approach, must result in a full revelation of all impacts of "the full range of Federal actions involved" and "should reflect the views of all participating agencies."

California has given the lead agency approach the force of law by incorporating the concept into its 1972 amendments to the CEQA. According to California law[110] the lead agency is "the public agency which has the principal responsibility for carrying out or approving a project which may have a significant effect on the environment." The California act places responsibility for preparation of the impact report on the lead agency[111] and requires consultation by the lead agency with other agencies that have jurisdiction over the project prior to completion of the environmental report.[112] The CEQA also assigns the task of resolution of disputes over which agency is properly the lead agency to the state's Office of Planning and Research.[113]

Although the California legislature in enacting its environmental quality act recognized the need to clarify the primary responsibility for preparation of EIRs when more than one agency is involved and further recognized that there might be conflicts among agencies as to which was properly the lead agency, it left some questions in the area of interagency coordination unanswered. For example, beyond requiring consultation by the lead agency with other agencies in any case where an impact statement is being prepared, it does not deal explicitly with the problem of disagreement between the lead agency and other agencies over the threshold decision as to whether an EIR is necessary at all. Whereas on the one hand the California legislation states that the lead agency is responsible for "the determination of whether the project may have a significant effect on the environment,"[114] on the other hand it states that "It is the intent of the Legislature that all agencies of the state government which regulate activities of private individuals, corporations, and public agencies which are found to affect the quality of the environment, shall regulate such activities so that major consideration is given to preventing environmental damage."[115] There is serious question as to whether a nonlead agency can accept a lead agency's decision not to prepare an EIR when the nonlead agency disagrees with that decision and still be in compliance with the law.

Delegation of Impact Statement Preparation

In addition to the issue of which is the lead agency, there is the issue of how much of the responsibility for preparation of the impact statement may be delegated to other parties, whether they are nonlead agencies with jurisdiction over the project, private project proponents, or consultants.

The first important judicial decision on this question was Greene County Planning Board v. FPC.[116] In that opinion the U.S. Court of Appeals for the Second Circuit ruled that the Federal Power Commission (FPC) could not adopt as its own an impact statement prepared by the Power Authority of the State of New York (PASNY). The only effort expended by the FPC on the impact statement in question was the collation of comments on PASNY's EIS from other federal agencies, the FPC's own staff, and environmental groups. The court disallowed this approach saying "The danger of this procedure, and one obvious shortcoming, is the potential, if not likelihood, that the applicant's statement will be based upon self-serving assumptions."[117]

Greene County gave little indication as to the degree of effort required on the part of the lead agency to immunize it from a claim that it was merely adopting the impact statement prepared by another party, and subsequent judicial decisions are of little help in this regard. When the Greene County decision was appealed to the Supreme Court, certiorari was denied, that is, the Supreme Court refused to rule in the case, thus allowing the decision of the Court of Appeals to stand. This is not a definitive decision on the part of the Supreme Court, and a large number of lower federal court decisions subsequent to Greene County have created a blurry picture of the boundaries of responsibility for an agency that wishes to delegate the preparation of an EIS. By far the majority of cases have held that delegation is proper.[118] However, in many of these cases the court seems to link the propriety of delegation to the level of participation of the lead agency in preparation and evaluation of the impact statement. For example, in Iowa Citizens v. Volpe the court stated:

The record is clear that FHWA (The Federal Highway Administration) did not merely rubber stamp the state's work. FHWA recommended changes in the draft statement and supplemented the final EIS by additional information.[119]

In Life of the Land v. Brinegar,[120] the Ninth Circuit Court of Appeals considered the delegation of impact statement preparation to a private party. The court approved such a delegation. The issue of delegation in that case was complicated by the fact that the private consulting firm which was assigned the EIS preparation had a financial interest in seeing the proposed project approved. However, the court dealt with that problem by viewing the private consulting firm as analogous to the Corps of Engineers when it prepares an EIR for one of its own projects. That is, the firm had an interest in seeing the project go ahead, but this did not necessarily mean that it would not have the good faith objectivity necessary to adequately evaluate the environmental impacts of the project.[121] Whether the Court would have taken this same approach had the Federal Aviation Administration (the lead agency) not taken an active part in preparation and review of the consulting firm's draft EIS is not known. However, it does appear that the court placed emphasis on the fact that the FAA did participate to a significant extent in preparation and review of the statement.[122] This, of course, puts the consulting firm in much the same position as a private party wishing to undertake a project itself which prepares a draft statement for the use of an agency in preparing a final statement.

The CEQ in its guidelines approves of the preparation of draft statements by an applicant for agency approval warning, however, that "In all cases, the agency should make its own evaluation of the environmental issues and take responsibility for the scope and content of draft and final environmental statements."[123]

THE ENVIRONMENTAL ANALYSIS AND THE PROJECT PLANNING PROCESS

A very important question that has not yet been discussed in detail is: how does the environmental analysis affect the planning and decision-making process? This question can be answered in two contexts: the actual and the theoretical.

The Federal Council on Environmental Quality in its fourth annual report to the President expressed the opinion that "because of internalization of NEPA's objectives, many of the most environmentally undesirable projects and alternatives are screened out of agency consideration prior to any formal action under section 102(2)(C)."[124]

The report goes on to enumerate modification or abandonment of projects reported by a number of federal agencies as a result of NEPA compliance. For example, the AEC reported shelving proposals to store radioactive wastes at two sites and changing the cooling tower design of several nuclear power plants, and the Corps of Engineers reported dropping 24 projects, delaying 44, and significantly modifying 197.

That all the changes in projects which were reported by the CEQ actually came about as a result of the requirements of NEPA is doubtful. Possibly, a number of them would have resulted from public pressures even without the impact statement legislation. There is no doubt, however, that NEPA does expand the information-gathering process which an agency must go through before undertaking a project and that the public has a right to participate in that information gathering. Whether the information thus obtained is absorbed into and actually influences the decision-making process is not known. It does appear that agencies will modify projects or undertake mitigation measures to avoid the delay and adverse publicity resulting from a court challenge of their impact analysis.

For projects that attract significant public attention it probably is of little consequence whether modifications occur as a result of the threat of delay or as a result of a change in the environmental understanding of the decision maker. For those projects that do not catch the public eye, however, the effectiveness of environmental laws depends on the good faith and environmental sensitivity of the decision makers. The size of this second class of projects and the extent to which NEPA and similar state laws have affected decision making in this type of case is unknown at this time.

Intertwined with the questions about whether the environmental analysis process actually affects project planning are a number of questions about what the law actually requires with regard to the relationships between environmental analysis and planning. The most important of these are the following:

1. At what point in the planning process must the analysis be completed, and

2. Does the discovery that a project will have serious environmental consequences require any particular response on the part of the decision maker, such as

(a) Mitigation?
(b) Choice of a less damaging alternative?
(c) Abandonment of the project?

Both questions are discussed more fully in the following paragraphs.

When in the Planning Process Must the Environmental Analysis be Completed?

This question will be answered differently depending on several factors. Recently, a number of writers have suggested that comprehensive ("program") impact statements may be appropriate for certain types of governmental activities. Such statements would discuss the overall effects of an entire governmental program, whether it be a regulatory or permit program, a grant program or a research program. Frederick Anderson, for example, in his book *NEPA in the Courts*[125] suggests that impact statements should be prepared in "tiers," with the earliest statement being completed prior to the initial policy decision that will eventually lead to individual actions which affect the environment. This would generally be at the legislation or cabinet decision-making stage. Later, as programs develop out of the policy decisions, a second-tier statement would be prepared for each program. Finally, statements would be prepared on each project within a particular program (e.g., each permit to construct in navigable waters issued by the Corps of Engineers, each construction grant given by the Department of Housing and Urban Development, or each research facility constructed by The Atomic Energy Commission).

The U.S. Court of Appeals for the District of Columbia has viewed the program statement approach as valid and, in fact, required for major research programs. In Scientists Institute v. AEC[126] the court ruled that the AEC was required to prepare an impact statement on its liquid-metal fastbreeder-reactor research program rather than wait to prepare a statement on each research facility built as a part of the program. The court was influenced by the fact that legislation was needed annually to continue funding for the program and that NEPA, by its own terms, applies to proposals for legislation. Further the court was wary of allowing the program to go forward knowing the investment necessary to carry it on without an advance assessment of environmental impacts. In the words of the court:

To wait until a technology attains the stage of complete commercial feasibility before considering the possible adverse environmental effects attendant upon ultimate application of the technology will undoubtedly frustrate meaningful consideration and balancing of environmental costs against economic and other benefits. Modern technological advances typically stem from massive investments in research and development, as is the case here. Technological advances are therefore capital investments, and, as such, once brought to a state of commercial feasibility the investment in their development acts to compel their application.[127]

The CEQ has also advocated program impact statements. Section 1500.6(d)(1) of its guidelines reads in part as follows:

Agencies should give careful attention to identifying and defining the purpose and scope of the action which would most appropriately serve as the subject of the statement. In many cases, broad program statements will be required in order to assess the environmental effects of a number of individual actions on a given geographical area (e.g., coal leases), or environmental impacts that are generic or common to a series of agency actions (e.g., maintenance or waste handling practices), or the overall impact of a large-scale program or chain of contemplated projects (e.g., major lengths of highway as opposed to small segments).

The guidelines go on to recognize that subsequent statements may be necessary for individual actions within a program when the program statement does not adequately cover the unique impacts of each particular action. It is likely that such follow-up statements would frequently be necessary, since at the program level it may not be possible to anticipate specific projects in enough detail to adequately foresee their impacts. On the other hand, each statement for the individual projects within a program would cover only those impacts not adequately described in the program statement and thus avoid the boiler-plate repetition of similar material in the statement for each project within a program.

Ideally, program statements would have the following advantages:

1. They would permit an evaluation of the overall effect of a program that individual project statements, when considered separately, might not adequately portray.

2. They would allow evaluation of the potential environmental effects of programs before the commitment of major material and human resources.

3. They would avoid the need for repetition of similar material in the impact statements for each project within a program.

We have been considering the timing of impact statement preparation. Even when a program statement is not prepared, there remains a question as to the appropriate time for preparation of the impact statement for an individual project. According to the CEQ guidelines: "Initial assessments of the environmental impacts of proposed action should be undertaken concurrently with initial technical and economic studies."[128] Assuming this initial assessment shows that the action in question is a "major federal action significantly affecting the quality of the human environment," a draft EIS and then a final EIS must be prepared. The CEQ guidelines give the following direction as to the proper timing for completion of the final statement.

To the maximum extent practicable no administrative action subject to section 102(2)(C) is to be taken sooner than ninety (90) days after a draft environmental statement has been circulated for comment, furnished to the Council (on Environmental Quality) and, except where advance public disclosure will result in significantly increased costs of procurement to the Government, made available to the public pursuant to these guidelines. . . .[129]

The guidelines go on to say that action should not be taken sooner than 30 days after the final EIS has been circulated.[130] The guidelines do make provision for an exception to this timetable for emergencies, after consultation with CEQ.

The guidelines do not distinguish (as far as EIS timing is concerned) between those projects that were begun either before or after the effective date of NEPA. They simply use the wording "to the maximum extent practicable" to qualify the prescribed schedule. To get a fuller picture of proper timing of compliance with NEPA for a project begun before the statute's effective date, we must look to judicial decisions.

For the most part, when courts have found NEPA to be applicable to an ongoing or continuing project, they have also found that NEPA had to be complied with before work could continue on the project. That is, they have issued injunctions or obtained commitments from the defendants to stop progress on the project involved until adequate compliance with NEPA has been achieved. Most courts have viewed arguments by agencies that the granting of an injunction pending preparation of an impact statement would greatly raise government costs as unconvincing in light of the NEPA mandate to consider environmental consequences prior to taking action. As was said by the Fourth Circuit Court of Appeals in Arlington Coalition v. Volpe:[131]

. . . The district court held and appellees claim that the question whether section 102(C) [sic] must be complied with is moot because the Secretary has agreed voluntarily to file an environmental impact statement. We disagree. Filing a report without suspension of work on Arlington I-66 until the report has been considered by the Secretary is not the sort of compliance that is likely to change the result. Section 102(C) [sic] contemplates not only that a report be compiled but also that the Secretary take into account the information contained therein in determining the final location and design of a highway.

In Committee to Stop Route 7 v. Volpe[132] the District Court for the District of Connecticut also recognized the temptation for an agency to give little genuine consideration to environmental factors if work on the project is allowed to continue during preparation of the impact statement. That court described the problem as follows:

When defendants ask me to weigh the possibility of increased cost of construction if these projects are delayed, they are assuming that the projects will be built, and that the preparation of an impact statement will have no effect whatever on the decision whether or not to build. I cannot accept that assumption.[133]

Although both cases involved projects on which only minor or no construction had been done prior to the plaintiff's motion for an injunction, $29 million had been expended on property acquisition in the Arlington case.

The courts have found injunctions appropriate even when projects were in advanced stages of construction. For example, in EDF v. Corps of Engineers[134] (the Gillham Dam case) the court found that an injunction would be appropriate, even though over $9 million of the total $14 million estimated construction cost had already been expended, and approximately two-thirds of the construction was completed. In Sierra Club v. Froehlke[135] the U.S. District Court for the Southern District of Texas enjoined further work on the Wallisville project and related dams and locks pending preparation of a satisfactory EIS, although construction on Wallisville was 87 percent complete.

There have been some cases in which a court has been unwilling to impose an injunction on an ongoing project, even though the court found that the agency in question had not complied with NEPA. In EDF v. Armstrong,[136] for example, the District Court for the Northern District of California refused to enjoin further work on the New Melones Dam saying that "a balance of the equities" convinced the court that the project should not be enjoined pending supplementation of an inadequate impact statement. On appeal, however, the Ninth Circuit Court of Appeals enjoined further work on the project pending a ruling by the District Court on the adequacy of the supplemented EIS,[137] although the Court of Appeals did not make any ruling on the propriety or legality of the District Court's failure to enjoin the project pending completion of the supplemental EIS.

In Natural Resources Defense Council v. Stamm[138], a case involving the Auburn Dam in California, the District Court for the Eastern District of California found the impact statement inadequate and issued an injunction but stayed its execution for six months, allowing efforts on the project to continue while the original impact statement was being supplemented.

The preceding discussion has concentrated on the court's approach to proper timing of impact statement preparation for ongoing projects as defined earlier in this chapter. Just as cases involving NEPA's applicability to ongoing projects should begin to decrease as the effective date of the act recedes, so too questions of the proper timing for compliance should decrease.

There have been very few cases dealing with the appropriate timing of compliance with NEPA for continuing projects, and no trend can really be distinguished to date. The major cases involving this issue are discussed briefly in the following paragraphs.

In Sierra Club v. Mason[139] the U.S. District Court for the District of Connecticut enjoined the planned dredging of New Haven Harbor and disposal of more than 1,000,000 tons of dredge spoil until an impact statement was prepared even though the dredging was part of a harbor maintenance dredging program going back more than twenty years.

In Lee v. Resor[140] however, the U.S. District Court for the Middle District of Florida refused to grant an injunction pending preparation of an EIS, although it found that the continuation of the Corps of Engineers program of spraying herbicide to eliminate water hyacinths (which impaired navigation) was a further major federal action having a significant effect on the environment. The court reached its decision not to issue an injunction after comparing the relative harm that, in its opinion, would result to navigation interests because of such an injunction with the harm to fish from allowing the spraying to go ahead during preparation of the EIS.

Finally, in Minnesota PIRG v. Butz[141] the U.S. District Court for the District of Minnesota found that the Forest Service's administration of timber sales contracts in the Boundary Waters Canoe Area after the effective date of NEPA required an impact statement, even though the administration was being undertaken in conformance with a plan adopted prior to NEPA's effective date. Further, and more important in terms of the present discussion, the court enjoined further logging in the area pending completion of a new management plan for the area and its accompanying EIS.

Does the Discovery of Serious Environmental Consequences Require Mitigation or Abandonment?

Several of the Federal Courts of Appeal have given conflicting answers to this question. It appears that the U.S. Supreme Court will have to resolve the issue of whether NEPA creates any judicially enforceable duty on the part of federal agencies to abandon a project that will have severe environmental consequences or to at least seek to mitigate those adverse consequences by providing counterbalancing environmental benefits. Another way of putting the same question is: does NEPA create a right to substantive judicial review (i.e., review of the correctness of an agency's decision) or merely to procedural review (i.e., review of the steps the agency took in reaching its decision)?

There is no doubt that NEPA was intended to modify the decision-making process in such a way that environmental factors would be taken into account and to result in modification, or, in some cases, abandonment, of environmentally damaging projects. As was said by the District of Columbia Court of Appeals in the Calvert Cliffs case:

NEPA requires that an agency must—to the *fullest* extent possible under its other statutory obligations—consider alternatives to its action which would reduce environmental damage. That principle establishes that consideration of environmental matters must be more than a *pro forma* ritual. Clearly, it is pointless to "consider" environmental costs without also seriously considering action to avoid them.[142]

The preceding language indicates the opinion of the District of Columbia Circuit that NEPA was intended to make a difference in governmental decision making, not simply to result in the preparation of impact statements. Although this particular language does not indicate whether that court sees NEPA as creating any judicially enforceable duty on the part of federal agencies to avoid adverse environmental impacts, elsewhere in its opinion the court states:

The reviewing courts probably cannot reverse a substantive decision on its merits, under Section 101, unless it be shown that the actual balance of costs and benefits that was struck was arbitrary or clearly gave insufficient weight to environmental values.[143]

The clear import of this language, of course, is that there are some instances in which an agency's decision on a project would be so irresponsible in view of the agencies' duties under NEPA as to be subject to reversal by the courts.

This latter language, however, was not central to the court's ruling in Calvert Cliffs; it was merely a statement of opinion by the court, known as dictum, and, therefore, is not binding on federal agencies or other courts. However, it does serve as an indication of the ruling that the Court of Appeals would make were it squarely faced with the question of whether an agency decision may be reversed for noncompliance with NEPA.

Other courts of appeal have made explicit rulings on the judicial reviewability of an agency's decision to proceed with a project in disregard of the revelation of serious environmental consequences in its impact statements. The Eighth, Fourth, and Seventh Circuit Courts of Appeal are presently in agreement that NEPA creates a duty to do more than merely prepare an impact statement and that the judiciary has the right to oversee and enforce compliance with this duty.

In EDF v. Corps of Engineers[144] the U.S. Court of Appeals for the Eighth Circuit became the first appeals court to explicitly rule on the question of substantive review under NEPA. In that decision the court ruled that NEPA required more than a full disclosure of environmental impacts. The court found that NEPA mandated on federal agencies a careful balancing process between economic and environmental costs and benefits. Most significantly, the court ruled that when it can be shown that the decision of an agency to go ahead with a project is erroneous in light of the balance of environmental and economic costs and benefits, the court may reverse that decision.[145]

The test which the Eighth Circuit said should be applied by the court to determine the correctness of an agency's decision to proceed with a project is as follows:

The reviewing court must first determine whether the agency acted within the scope of its authority, and next whether the decision reached was arbitrary, capricious, an abuse of discretion or otherwise not in accordance with law. In making the latter determination, the court must decide if the agency failed to consider all relevant factors in reaching its decision, or if the decision itself represented a clear error in judgment.

Where NEPA is involved, the court must first determine if the agency reached its decision after a full, good faith consideration and balancing of environmental factors. The court must then determine, according to the standards set forth in sections 101(b) and 102(1) of the Act, whether "the actual balance of costs and benefits that was struck was arbitrary or clearly gave insufficient weight to environmental values." (Citing Calvert Cliffs)[146]

The court goes on to clarify this standard by saying that a court could not properly reverse an agency's decision merely because the court would not have made the same decision based upon the facts available to the agency. That is, the agency's decision must represent a clear error in judgment, not merely a different but reasonable balancing of environmental and economic factors than the court itself would have made.

The Fourth Circuit Court of Appeal in Conservation Council v. Froehlke,[147] a case involving the New Hope Dam in North Carolina, and the Seventh Circuit in Sierra Club v. Froehlke,[148] involving the Kickapoo River in Wisconsin, have also ruled that NEPA creates a right to judicial review of an agency's substantive decisions.

The standard of review adopted by the Fourth Circuit[149] was virtually the same as that adopted by the Eighth Circuit. The Seventh Circuit explained the standard it felt should be applied in somewhat less broad terms, saying merely that the review "should be limited to determining whether the agency's decision is arbitrary or capricious"[150] and that "the court is not empowered to substitute its judgment for that of the agency."[151] That court does not appear to accept the approach of the Eighth and Fourth Circuits that a court may reverse when the agency gives "insufficient weight to environmental values." The Seventh Circuit went on to evaluate the Corps' decision and found "that the Corps 'reached its decision after a fair, good faith consideration and balancing of environmental factors' and that its decision is neither arbitrary nor capricious."[152]

The particulars of these rather broadly stated standards for substantive review under NEPA have not yet been defined by the courts. Clear definition must await further judicial interpretation and, particularly, cases which hold that specific agency decisions were not proper.

To date, only one court has made such a ruling. In Montgomery v. Ellis the U.S. District Court for the Northern District of Alabama ruled that the interest rate used by the Soil Conservation Service in computing the cost of a proposed creek channelization project was too low and the projected project life too long. According to the court:

It seems clear that in light of present economic conditions and the continuing policy and responsibility of the Federal Government to protect the environment "to the fullest extent possible" as required by NEPA, the courts should review any determination striking a balance of benefits and costs that employs an historically arbitrary interest rate or project life such as is being used in this case. . . ."[153]

The court goes on to describe the role of courts in undertaking substantive review as one of determining the reasonable bounds for the exercise of administrative discretion, saying:

The Court recognizes that there must necessarily be a zone of administrative discretion where administrative action will not be reversed by the courts. Borrowing from the example set forth by plaintiff, the Court agrees that if there is some dispute as to the value to be assigned for the benefit of a man-day of fishing, as long as that benefit is computed within reasonable bounds, court should accept the administrative decision . . . . Where the administrative decision appears to be within such reasonable bounds, it should be left undisturbed; but where, as here, it is highly out of line as respects the interest rate and project life, it is the courts function to reverse that determination.[154]

Early Fifth Circuit Court of Appeals decisions indicated that that court would not review a substantive agency decision.[155] However, in a more recent case, EDF v. Corps of Engineers,[156] involving the Tennessee-Tomligbee waterway project of the Corps of Engineers, the court, citing the Fourth and Eighth Circuits' positions and the Calvert Cliff decision in the District of Columbia Circuit, stated that "the majority and better reasoned rule favors such review."[157]

In this same decision the Fifth Circuit also ruled on one further issue that may in the future essentially negate any right to judicial review of many substantive agency decisions. The Corps argued against substantive review of the Corps' decision to proceed with the project on the grounds that the Congress continued its approval of the project after considering the EIS,[158] and the court accepted this argument. The court recognized that a number of other courts before it had dealt with similar questions and determined that congressional action on a project (particularly appropriations for further work on the project) did not necessarily constitute an implied waiver of NEPA responsibilities for the agency involved.[159] However, the court distinguished this particular case on the grounds that the Tennessee-Tomligbee impact statement was explicitly considered by Congress in deciding to go ahead with the project, whereas the argument which had been rejected in the previous decisions was that further appropriations by Congress without benefit of an EIS impliedly constituted a waiver by Congress of the NEPA requirements.

Whereas the Fourth, Fifth, Seventh, and Eighth Circuits have ruled that NEPA does create a right to judicial review of substantive agency decisions, the Tenth Circuit has indicated that such a right is not created by NEPA. In an early decision concerning termination of government helium purchase contracts by the Department of Interior, the National Helium case, the Tenth Circuit Court of Appeal cited favorably the District Court's opinion in the Gillham Dam case, EDF v. Corps of Engineers, holding that NEPA did not create substantive rights. That decision was subsequently overturned by the Eighth Circuit's opinion in the same case, as discussed previously. This left a hiatus in which it was difficult to reach any firm conclusion as to what the Tenth Circuit's opinion concerning the substantive rights issue was. In a later decision in the same National Helium litigation the District Court cited the Eighth Circuit's substantive rights decision with apparent approval[160] and implied that it would consider whether the Department of Interior's substantive decision was appropriate if given an opportunity,[161] but found that the EIS was so defective that it had to be upgraded, thus delaying any necessity for substantive review.

Subsequent to this later District Court opinion, the Circuit Court overturned the District's ruling that the impact statement was inadequate. This latest Circuit Court opinion went on to indicate that the Tenth Circuit continues to believe substantive review is not appropriate under NEPA.[162]

Finally, several Ninth Circuit Court of Appeal cases indicate as dictum that the Ninth Circuit does not believe it has the authority to overturn a substantive agency decision under NEPA.[163]

Regardless of how the Supreme Court ultimately resolves the dispute among the Circuits as to the availability of substantive review under NEPA, it is interesting to speculate on the ultimate impact of a determination that such a right does exist. As noted earlier, there has been only one judicial decision to date, Montgomery v. Ellis, decided by the U.S. District Court for the Northern District of Alabama which has held that an agency decision was in fact arbitrary or capricious in light of NEPA's substantive provisions view. It should not be assumed, however, that because agency decisions have as yet been infrequently overturned under NEPA, the right to substantive review is nugatory. A judicial decision to overturn an agency's substantive decision in even a small minority of cases should be influential in encouraging agencies to look at NEPA compliance on a day-to-day basis as more than a pro forma ritual.

In some states it is clear that state courts do have the power to undertake substantive review of agency decisions for compliance with the state's environmental quality act. For example, as previously mentioned, the Washington Supreme Court ruled, in Eastlake Community Council v. Roanoke Associates, that Washington's State Environmental Policy Act permits substantive review. And in California, amendments to the CEQA adopted in 1976 (specifically, Public Resources Code Section 21081) provide, in essence, that a state agency approving or carrying out a project must see that mitigation measures identified in an environmental impact report are implemented unless the agency makes findings that implementation of the mitigation measures would be infeasible as a result of specific economic, social or other considerations. This legislation appears to lay the foundation in California for substantive judicial review of agency decisions, at least to the extent that mitigation measures mentioned in an impact report are not implemented in carrying out a project.

NEPA AND SOCIAL IMPACTS

There are frequent mentions of social impacts and social sciences in the statutory language of NEPA. For example, Section 101(a) contains the declaration that ". . . it is the continuing policy of the Federal Government . . . to use all practicable means and measures . . . in a manner calculated to foster and promote the general welfare, to create and maintain conditions under which man and nature can exist in productive harmony, and fulfill the *social,* economic and other requirements of present and future generations of Americans." (emphasis added)

In Section 102(2)(A) the act requires that all agencies of the federal government shall—

(A) Utilize a systematic, interdisciplinary approach which will insure the integrated use of natural and *social sciences* and the environmental design arts in planning and in decisionmaking which may have an impact on man's environment. (emphasis supplied)

The clear indication here, of course, is that in analyzing the potential environmental impacts of projects, the social sciences (e.g., psychology and sociology) should be utilized along with the natural sciences (e.g., biology, physics, chemistry) and that the effects of projects on the human psychological condition are to be analyzed and considered under NEPA along with the effects on the natural environment. The purpose of this book is to enhance the degree to which Congress' intent in this section is realized in real EIS and agency planning efforts.

The theme that social impacts should be an important component of agency decision making is carried through in Section 102(2)(C) in which the charge to agencies is to prepare an impact statement that will disclose the impacts of a proposed project on the "human environment." "Human environment" as used here apparently means something more than the biological and physical surroundings that we normally think of as the natural environment, since elsewhere in the act there is specific reference to the "natural environment."

Further, throughout the act there are references to effects of federal activities that we would normally consider social or socioeconomic. For example, in Section 101(b)(2) there is a reference to "esthetically and culturally pleasing surroundings." Section 101(b)(4) discusses the necessity to "preserve important historic, cultural and natural aspects of our national heritage," and Section 101(b)(5) discusses as a goal "high standards of living and a wide sharing of life's amenities."

Taken together these references to social sciences, social impacts, and the social needs of the country indicate that Congress had in mind in passing NEPA more than the necessity to study and preserve the natural environment. Congress was also directing federal agencies and the CEQ to consider the effects of federal actions on the human psyche and human social interrelationships.

The CEQ guidelines are consistent with the idea that the social as well as the biological and physical consequences of federal action are to be considered in EISs and in decision making based on them. In Section 1500.2(b)(3), for example, the guidelines state that

In particular, agencies should use the environmental impact statement process to explore alternative actions that will avoid or minimize adverse impacts and to evaluate both the long- and short-range implications of proposed actions to man, his physical and social surroundings, and to nature.

Further support for the idea that social impacts are among those to be considered under NEPA is found in journals and judicial decisions. The following list, for example, is part of a table listing possible impacts of highway construction in a well-known transportation journal.[164] Many of these variables are discussed by Schott in Chapter 6:

Recreation	Hunting
	Fishing
	Boating
	Swimming
	Camping and hiking
	Picnicking
Aesthetics and human interests	Open spaces
	Parklands
	Historical and archeological sites
	Monuments
	Cemeteries
Socioeconomic	Employment
	Sanitation and waste disposal
	Health and safety
	Income
	Parking
	Population concentration
	Crime
	Availability of drugs
	Overburdened mass transportation
	Rehousing problems
	Tax burden
	Lighting an area at night
	Load on public services
	Property values
	Effects on schools
	Noise
	Energy

There are a number of judicial decisions dealing with the matter of social impacts. In Hanly v. Mitchell,[165] for example, the Second Circuit Court of Appeals undertook the following informative discussion of the social impacts of the construction of a jail in Manhattan:

Plaintiffs claim that the living environment of all the families in this area will be adversely affected by the presence of the jail and by the fears of "riots and disturbances" so generated. In particular, plaintiffs argue that the city prison formerly located at Sixth Avenue and Eighth Street has been vacated because the noise of the inmates, their demonstrations, and the beckoning and signaling between them and their visitors caused disturbances in the neighborhood. The Paduano memorandum [a memorandum prepared by the General Services Administration in an attempt to comply with NEPA] contains no hint that such possible disturbances were considered. Nor is there any mention of the potential dangers of housing an out-patient treatment center in this area. Moreover, even as to more routine considerations, there is a conspicuous absence of a thoughtful discussion of possible parking problems caused by trucks delivering food and supplies, vans taking prisoners to and from the Eastern District and New Jersey courts, the need for parking space for prison personnel, and the need to accommodate those visiting the prisoners, whether lawyers or family.

Defendants argue to us that these are not "environmental considerations as they are defined in" the Act and that the injuries plaintiffs envision are speculative at best. As to the latter point, it may be that some of plaintiffs' fears are vague and speculative, but clearly all of them are not and the "responsible official" of GSA has apparently never considered any of them. As to defendants' argument that plaintiffs' concerns are irrelevant under the Act, this assertion, characterized most charitably, is simply incorrect. The National Environmental Policy Act contains no exhaustive list of so-called "environmental considerations," but without question its arms extend beyond sewage and garbage and even beyond water and air pollution . . . (citations omitted). The Act must be construed to include protection of the quality of life for city residents. Noise, traffic, overburdened mass transportation systems, crime, congestion and even availability of drugs all affect the urban "environment" and are surely the results of the "profound influences of . . . high density urbanization [and] industrial expansion." Section 101(a) of the Act. . . . Thus, plaintiffs do raise many "environmental considerations" that should not be ignored. . . .[166]

Likewise, in First National Bank v. Richardson[167] the Seventh Circuit Court of Appeals found that "NEPA must be construed to include protection of the quality of life for city residents" but allowed construction of a jail facility in a nonresidential area of Chicago to go ahead without preparation of an impact statement after determining that the chosen location was the most beneficial. Further, in Tierrasanta Community Council v. Richardson[168] the U.S. District Court for the Southern District of California found that construction of a youth detention facility adjacent to a public school required preparation of an EIS. According to the District Court, the environmental "assessment" prepared by the GSA did not, among other things, "adequately consider the psychological and sociological effects of the proposed youth facility on the families residing in the community adjoining the proposed facility, surrounding property values, the character of the adjoining residential neighborhoods, or the education of elementary school children attending a school adjacent to the facility."[169]

In contrast to the cases indicating that the social impacts of jail facilities in residential areas must be considered by federal agencies is Nucleus of Chicago Homeowners v. Lynn,[170] a Northern District of Illinois case. This case holds that "there is no evidence to support the plaintiffs' allegations that prospective tenants of public housing are more likely to engage in anti-social conduct than present community residents." After listening to sociologists appearing as expert witnesses for both plaintiffs and defendants, the court concluded that there would be no significant environmental impacts as a result of construction of a public housing project. This case differs from the jail cases, however, in that the court was ruling on the weight of the evidence (i.e., whether a public housing project would in fact have an adverse environmental impact) and not on the issue of whether social impacts are environmental impacts as that term is used in NEPA.

Another case which required an in-depth look at social impacts involved a plan by the Postal Service to build a vehicle maintenance facility on one square block in New York City with a public housing apartment complex to be built on the roof. The vehicle maintanance facility would have concrete walls rising 80 feet from the street and the apartment complex would have approximately 860 units. In this case, Chelsea Neighborhood Association v. U. S. Postal Service,[171] the court found that the following types of impacts had not been (and must be) discussed:

(1) possible overcrowding of local elementary schools
(2) the need for future expansion of local health services
(3) effects on park usage
(4) increased need for parking
(5) the need for garbage collection and other support services

The court went on to say:

A possibly more serious shortcoming of the project lies in the social, not physical, sciences. What effect will living at the top of an 80-foot plateau have on the residents of the air-rights housing? Will there be an emotional as well as physical isolation from the community? Will that isolation exacerbate the predicted rise in crime due to the increase in population density? That an EIS must consider these human factors is well established . . . We do not know whether informed social scientists would conclude that the top of the VMF would likely become a human jungle, unsafe at night and unappealing during the day. The question must be faced, however, by those who plan the project.[172]

Several other judicial decisions have dealt to a minor extent with the place of the social sciences and social impacts under NEPA. In Town of Groton v. Laird,[173] for example, the court listed a number of social factors that were taken into account by the Navy in making its decision to construct military housing near a private residential area. These factors included "health, safety, local socioeconomic factors, transportation systems, vehicular and air traffic patterns, utility systems, public services, and aesthetics."[174] The court stated in a footnote that "Anything that influences urban dwellers' quality of life is relevant when weighing significance. Crime, noise, stench, congestion, and even existence of drug traffic, are all to be considered as environmental factors."[175]

Few cases involving rural areas have explicitly considered the issue of the attention that should be accorded social impacts under NEPA. However, this is most likely a result of the fact that the effects on the natural environment in these cases are the major concern of the plaintiffs. When projects in rural areas may have demonstrable social impacts, these should be considered. In EDF v. Corps of Engineers[176] (involving the Tennessee-Tomligbee waterway) the court did mention that "The systematic interdisciplinary approach of 102(2)(A) is designed to assure better programs and a better environment by bringing together the skills of the biologist, the geologist, the ecologist, the engineer and the landscape architect, the economist, the sociologist, and the other disciplines relevant to the project."[177] Further, in its discussion of the particular environmental impacts of the waterway, the court considered effects on historical and archeological sites.

In summary, although courts have differed as to whether the social impacts of particular projects will be significant, there has been little disagreement with social impacts are among those effects of federal projects which should be considered under NEPA. The major problem remaining with regard to consideration of social impacts is the development of proper techniques for predicting and evaluating them. As was said, for example, in Nucleus of Chicago Homeowners v. Lynn:[178]

Predictions of behavior of prospective tenants whose identity is not yet known, made by the expert witnesses in this case, and the data upon which these predictions are based is uncertain and unconvincing. The conclusions of the expert witnesses are difficult, if not impossible, to verify and substantiate.

The development and application of sound techniques for evaluation of the potential social impacts of government projects is the focus of the remainder of this book.

NOTES

1. All citations to judicial decisions in this chapter refer the reader to a Bureau of National Affairs publication, *Environment Reporter—Cases* (ERC). This is a compilation of judicial

decisions concerning the environment from federal and state courts throughout the country and was thought to be the most available source of these decisions to nonattorney readers. Citations to these volumes include: (1) the volume number, (2) the initials ERC, and (3) the page number.

2. The U.S. Supreme Court has handed down a decision in a case involving-NEPA, Students Challenging Regulatory Agency Procedures v. United States, 5 ERC 1449 (1973). The case involved a challenge to the Interstate Commerce Commission's decision to allow a rate increase for the transportation of scrap material prior to preparation of an impact statement. However, the decision avoided interpreting NEPA; rather, it rested on an interpretation by the court that it had no jurisdiction under the Interstate Compact Act to review the ICC's decision.

3. 4 ERC 1593 (1972), modified 4 ERC 1705 (1972).

4. Eastlake Community Council v. Roanoke Associates, 5 ERC 1897 (1973).

5. For the most recent version, see Preparation of Environmental Impact Statements: Guidelines, Volume 38, Federal Register Number 147, Part II, August 1, 1973.

6. Bucklein v. Volpe, 2 ERC 1082 at 1083 (1970).

7. Calvert Cliffs Coordinating Committee v. AEC, 2 ERC 1779 at 1784–1785 (U.S. Court of Appeals, District of Columbia Circuit 1971).

8. These cases include Portland Cement v. Ruckleshaus, 5 ERC 1593 (U.S. Court of Appeals, District of Columbia Circuit 1973), involving the Clean Air Act, and Environmental Defense Fund (EDF) v. EPA 6 ERC 1112 (U.S. Court of Appeals, District of Columbia Circuit 1973), involving the Federal Insecticide, Fungicide and Rodenticide Act. In spite of these judicial decisions, however, EPA has recently decided to prepare voluntary impact statements on many of its activities.

9. 1 ERC 1449 (1971).

10. 4 ERC 1966 (U.S. District Court for the Western District of Tennessee 1972).

11. *Id.*, at 1967–1968.

12. *Id.*, at 1968.

13. EDF v. Corps of Engineers, 2 ERC 1260 at 1266 (1971).

14. 4 ERC 1408 at 1415–1416 (1972).

15. National Helium v. Morton, 3 ERC 1129 (U.S. Court of Appeals for the Tenth Circuit, 1971).

16. See Note 5.

17. Title 14, California Administrative Code, Chapter 3, Section 15000, et seq.

18. Public Resources Code Sections 21100(c) and 21100(g).

19. 5 ERC 1418 at 1423 (U.S. Court of Appeals for the District of Columbia Circuit, 1973).

20. Environmental Defense Fund v. Hardin, 2 ERC 1425 (U.S. District Court for the District of Columbia, 1971).

21. Goose Hollow Foothills League v. Romney, 3 ERC 1087 (U.S. District Court, District of Oregon, 1971).

22. City of New York v. U.S., 3 ERC 1571 (U.S. District Court for the Eastern District of New York, 1972).

23. National Helium v. Morton, see Note 15.

24. See Note 5, Section 1500.5(a)(1).

25. NEPA Section 102(2)(C).

26. 5 ERC 1910 (1973).

27. 5 ERC 1383 (1973).

28. *Id.,* at 1384.

29. 3 ERC 1280 (U.S. Court of Appeals for the Fourth Circuit, 1971).

30. See Note 5, Section 1500.5(a)(2). In a decision handed down since the mainbody of the text of this chapter was prepared, the U. S. District Court for the Middle District of North Carolina has confirmed the CEQ's position. This decision is Carolina Action v. Simon, 7 ERC 1807.

31. Lathan v. Volpe, 3 ERC 1362 (U.S. Court of Appeals for the Ninth Circuit, 1971), La Raza Unida, v. Volpe, 3 ERC 1306 (U.S. District Court for the Northern District of California, 1971).

32. 2 ERC 1871 (U.S. Court of Appeals for the Fifth Circuit, 1971).

33. See San Antonio Conservation Society v. Texas, 6 ERC 1273 (U.S. District Court for the Western District of Texas, 1973).

34. 5 ERC 1658 (1973).

35. See Note 29.

36. Ely v. Velde, 6 ERC 1558 (1974).

37. See Note 5.

38. 4 ERC 1153 (1972).

39. *Id.,* at 1155.

40. 4 ERC 1952 at 1965 (1972).

41. 3 ERC 1883 (U.S. District Court for the Eastern District of North Carolina, 1972).

42. 4 ERC 1862 (U.S. District Court for the District of Iowa, 1972).

43. Transcontinental Gas v. Development Commission, 4 ERC 1441 at 1447 (1972).

44. See Note 5, Section 1500. 6(b).

45. 4 ERC 1785 at 1789 (1972).

46. *Id.,* at 1790.

47. Citizens v. Volpe, see Note 40, at 1965.

48. 3 ERC 1421 (U.S. Court of Appeals for the Third Circuit, 1971). The Ninth Circuit Court of Appeals reached a similar result in Robinswood Community Club v. Volpe, 6 ERC 1401 (1974) as did the Third Circuit in Concerned Citizens of Marlboro v. Volpe, 4 ERC 1042 (1972).

49. 2 ERC 1260 (U.S. District Court for the Eastern District of Arkansas, 1971.)

50. 4 ERC 1579 (U.S. District Court for the Middle District of Florida, 1972).

51. 5 ERC 1251 (U.S. District Court for the District of Minnesota, 1973); upheld 6 ERC 1694 (U.S. Court of Appeals for the Eighth Circuit, 1974).

52. 4 ERC 1678 (U.S. District Court for the Northern District of Alabama, 1972).

53. See Note 48.

54. 4 ERC 1686 (U.S. District Court for the District of Connecticut, 1972).

55. See Note 18.

56. Chapter 274, Wisconsin Laws of 1971, Section 1.11(2)(C)(6); Connecticut Public Act No. 73-562, Section 2(C).

57. See Note 5, Section 1500.8(a)(1).

58. *Id.*

59. *Id.*

60. *Id.*, Section 1500.8(a)(3)(ii).

61. *Id.*, Section 1500.8(a)(2).

62. *Id.*, Section 1500.8(a)(3)(ii).

63. *Id.*

64. Requirements for discussion of social impacts are considered in detail in the portion of this chapter entitled "NEPA and Social Impacts" beginning at p. 52.

65. See Note 49.

66. 3 ERC 1126 (1971).

67. EDF v. Corps of Engineers, 4 ERC 1408 (U.S. District Court for the Northern District of Mississippi, 1972).

68. *Id.*, at 1419.

69. *Id.*

70. See Note 49 at 1269.

71. See Note 20.

72. See Note 5.

73. *Id.*, Section 1500.8(b).

74. *Id.*, Section 1500.8(a)(1).

75. Natural Resources Defense Council v. Grant, 5 ERC 1001 at 1004–1005 (U.S. District Court for the Eastern District of North Carolina, 1973). A similar ruling was made by the U.S. Court of Appeals for the Fifth Circuit in Silva v. Lynn, 5 ERC 1654 at 1656 (1973) and by the U.S. District Court for the Western District of Washington in Lathan v. Volpe, 4 ERC 1487 at 1490 (1972). In the Lathan case the court ruled that the defendants failed to back up their conclusion as to the noise levels expected as a result of freeway operation with scientific data or references to studies.

76. Sierra Club v. Froehlke, 5 ERC 1033 at 1068 (U.S. District Court for the Southern District of Texas, 1973).

77. See Note 49.

78. See Note 5, Section 1500.8(A)(5).

79. See, e.g., National Helium v. Morton, 5 ERC 1545 at 1559 (U.S. District Court for the District of Kansas, 1973) and Daly v. Volpe, 4 ERC 1481 at 1484 (U.S. District Court for the Western District of Washington, 1972).

80. *Id.*, at 1484. The issue of minimizing or mitigating adverse impacts is discussed more fully in the following section concerning alternatives.

81. See Note 7, at 1788.

82. See, e.g., EDF v. Corps of Engineers (Gillham Dam case on appeal), 4 ERC 1721 at 1724 (U.S. Court of Appeals for the Eighth Circuit, 1972) and Sierra Club v. Froehlke, 5 ERC 1920 at 1922 (U.S. Court of Appeals for the Seventh Circuit, 1973).

83. See Note 7, at 1782.

84. See Note 49, at 1269.

85. 4 ERC 1562 at 1565 (U.S. District Court for the Central District of California, 1972).

86. See Note 5, Section 1500.8(a)(5)

87. For a detailed discussion of the problems surrounding delegation of impact statement preparation, see the section of this chapter entitled "Delegation of Impact Statement Preparation."

88. 5 ERC 1939 at 1945 (1973).

89. See Note 5, Section 1500.8(a)(4).

90. *Id.*

91. 6 ERC 1008 at 1013 (U.S. District Court for the Eastern District of Tennessee, 1973), upheld by the U. S. Court of Appeals for the Sixth Circuit, 6 ERC 1367.

92. 3 ERC 1558 (1972).

93. *Id.,* at 1564.

94. *Id.*

95. *Id.*

96. The reader should keep in mind that, as pointed out previously, the fact that an alternative project must be done by another agency or that it cannot be accomplished without legislation does not mean that an agency may conclude the alternative is not feasible.

97. See Sierra Club v. Froehlke, Note 76, at 1075; Farwell v. Brinegar, Note 88, at 1945; Natural Resources Defense Council v. Morton, Note 92, at 1564; Silva v. Lynn, Note 75, at 1657; and Iowa Citizens v. Volpe, 6 ERC 1088 at 1089–1090 (U.S. Court of Appeals for the Eighth Circuit, 1973). A good discussion of the material contained in a proper revelation of the effects of alternatives may be found in a decision by the District Court for the Southern District of Florida: City of North Miami v. Train, 6 ERC 1841 (1974).

98. EDF v. Corps of Engineers, Note 49 at 1267.

99. See Note 5, Section 1500.8(a)(7).

100. See Note 18.

101. Chapter 274, Laws of 1971, Section 1.11(2)(c)(6).

102. Public Act No. 73–562, Section 2(c).

103. Laws of 1973, Chapter 412, Section 4(b) reads as follows: "No state action significantly affecting the quality of the environment shall be allowed, nor shall any permit for natural resources management and development be granted, where such action or permit has caused or is likely to cause pollution, impairment, or destruction of the air, water, land or other natural resources located within the state, so long as there is a feasible and prudent alternative consistent with the reasonable requirements of the public health, safety and welfare and the state's paramount concern for the protection of its air, water, land and other natural resources from pollution, impairment or destruction. Economic considerations alone shall not justify such conduct."

104. Public Resources Code Section 21155.

105. Guidelines, see Note 5, Section 1500.8(a)(5).

106. 6 ERC 1056 (1973).

107. *Id.,* at 1057.

108. See Note 5, Section 1500.7(b).

109. *Id.*

110. Public Resources Code Section 21067.

111. *Id.,* Section 21165.

112. *Id.,* Section 21104, 21153.

113. *Id.,* Section 21165.

114. *Id.*

115. *Id.,* Section 21000(g).

116. 3 ERC 1595 (1972).

117. *Id.,* at 1599–1600.

118. Cases holding that delegation of authority to prepare an EIS is not consistent with NEPA include, in addition to Greene County: Northside Tenants Rights Coalition v. Volpe, 4 ERC 1376 (U.S. District Court for the Eastern District of Wisconsin, 1972); Scherr v. Volpe, 4 ERC 1435 (U.S. Court of Appeals for the Seventh Circuit, 1972); Conservation Society v. Secretary, 5 ERC 1683 (U.S. District Court for the District of Vermont, 1973); and I-291 Why? Association v. Burns, 6 ERC 1275 (U.S. District Court for the District of Connecticut, 1974). Cases holding that delegation is acceptable include: Iowa Citizens for Environmental Quality v. Volpe, 4 ERC 1755 (U.S. District Court for the Southern District of Iowa, 1972) which was upheld on appeal (see 6 ERC 1088); National Forest Preservation Group v. Volpe, 4 ERC 1836 (U.S. District Court for the District of Montana, 1972); Citizens Airport Committee v. Volpe, 4 ERC 1738 (U.S. District Court for the Eastern District of Virginia, 1972); Finish Altoona's Interstate Right v. Volpe, 5 ERC 1205 (U.S. District Court for the Northern District of Georgia, 1973); Citizens Environmental Council v. Volpe, 5 ERC 1989 (U.S. Court of Appeals for the Tenth Circuit, 1973); Movement Against Destruction v. Volpe, 5 ERC 1625 (U.S. District Court for the District of Maryland, 1973), and Life of the Land v. Brinegar, 5 ERC 1780 (U.S. Court of Appeals for the Ninth Circuit, 1973).

119. Iowa Citizens v. Volpe, see Note 118, at 1759. This view was upheld by the Eighth Circuit Court of Appeals upon appeal (6 ERC 1088). However, there was a vigorous dissent by Judge Lay who argued that allowing the project proponent (the state highway agency) to prepare a draft statement would create a danger that statements for such projects would be self-serving. This dissent fails to recognize, however, that the federal agency involved may have the same institutional biases in favor of the project as the state agency. Therefore, requiring preparation of the draft as well as final statement by the federal agency may be no guarantee that the statement will not be self-serving.

120. See Note 118.

121. *Id.,* at 1784.

122. *Id.,* at 1784–1785.

123. See Note 5, Section 1500.7(c).

124. *Environmental Quality, the fourth annual report of the Council on Environmental Quality,* September, 1973, at 246.

125. Johns Hopkins University Press, Baltimore, Maryland, 1973, Page 290.

126. 5 ERC 1418 (1973).

127. *Id.,* at 1424.

128. See Note 5, Section 1500.2(b).

129. *Id.,* Section 1500.11(b).

130. *Id.*

131. 3 ERC 1995 (1972) at 2001.

132. 4 ERC 1329 (1972).

133. *Id.,* at 1333.

134. See Note 49.

135. See Note 76.

136. 5 ERC 1153 (1973).

137. *Id.,* at 1154.

138. 6 ERC 1525 (1974).

139. See Note 54.

140. 4 ERC 1579 (1972).

141. 5 ERC 1251 (1973).

142. See Note 7, at 1792.

143. *Id.*, at 1783.

144. See Note 82.

145. *Id.*, at 1728.

146. *Id.*

147. 4 ERC 2039 (U.S. Court of Appeals for the Fourth Circuit, 1973).

148. See Note 82.

149. 4 ERC 2039, clarified at 6 ERC 1063.

150. See Note 82 at 1924.

151. *Id.*

152. *Id.*

153. 5 ERC 1790 at 1800 (1973).

154. *Id.*, at 1801.

155. Save our Ten Acres v. Kreger, 4 ERC 1941 (1973); and Hiram Clarke Civic Club, Inc., v. Lynn, 5 ERC 1177 (1973).

156. 6 ERC 1513 (1974).

157. *Id.*, at 1523.

158. *Id.*, at 1524.

159. *Id.* For example, in Committee for Nuclear Responsibility v. Seaborg, 3 ERC 1126 at 1127, the District of Columbia Court of Appeals stated: ". . . it is well settled that repeal by implication is disfavored, and the doctrine applies with full vigor when, as here, the subsequent legislation is an appropriations measure. . . . There is, of course, nothing inconsistent with adoption of appropriation and authorization measures on the *pro tanto* assumption of validity while leaving any claim of invalidity to be determined by the courts."

160. See Note 79, at 1555.

161. *Id.*, at 1564.

162. 6 ERC 1001 at 1005 (1973).

163. Jicarilla Apache Tribe v. Morton, 4 ERC 1933 at 1936 (1973); EDF v. Armstrong, 6 ERC 1068 at 1074 (1973).

164. Mattson, Foster A. and Eugene M. Wilson, NEPA: Legal Interpretations and Suggested Direction, Traffic Q., January 1974, 119 at 135.

165. 4 ERC 1152 (1972).

166. *Id.*, at 1156–57.

167. 5 ERC 1830 (1973).

168. 6 ERC 1065 (1973).

169. *Id.*, at 1067.

170. 6 ERC 1094 (1973).

171. 7 ERC 1957.

172. *Id.*, at 1963.

173. 5 ERC 1217 (U.S. District Court for the District of Connecticut, 1972).

174. *Id.*, at 1220.
175. *Id.*
176. See Note 14.
178. *Id.*, at 1415.
177. See Note 170 at 1096.

Demographers who know enough to forecast migration also know better.

PETER A. MORRISON
(1969)

Theoretical Issues in the Design of Population Mobility Models

What really matters is not whether . . . forecasts . . . are "right" or "wrong" but rather that they focus concern where it should be focused.

OTIS DUDLEY DUNCAN
(1969)

Social Forecasting—The State of the Art

THREE
Demographic Perspectives on Impact Assessment

THOMAS M. DIETZ

Demography is the study of human populations. As a science it focuses on the empirical, mathematical, and statistical analysis of birth, death, and migration processes and their effects on population size, structure, composition, and distribution, and on the causes and consequences of changes in these variables. Changes in population size, composition, and distribution represent significant social impacts in themselves and may lead to a wide variety of changes in other components of the social system. This chapter is a very general attempt to suggest approaches for the consideration of demographic change in the impact assessment process and to outline some results of demographic research that may be of use to the social impact analyst.

At local and regional levels projected growth often plays a crucial role in causing environmental change. A quick perusal of project proposals reveals that a significant part of the projected benefits used to justify the action result from meeting the demands of future population growth. The anticipated demand is in part the result of demographic projections for the areas to be serviced, so the ultimate rationale for many projects is underpinned by demographic analyses. As noted in the second and fourth sections that follow, such analyses often rest on assumptions not made explicit in the project analysis, and they may take on the character of self-fulfilling prophecies that can short-circuit the policy formulation process.

Population changes at the local level may follow as direct and indirect consequences of a given project or policy and will in turn influence other aspects of the overall socioeconomic system. The construction of a limited access highway has obvious influences on air quality, vegetation, and landform in a given area. Such effects are routinely discussed in EISs. But a highway also influences the desirability of various residential areas by altering their accessibility. This may lead to changes in local population size, density, and composition, changes that may in turn alter local commercial patterns. Such impacts are all too often ignored in impact statements. This chapter is concerned with providing the writers and reviewers of impact statements with information that will allow them to move beyond the uncritical use of population projections to identify and assess the impacts of a given project or policy on population size, density, and composition.

An impact identification checklist is presented in the second section. This outline, which focuses attention on those aspects of a project that may lead to changes in population, can serve as a first step in the assessment process. As a step beyond simple identification, this section also examines various qualitative aspects of impact assessment.

The third section is a brief and general introduction to sources of demographic data. Acquiring useful information for impact reviews is never an easy task and will always be dependent on local sources. The discussion here serves as an introduction to the most basic data resources and also suggests some less obvious sources.

The fourth section provides a brief summary of commonly used techniques of population projection and estimation. It provides information on the weaknesses and assumptions of various techniques and should be useful in examining project proposals and in the development and review of impact statements.

The fifth section examines three general approaches to quantitative impact assessment: simulation modeling, regression analysis, and Delphi surveys. None of these methods is limited to use with demographic variables but may be applied as readily to other social factors and to biological and physical variables. Unfortunately, none of these techniques has been extensively applied to the impact review process, so this last section must be viewed in part as a suggestion for further research.

Throughout this chapter the discussion focuses on population movement. Of the three basic demographic processes (births, deaths, and movement), most projects or policies will have significant influences only on changes in residence. Unfortunately, migration is probably the least understood of all three processes and, for the most part, demographers have been interested in population movements across greater distances than are typically relevant for impact assessment. As a result there is less theoretical and empirical literature that can be cited here for guidance. However, interest in short-distance migration is increasing and, hopefully, it will be possible in a few years to utilize a larger body of background research in assessing demographic impacts.

Throughout this chapter it is necessary to employ a variety of terms whose precise definition is dependent on the project or policy analysis. Thus project area, area of relevance, and affected area can only be precisely specified in relation to local administrative boundaries, data sources, and the specific nature of the project under consideration. Similarly, a definitional problem arises with regard to mobility and migration. As Bogue[1] (p. 752) notes:

Residential mobility is defined as any change of usual residence that involves movement from one structure (house, apartment, hotel, barracks, dormitory, etc.) to another. Demographers classify this mobility into two classes:

1. *Local movement:* change of residence within the same community,
2. *Migration:* change of residence involving movement between communities.

The difference between local movement and migration obviously lies in the definition of "community". In much research on population movement the definition of community is highly dependent on the available data set, thus migration may alternatively be designated as a move across municipal, county, or state boundaries. As is briefly noted subsequently, the determinants of local movement and those of migration are somewhat different. In impact assessment it will sometimes be clear whether long- or short-distance moves are of importance; a residential housing development will usually draw only from within a fairly short radius, whereas a major economic addition to the community, perhaps requiring a highly specialized work force, may draw in migrants from thousands of miles away. But within a recreational second-home subdivision (or a primary-home subdivision located in a particularly scenic area) some owners may be local residents, others may be from a broader surrounding area, and still others may maintain a permanent residence hundreds of miles away. The distinction between local movers and migrants is arbitrary. These problems cannot be resolved for the general case. Throughout the chapter mobility is used to refer to movement across some boundary relevant to the project area, and local mobility or local movement refers to moves within the boundaries of the area of relevance. But since the spatial boundaries involved cannot be generalized, the use of the terms is somewhat arbitrary.

IMPACT IDENTIFICATION AND THE QUALITATIVE APPROACH TO ASSESSMENT

Impact assessment and review is normally carried out under substantial temporal and fiscal restraints. These constraints frequently make it impossible to apply techniques for quantitative impact assessment discussed elsewhere in the chapter. The goal of this chapter, and of this book, is to make broadly available practical approaches to the review of social impacts. Since quantitative techniques cannot always be employed, the present section is an attempt to deal with the problems of identification and display of demographic impacts at a level that should be of some utility for all projects. Much of what follows is simply a systematic approach to the use of available data, tempered with common sense; even with a limited budget and time horizon such an approach may substantially improve the quality of an impact review.

Predevelopment Period

The first stage in any impact assessment should be a presentation of the current situation in the area of relevance. Basic figures on population size are usually included in impact statements, but their use is frequently inadequate in two regards. First, they only include aggregate measures of population size. However, the characteristics of a population with regard to any of a number of variables are important in developing an understanding of local conditions. Given the amount of detail available from the U.S. Census and other sources, an impact statement should, wherever possible, include a breakdown of the population by age, race, and socioeconomic status or income. Population density and distribution should likewise be presented on a reasonably fine scale. This sort of data display gives the reader a much clearer picture of the present state of affairs than do simple population size figures. A population of 50,000 that is 80 percent white and has a median income of $10,000 and a median age of 35 is far different than a similar-sized population composed of 20 percent whites, 20 percent blacks, and 60 percent Spanish-speaking persons with a median income of $5000 and a median age of 25. Even far more subtle differences in population composition may carry a great deal of relevant information.

A second important aspect of the presentation of the current situation is the use of adequate comparative data. Most readers of an impact statement are not likely to be familiar with demographic measurements so that the data for the project area will in itself be of relatively little value. This problem may be remedied by the use of comparisons. City A may be compared with a similar city B and with the county, the state, and the nation in which it is located. This permits the reader to develop a feel for the demographic situation and provides a better background for understanding anticipated changes. Additionally, time-series data for the project area may add perspective. Given a 30-year record of age, racial, and economic composition; population size; and distribution, the dynamics of demographic change become more evident. In such time-series displays, the analysis should become increasingly fine-grained as it approaches the present time period, so that very recent trends can be discerned and given due attention.

It will often be the case that for either critical populations (e.g., those directly affected by a proposed project) or for certain critical points in time (particularly for the recent past and present in projects being assessed a substantial time period after a census), data will not be available. It is in this situation that the estimation techniques discussed in the fourth section are useful. The results of applying such methods should be clearly labeled as estimates rather than simply presented as actual counts. The use of estimates in an impact report should be accompanied by a brief discussion of the technique(s) employed and the assumptions made. Whenever possible, several alternate methods of estimation should be employed, their results presented, and differences among them discussed.

The "No-Project" Option

The no-project option is always problematic in social impact assessment. Social systems have complex internal dynamics, and many techniques are not sufficiently sensitive to detect differences caused by the presence or absence of a single project or policy. Further, for many demographic variables the separation of causes from effects is very difficult or impossible. Water resources developments, for example, have usually been planned as a necessary response to population growth. But as Hollis and McEvoy[2] point out, it is equally reasonable to consider regional population growth as an effect induced by the availability of water in an otherwise arid area. Similarly, it is traditional to look on residential developments as a response to demand for housing by a given population. But one may also consider such developments as largely external, speculative investments that may induce the residentially mobile to settle in the project area. The most reasonable approach seems to be one that acknowledges the multicasual aspects of social systems recognizing that feedback loops are complex and powerful and that separating causes from effects is a difficult task.

Impact Identification

How can the analyst attempt to separate the influence of the project from the overall prospects for the future? Clearly, no existing techniques of assessment allow the easy development of clear-cut with-project and without-project alternative projections. But as Duncan[3] points out, the goal of forecasting is not so much estimation as identification. This is as true of social impact assessment as of any other attempt to foresee the future. The current state of the art allows the investigator to make only exploratory estimates of the quantitative consequences of a project. The development of an awareness of social impacts is crucial. A list of sensitive variables, possible consequences, and critical subsystems associated with a given project represents a substantial step forward. It provides the decision maker with a new information set, one that can be integrated with the harder statements of the natural scientist. It alerts those concerned with the project to sensitive areas that bear careful monitoring. Although not a final solution simple identification represents a substantial improvement over ignoring social dimensions altogether.

This perspective, which focuses on the identification of potential impacts (with quantitative and semiquantitative estimations employed where possible) allows the analyst to deal with the project/no project problem. Two discreet estimates of effects are not possible. But present trends can be examined, the variables which are underlying causes of observed migration patterns may be identified, and the effects of migration can be distinguished from those of natural increase so that the potential relative impact of migration may be made more clear. This overall picture of the preproject state allows the analyst to develop a perspective on what the future will be like if present trends continue. It is then possible to turn to the characteristics of the project at hand. Using an elaboration of the approach suggested below, the effects of the project on migration can be identified and described. These presumed effects of the project may then be compared with existing trends. The project may tend to accelerate or to decelerate current dynamics or have negligible effect.

From such a perspective it is possible to develop an approach for elucidating the likely effects of a given project on migration. A number of treatments of

impact assessment, faced with a similar problem, have employed either matrices or checklists (Examples may be found in Chapters 4, 5, and 6.) A
preliminary checklist for demographic impacts is presented in Table 1. Application of this checklist to a specific project would require considerable "fleshing
out" of the format.

The distinctions between categories are purposefully somewhat arbitrary,
since the goal of the checklist is not taxonomic but rather to insure that few if
any potential sources of demographic change are ignored. It is better that a
given impact fall under multiple categories than for it to be overlooked.

CONSTRUCTION PHASE EFFECTS

The first category of impacts are those related to construction. If these effects
are substantial, it should be possible to obtain fairly firm estimates of the
number of persons to be displaced and the required amount of labor for the

Table 1   Checklist for Demographic Impact Assessment

I Construction Phase Effects

   1. Relocation
   2. Direct effects of construction (influx of workers)
   3. Indirect Effects of Construction (economic growth due to worker salaries and
       the purchase of goods and services, temporary changes in local amenities, traffic
       patterns, etc.)

II Changes in carrying capacity

   4. Physical (air, water, etc.)
   5. Formal (zoning ordinances, land use plans, etc.)

III Economic and employment effects

   6. Direct (persons employed from within and without the local area)
   7. Indirect (new employment created by economic growth effects)

IV Housing and site characteristics

   8. Housing availability, quality, and cost
   9. Trip times and costs and traffic flow patterns
  10. Aesthetic and health considerations
  11. Sociocultural factors
  12. Area characteristics (schools, shopping facilities, etc.)

---

project. When considering displaced persons it is critically important to examine the exact composition of the relevant population and the effects displacement may have on them.[4]

Estimates of the requisite labor force for construction can usually be obtained directly from the project plans or from discussion with project engineers or contractors. Given some information on the number of workers and the job skills required over a time period, it is then necessary to determine whether labor will be drawn from a local pool of under- and unemployed, whether some workers will commute from other areas, or whether some in-migration of labor may be expected. This last situation should be given due consideration; the influx for 2 years of 200 construction workers to a city with a normal population of 2000 represents a very substantial impact.

In the case of sizable projects the construction phase activities may induce substantial secondary impacts. Increased local employment and the local purchase of goods and services may substantially alter the economy of the project area. If these effects are temporary, it is important to consider not only permanent but also transitory changes in local population size and composition.

CHANGES IN CARRYING CAPACITY

It can be argued that influences such as increased water supply and upzoning should be treated as responses to population pressure. Arguments relating to community growth-control measures often center around limiting the local carrying capacity in some fashion. These issues are still in flux and cannot be effectively reviewed here. However, the concept of a population carrying capacity is a relevant one for the impact assessor. Various projects and policy decisions must minimally be seen as accomodating growth, and the assessor needs to consider this fact in examining them.

For the purposes of this chapter, a distinction has been made between changes in physical carrying capacity and changes in formal carrying capacity. The former refers to the development of facilities to meet anticipated population demands such as the enlargement of wastewater treatment facilities and utility grids. The latter represents policy decisions that allow alteration in growth patterns including zoning, land use ordinances and ambient air-quality standards. The distinction is of heuristic value only; it should be clear that plans for a water treatment plant must consider legal requirements on effluent discharge as well as the size of the population to be serviced. Similarly, the enactment of stricter regulations on ambient air quality in a given airshed may be met with either more effective control technologies or with a smaller ultimate population, or by a mix of both strategies.

Water projects are probably the most common source of change in physical carrying capacity. A developer may initially plan to build 50 dwelling units but provide water and sewage capacity adequate for 100 units. Similarly, municipalities and states often design water facilities to meet substantial amounts of projected growth with little analysis of the causes or desirability of the growth. It seems more reasonable to treat the planning of water projects whose capacities substantially exceed present needs as a conscious decision to opt for the pattern of growth implied. This pattern can then be compared with other plans and policies. Given a present population of size X, proposed water plans may call for a capacity adequate to handle a population of size $X + Y$. What will happen to the air quality in the area if Y individuals are added to the population, given reasonable assumptions about control technology and auto usage? Can current and projected parks, schools, and roads handle a population of $X + Y$? In an area with adequate planning it should be possible to examine plans to change one element of physical carrying capacity by comparison with the constraints imposed by other limits.

In considering a project's alteration of physical carrying capacity, it is also wise to consider the cost of error due to inadequate population projection. A park may be planned to sustain intensive use over the next 25 years. If the anticipated growth does not occur, it may have been more satisfactory to have employed a design focused on more extensive use by a smaller population. A wastewater treatment plant may be highly effective at a given level of population; at half or twice that level it may be grossly inefficient. Population projections are not perfect, as is noted in the following sections, and their use in planning should give due consideration to the costs of errors.

Formal limits on carrying capacity refer to changes in land use plans, zoning restrictions, and other legal or administrative constraints on growth. Some changes may facilitate growth by allowing higher densities and more intensive use, others may act to sharply curb existing growth trends by placing upper bounds on population size or density. Changes in such factors are, of course, intimately related to land use analysis and must be considered in the context of land use planning (see Chapter 3). As with changes in physical carrying capacity, assessing the impacts of such formal alterations in policy should attempt to account for both direct and indirect effects. Changing zoning and land use plans usually affects property values, which in turn may alter tax rates, making the land either more or less expensive for a given use. Higher tax rates may force owners to sell, generating a turnover in local population. Area A may be downzoned from X to Y units per acre. This may substantially increase land values, prices, and taxes, inducing some present owners to sell for an immediate profit and/or to avoid a heavy tax burden. Some prospective buyers may be deterred by the higher costs, others may find the lower density appealing. Surrounding areas will be similarly affected as land values shift in response to the change in overall land use mix, and assessment under such circumstances is complex. The impacts of zoning and land use plans on land values and tax structures should be considered. These changes can then be compared to the economic characteristics of the present population of the area, and some estimate can be made of changes in population size, structure, and distribution that may follow. Here again, the compatability of the specific change with overall plans and trends must be given due consideration.

ECONOMIC AND EMPLOYMENT EFFECTS

Economic and employment effects are frequently considered in impact assessments. The basic approach employed is to first consider the direct employment effects of a project. The number and skills of workers required may then be compared to the local pool of under- and unemployed. This should allow some estimate of the number of workers who will be hired locally and the number who may be expected to migrate to the area. The increased income from new jobs and from goods and services purchased locally may produce secondary increases in employment. Again, the anticipated employment opportunities (which may be estimated by multiplier analysis, see Chapter 5) must be compared with the current pool of unemployed and then some estimate of induced in-migration developed.

HOUSING AND SITE CHARACTERISTICS

The housing and site characteristics category covers a wide range of variables that may be altered by a project and that may in turn affect population size, distribution, or composition. Economic factors are certainly of critical importance to those moving a substantial distance, but local-level movements tend to be strongly influenced by site characteristics. Thus changes in site characteristics are critical influences in local mobility.

An obviously important facet of site desirability is the character of the dwelling unit. The present scheme lumps together the interrelated elements of availability, cost, and quality. All three factors must be given due consideration in assessing project impacts. Clearly, a development of $50,000 single family dwelling units will be inhabited by a far different population than a group of $15,000 condominiums. Further, dwelling types and costs taken in combination with interest rates and income levels will in large part determine the build-out rate for a development. Recreational second-home purchases are likely to drop off sharply in times of economic stress, whereas the demand for housing located within easy access of public transportation systems is likely to rise, as will demand for trailers and other moderately priced housing. Again, adequate impact assessment must consider the costs of inaccurate projection. A half-filled residential subdivision represents a far different and perhaps more severe impact than a fully occupied one. Considerations of market factors, cost, and quality should be used to develop estimates both of the number of new occupants that may realistically be expected and also of the characteristics of those individuals.

The location of a given site, in relation to the region of which it is a part, is important in examining demographic impacts. Access to freeways, for example, has traditionally been an important site characteristic. This is likely to continue to be true, but with rising fuel costs, access to existing or proposed public transportation networks should be given increased weight. Comparisons of the relative desirability of two sites should continue to consider trip time to places of employment, shopping areas, and the like. Trip costs estimates, although correlated, are likely to become important independently and should be given due consideration.

Aesthetic and health amenities may be enhanced or diminished by a given project. Obvious examples are readily available. Construction of freeways or airports may increase noise and pollution levels of nearby dwellings, leading to substantial out-migration and the lessening of property values. Development or improvement of park facilities and open-space areas may greatly enhance the desirability of adjacent areas, leading to higher occupancy rates and higher housing costs. It is often the case that aesthetic and health values are in conflict with other site characteristics, presenting a problem for the analyst. For example, the aforementioned freeway, although increasing noise and pollution levels, may substantially decrease trip time from the area in question to areas of employment, recreation, and so on. To further complicate the situation different subgroups within the population are likely to attach different relative weights to different components of desirability. Thus the affluent are likely to place a high value on the aesthetic, whereas the less affluent will place it on access to transportation systems. The project analyst, as is so often the case, must use judgment in balancing aesthetic and health factors against other site characteristics.

Sociocultural factors refer to the composition and dynamics of the community in the area of relevance. Communities may differ with respect to the degree of integration and communication among members and with regard to their relative heterogeneity. The construction of an apartment dwelling in a single family dwelling unit area may serve to increase the heterogeneity of the local population, but it may also detract from community integration. Some current residents may leave because of the loss of integration and the presence of "strangers," other potential immigrants may be attracted by the diversity of the community. The development of pedestrian shopping areas may increase contact among local residents and thus serve to increase community solidarity. Neither diversity nor solidarity are good or bad per se, but they are affected by various types of projects and may in turn effect the desirability of a site. Thus they should be given consideration in impact assessment.

Characteristics of an area such as access to and quality of schools, access to commonly used shopping facilities and entertainment centers, and the overall levels of services and amenities have a substantial influence on the perceived desirability of a site. Projects and policies that affect such area characteristics as the construction of new schools or the improvement of police and fire protection alter the desirability of a site and may attract potential immigrants. Similarly, deterioration of such services may lower desirability and lead to positive feedback situations in which those most able to support such services will move elsewhere, leaving the area to those who have little political or financial resources with which to improve the characteristics of the area (see also the fifth section).

There are no easy methods for the identification of demographic impacts. The process is one of informed judgment by the analyst. Tools such as the checklist presented here may be useful in organizing the analyst's task and reducing the risk of ignoring critical factors, but the heart of this portion of the impact assessment process remains the presentation of whatever information and estimates exist, along with an attempt to identify areas of uncertainty.

SOURCES OF INFORMATION

Any attempt to utilize demographic information in impact assessment must begin with the collection of such information. The sources available to the investigator are highly diverse, ranging from original field surveys to published census data. It would be impossible to cover all approaches to data collection here. In any event the sources available vary greatly from area to area, and each project will involve slightly different needs and temporal and fiscal restrictions. This section of the chapter is meant to serve as an introduction to some of the more commonly available sources and should help get the investigator started. As always, imagination and perseverance are the keys to success.

U.S. Census Data

Within the United States consideration of population-related problems is greatly facilitated by the accessibility, abundance, and quality of the efforts of the Bureau of the Census of the U.S. Department of Commerce. An examination of published census reports should always be the first step in the data collection process. A brief outline of the information available in published form from the 1970 Census of Population and Housing is presented in Table 2. These reports contain a wealth of information and are, in many cases, a principle source of data for any later work.

Before turning to noncensus data sources, it should be emphasized that the published materials described in Table 2 are not the only useful information

Table 2   1970 Population Census Reports

Series PC(1)-A

Volume I. Characteristics of the Population.   This volume consists of 58 "parts"—number 1 for the United States, numbers 2 through 52 for the 50 states and the District of Columbia in alphabetical order, and numbers 53 through 58 for Puerto Rico, Guam, Virgin Islands, American Samoa, Canal Zone, and Trust Territory of the Pacific, respectively. Each part, which is a separate clothbound book, contains four chapters designated as A, B, C, and D. Each chapter (for each of the 58 areas) is first issued as an individual paperbound report in four series designated as PC(1)-A, B, C, and D, respectively. The 58 PC(1)-A reports are specially assembled and issued in a clothbound book, designated as Part A.

Number of Inhabitants.   Final official population counts are presented for states, counties by urban and rural residence, standard metropolitan statistical areas (SMSAs), urbanized areas, county subdivisions, all incorporated places, and unincorporated places of 1000 inhabitants or more.

Series PC(1)-B

General Population Characteristics.   Statistics on age, sex, race, marital status, and relationship to head of household is presented for states, counties by urban and rural residence, SMSAs, urbanized areas, county subdivisions, and places of 1000 inhabitants or more.

Series PC(1)-C

General Social and Economic Characteristics.   Statistics are presented on nativity and parentage, state or country of birth, Spanish origin, mother tongue, residence 5 years ago, year moved into present house, school enrollment (public or private), years of school completed, vocational training, number of children ever born, family composition, disability, veteran status, place of work, means of transportation to work, occupation group, industry group, class of worker, and income (by type) in 1969 of families and individuals. Each subject is shown for some or all the following areas: states, counties (by urban, rural-nonfarm, and rural-farm residence), SMSAs, urbanized areas, and places of 2500 inhabitants or more.

Series PC(1)-D

Detailed Characteristics.   These reports cover most subjects shown in Series PC(1)-C, presenting the data in considerable detail and cross-classified by age, race, and other characteristics. Each subject is shown for some or all the following areas: states (by urban, rural-nonfarm, and rural-farm residence), SMSAs and large cities.

Series PC(2)

Volume II. Subject Reports.   Each report in this volume concentrates on a particular subject. Detailed information and cross-relationships are generally provided on a

Table 2   (Continued)

national and regional level; in some reports data for states or SMSAs is also shown. Among the characteristics to be covered are national origin and race, fertility families, marital status, migration, education, unemployment, occupation, industry, and income.

Series HC(1)-A

Volume I. Characteristics for States, Cities, and Counties.   This volume consists of separate reports for the United States, each of the 50 states, the District of Columbia, Puerto Rico, Guam, Virgin Islands, American Samoa, Canal Zone, and the Trust Territory of the Pacific. For each of these 58 areas, the data is first issued in two separate paperbound chapters, designated as A and B. The two chapters are then assembled and issued in a hardcover "part." These parts are mostly issued in the Fall of 1971. (For the outlaying areas other than Puerto Rico, all the housing data is included in chapter A.)

General Characteristics for States, Cities, and Counties.   Statistics on kitchen facilities, plumbing facilities, number of rooms, persons per room, units in structure, mobile home, telephone, value, contract rent, and vacancy status are presented for states (by urban and rural residence), SMSAs, urbanized areas, places of 1000 inhabitants or more, and counties.

Series HC(1)-B

Detailed Characteristics for States, Cities, and Counties.   Statistics are presented on a more detailed basis for the subjects included in the Series HC(1)-A reports as well as on such additional subjects as year moved into unit, year structure built, basement, heating equipment, fuel, air conditioning, water and sewage, appliances, gross rent, and ownership of second home. Each subject is shown for some or all the following areas: states (by urban, rural-nonfarm, and rural-farm residence), SMSAs, urbanized areas, places of 2500 inhabitants or more, and counties.

Series HC(2)

Volume II. Metropolitan Housing Characteristics.   These reports cover most 1970 census housing subjects in considerable detail and cross-classification. There is one report for each SMSA, presenting data for the SMSA and its component large cities, as well as a national summary report.

Series HC(3)

Volume III. Block Statistics.   One report is issued for each urbanized area showing data for individual blocks on selected housing and population subjects. The subjects also include reports for the communities outside urbanized areas that have contracted with the Census Bureau to provide block statistics from the 1970 Census.

Series HC(4)

Volume IV. Components of Inventory Change.   This volume contains data on the disposition of the 1960 inventory and the source of the 1970 inventory, such as new

Table 2 (Continued)

construction, conversion, mergers, demolitions, and other additions and losses. Cross-tabulations of 1970 and 1960 characteristics for units that have not changed and characteristics of the present and previous residence of recent movers are also provided. Statistics are shown for 15 selected SMSAs and for the United States.

Series HC(5)

Volume V. Residential Finance. This volume presents data regarding the financing of privately owned nonfarm residential properties. Statistics are shown on amount of outstanding debt, manner of acquisition of property, homeowner expenses, and other owner, property, and mortgage characteristics for the United States and region.

Series HC(6)

Volume VI. Estimates of "Substandard" Housing. This volume presents data on "substandard" housing units for counties and cities, based on the number of units lacking plumbing facilities combined with estimates of units with all plumbing facilities but in "dilapidated" condition.

1970 Population Housing Census Joint Report

Series PHC(1)

Census Tract Reports. This series contains one report for each SMSA, showing data for most of the population and housing subjects included in the 1970 Census.

From U.S. Bureau of the Census[5]

available from the bureau. Population and housing census data are available in a variety of forms, including microfilm and computer tape (see *1970 Census User's Guide*).[5] The Census Bureau also publishes a series of basic projections,[6] methodological studies,[7] and a variety of materials that serve as useful introduction to census data (see *The 1970 Census And You, A General Introduction to Census Data*[8]; *Census Data For Community Action*,[9]). If adequate funds exist, it is possible to contract with the bureau (or sometimes with private firms or state agencies) for special compilations of census data to meet specific user needs. An examination of published census data should be preceded by a careful perusal of the *Census User's Guide* Part I and a review of available census publications.

It will often be the case that available census data, although necessary, will not be sufficient for impact assessment. Differing administrative boundaries, the small size of affected areas, and the decennial sampling frame of the census will often make it necessary to turn to other sources for both data and projections.

An exhaustive list of such sources is not possible; public and private institutions are constantly finding needs for population information, and each time data are collected, they are for a slightly different set of purposes and subjected to a slightly different framework of analysis. The remainder of this discussion should be taken as a starting point that may be adapted to the local data environment.

State Agencies

State agencies are extremely useful sources of demographic information. In most states a single office or agency is designated as the lead agency for population information. Usually, this agency will publish periodic estimates and projections for areas of administrative relevance, coordinate and inventory demographic data collection and analysis efforts throughout the state, and monitor information available from federal agencies. Contacting these lead agencies is a logical next step after the examination of federal census data. They can provide information directly and suggest possible sources of further information useful for demographic impact assessment. For general information on possible state-level data sources, consult the U.S. Bureau of the Census, *Current Population Reports: Federal-State Cooperative Programs for Population Estimates Series P-26*[10]; *Current Population Reports, Special Censuses Series P-25*[11]; *Directory of Federal Statistics for Local Areas: A Guide to Sources*[12]; *Directory of Federal Statistics for States: A Guide to Sources,*[13]; *Directory of Federal Statistics, Non-Federal Statistics for State and Local Areas: A Guide to Sources.*[14]

There are several additional sources to be considered at the state level. Fiscal, commerce, and labor agencies are the logical source of employment and other economic statistics. Health agencies maintain birth, death, and marriage statistics that are critical to most estimation and projection techniques. Specialized agencies may have useful symptomatic data on utility hookups, motor vehicle registrations, number of tax returns, and so on. Other agencies may monitor special populations such as school-aged and preschool youth, the aged, migrant laborers, minorities, and the poor. Some of these subpopulations such as minorities, the poor and the aged are important when considering impacts on population composition. Other data, such as that on school-aged and preschool youth, are useful both as inputs to estimations and projection techniques discussed in the fourth section and as measures of population composition.

Other Sources

County, regional, and municipal agencies may find both federal and state data sources inadequate for their administrative needs. In such cases the agency with overall planning authority or with specific data requirements may conduct special studies to develop the necessary data base. At the local level the planning agency or its equivalent is the logical starting place in a search for fine-grain data. Other possible sources include any agency which involves either planning functions or which is expected to actively seek out its clientele. Thus school boards usually have good information regarding the present and future school-aged population, and health agencies are aware of the size and characteristics of the medically indigent population.

The private and semipublic sectors may also provide data. Public utilities are frequently utilized sources of symptomatic data for estimation techniques, zoning boards can provide data to develop maximum density models, and agricultural agencies may have aerial photographs useful for some estimation techniques. Chambers of commerce and major financial institutions maintain information on present and anticipated economic activity, and these and other commercial institutions often have useful data bases resulting from their marketing research. Planning, fire, and police departments may be sources of up-to-date maps.

Several notes of caution should be heeded when attempting to develop an information base. First, the investigator must take care to ascertain the original source of the data and the method employed in collection, analysis, estimation, or projection. It is not uncommon for the same set of projections to be used by a number of institutions, each time appearing in a slightly different guise. It is often the case that such uses do not provide information on the methodology originally employed. This may render the secondary sources essentially useless for impact assessment purposes. At the very least it increases potential error substantially. A move away from "magic numbers taken as givens" such as long-range (50 years or more) projections requires some understanding of and concern with the methodology of quantitative demography. It is worth a good deal of extra effort to learn the origin and validity of a particular figure. Beyond that, data that are obviously politically sensitive must be viewed with caution. An agency may choose definitions and data collection techniques that bias statistics so as to increase budget allocations or make programs look successful. The researcher must view such data with caution and compare alternate sources and measures wherever possible. Finally, before attempting to collect data from a half-dozen different sources, the analyst should decide which specific data sets would be ideal for the task as hand and which would be minimally adequate. If specific strategies of data analysis and interpretation are not used to define the data sets required, a great deal of time can be wasted collecting useless information. Some minimal data needs were discussed in the second section. The fourth and fifth sections examine more quantitative techniques and their data requirements.

POPULATION ESTIMATION AND PROJECTION TECHNIQUES

The use of demographic information in impact assessment involves a logical sequence of activity. First, the best data available on the population of relevance is gathered. These data are used to produce a description of current conditions, including the character of the population and an analysis of recent trends and their likely causes. Then projections of the likely future population of the area are developed, the causes of change between present and anticipated future are considered, and the effects of the project on thoes changes are considered.

This section deals with two aspects of the assessment sequence: the development of estimates of current population size and composition for points in time from the last actual enumeration to the present and the development of projections of future population based on traditional methodologies. For mastery of the techniques outlined here the reader should consult a handbook such as Morrison's *Demographic Information for Cities*,[15] his *Small Area Population Estimates for the City of St. Louis, 1960–1972, With a Method for Updating Them*,[16] Atchley's *Population Projections and Estimates for Local Areas*,[17] Pittenger's *Projecting State and Local Populations*[18] and Shryock, Siegel, and Associates' *The Materials and Methods of Demography*.[19] This chapter sketches in broad terms the battery of methods available and briefly considers the advantages, disadvantages, and underlying assumptions of each.

Direct Trend Extrapolation

The simplest method of estimation and projection is the direct extrapolation of known patterns of population change to some future point in time for which actual data is not available. The researcher first gathers available population counts for the area of relevance. Given a time series of data points:

$$P_{A,t}, P_{A,t+1}, P_{A,t+2}$$

where $P_{A,t+1}$ is the population of area A at time $t + 1$ and so on, an expression for the pattern of change in population can be developed. Thus it is possible to calculate the number of people added to or subtracted from the population each year. A slightly more sophisticated approach would be to calculate the percentage change per year. In the former case population growth past the last data point could be calculated and projected by simple addition; in the latter compound interest formulas could be applied. If the empirical time series is to be extended only to the present, the researcher is involved in estimation, that is, updating a previous census to the present. If future points are to be calculated, projection is involved, that is, trying to forecast what the population will be in the future. In either case the basic methodology is the same.

The underlying logic of this approach is that the population of the area in question can be expressed as a function of time and that, given the appropriate relationship between time and population, all other factors may be ignored. Although the two approaches just described represent simple linear and exponential growth patterns, a wide variety of other functional forms can be employed via the use of polynomial regression approaches and the addition of maximum population size constraints. But the essential logic remains unchanged. A population is estimated and projected without any consideration of the causal mechanisms underlying its changes. The age structure of the population and the various forces that may influence rates of migration cannot be readily incorporated into a direct-trend extrapolation model. The technique is easy to apply but has only very limited utility. It may be helpful in providing a very simple, comparative, "if this goes on" projection, but it cannot play any extensive role in impact assessment, since it ignores any factors causing or underlying change. Unfortunately, many EIRs and public works plans have employed only this simple projection technique and have given inadequate consideration to the causes and consequences of demographic change. Also, trend extrapolation ignores basic demographic information regarding age structure and vital rates of the population being considered and thus tends to be less accurate for both estimation and projection than techniques discussed below. It also is a method that utterly ignores uncertainty.

Prorating (Area Ratios)

The prorating or area-ratio approach to population estimation and projection may be seen as something of a middle ground between direct-trend extrapolation and more complex methods. With this method a time series of population data is required for the areas of relevance, A, and for a larger area, B, which includes A. Census counts, estimates, or projections are also required for area B for the points in time to be estimated for A. The time series is used to formulate a relationship between the population of area A and that of area B (most commonly given as the ratio of A to B). The estimated relationship is then applied to the given census data, estimates, or projections for area B to form estimates or projections of the population of area A.

This method is one of the most frequently used techniques for small-area population projections. It is computationally simple and has the advantage of at least partially utilizing the demographic information contained in the projections and estimates for the larger area, which are usually developed by more sophisticated methods. When projections or estimates are not available for an immediately larger area, say for a county in which the area of relevance is contained, it is possible to start with state-level data and prorate to the county first and then work from the county to the city or area of relevance. If several small areas are to be considered, all contained in a single larger area, a priori restrictions may be placed on peak population sizes or rates of growth for the smaller areas, thus allowing for saturation effects, zoning controls, and so on. Greenberg, Krueckenberg, and Mautner[20] have incorporated a number of options of this type into a computer program for small-area population projection.

As an example of the possible application of the prorating method, consider two hypothetical projects. The first will be the construction of a major reservoir in a rural agricultural area within 2-hours driving time of a major metropolitan area. The focus of concern here will be the effects of the reservoir on a small town that will be near the eventual shoreline. The second hypothetical project will be the construction of an overpass that will divert traffic away from the downtown sections of a small city in a major metropolitan region.

For the first example prorating approaches might be useful for estimating the current population of the town from existing estimates of the population of the surrounding county. A projection may also be developed, assuming that projections already exist for the county. These projections and estimates must be used with great care, for they assume that changes in the town are and will continue to be linked to that of the county in some simple fashion. In a rather homogeneous rural county this might be a useful assumption for comparative purposes, but this rationale should be stated explicitly in any presentation of estimates and projections.

In the case of the small city, population estimates and projections could similarly be developed by prorating county growth. If estimates and projections already exist or could be developed for the city as a whole, it might be useful to develop such data for smaller areas within the city that may be affected differently by the construction of the overpass. A simple prorating approach to projection would be of limited utility here, since growth is likely to shift to other areas as one area of a community becomes densely populated. An approach incorporating saturation effects, such as that of Greenberg, Krueckenberg, and Mautner, (noted previously) may allow a more sophisticated application of prorating in such situations.

As may be seen from the foregoing discussion, the principal problems with the prorating approach is that, like trend extrapolation, it makes only minimal use of any information available about the population changes in areas of relevance. A causal relationship is imputed to population change in the larger area and that in the smaller. The more elaborate extensions of prorating (such as that employed by Greenberg et al.) move toward consideration of various growth-rate limitations but cannot adequately deal with changes that may be presumed to flow from a typical project. Prorating is a simple but crudely empirical approach to quantitative estimation and projection. It does not disaggregate growth sufficiently to be useful for more than comparative purposes in impact assessment.

The Vital Rates and Composite Methods

The vital rates method and the similar composite method are techniques limited to the task of population estimation and thus are not directly useful for assessing the future effects of a project. They are among the most precise methods for developing a picture of the current population situation, and despite their relative computational complexity and substantial data requirements, they are frequently employed. For this reason they are reviewed here.

The vital rates method was developed by Bogue.[21,22] The required input data consists of crude birth- and death-rate estimates for the population under consideration and data on the number of births and deaths that actually occurred over the time period of the estimate. The birth and death rates may be estimated from state-level data with corrections applied for traditional differences between the state and local area. Actual counts of births and deaths may be obtained from local health records. Since $BR = B/POP$, where BR is the birth rate for a given period, B is the number of births occurring during that period, and POP is the size of the population during that period, it follows by simple algebra that $POP = B/BR$. We now have an expression for the population of the area to be explained in terms of two other quantities. Taking a figure from local health records for the number of births for the period to be estimated and dividing by an estimate of the local birth rate yields an estimate of the size of the local population. The use of accurate estimates of the local birth rate is, of course, critical. They may be developed by using state-level estimates after making adjustments based on historical records and information on expected socioeconomic composition for differences between the state and the local area. Death-rate estimates and registered deaths may be employed in a similar fashion to yield an additional population estimate that may be combined with the birth-rate estimate to yield an overall estimate.

There are several problems associated with the vital rates method. First, it is sensitive to registration errors. This is not a substantial problem when large aggregates are considered, but in fairly small areas it may introduce serious bias. A second problem is that it does not take account of the structure of the population. It is this defect that the more general composite method attempts to correct.

Composite Methods of Estimation

The composite method was developed by Bogue and Duncan[23] and has been modified to fit a wide variety of particular circumstances. It may be seen as a refinement of the vital rates method, which uses symptomatic data to estimate different components of the population. Obviously, the number of deaths is a sensitive indicator of the number of elderly persons in the population but is insensitive to the number of children. Similarly, school enrollments are linked to the number of school-age children, but are not related to the number of elderly persons. The composite method seeks to find readily available data sets that are sensitive to the size of various age, sex, and racial groups and to use these data to estimate the size of that subpopulation using the same computational scheme that was employed in the vital rates method. A typical approach (following Morrison[16]) would be to use

- Death data (age, sex, and race specific) to estimate the age 45+ population;
- Birth data to estimate the age 15–44 female population;
- Sex ratios and the estimate of the age 15–44 female population to estimate the 15–44 male population;
- School enrollment data (adjusted for underenrollment) to estimate the 5–14 population;
- Race-specific fertility data to estimate the population under 5.

Consider again the example of the small town near a dam site. State estimates of vital rates may be obtained and adjusted to better match the age and socioeconomic composition of the population to be estimated. County-level birth and death registration may be sorted by addresses to determine the number of births and deaths occurring in the town in the year for which the population is to be estimated (assuming such figures are not directly available for the town). Similarly, local and county school records may be examined to obtain the number of students enrolled from the town. Death rates for given age groups may be divided into the number of deaths occurring in that age group to obtain estimates of population size, particularly of the size of the elderly population, for which the measure is most sensitive. Birth data may be used to estimate the female population of reproductive age, sex and fertility ratios to derive estimates of the reproductive male and preschool populations, respectively. The schoolage populations may be estimated by dividing the number of students in the town by an enrollment-rate estimate that may be obtained from education departments. Since it is likely that a rural community has more elderly persons and fewer young adults than might otherwise be expected, extra indicators should be employed to supplement the estimates of these subpopulations. Military enlistments and draft records, marriage records and medicare records may be possible indicators, although the utility of each measure must be tested for points in time with known data before it is actually used in an estimate. A similar approach could be used for the small city of our previous example. Estimates of the population of the city as a whole and of relevant sections of the city could be generated.

There are an unlimited number of potential variations that the researcher may employ to fit particular circumstances. Any symptomatic variables for which local rates can be estimated and the number of "events" occurring locally can be determined are candidates for inclusion. Only the data base and the imagination of the investigator limit the use of the technique. As fine a level of compositional detail as desired may be generated, and estimates may be readily updated a segment at a time as new symptomatic data become available. The technique is not, of course, without error, and previous studies have shown that estimates at the state level may be off by 1–3 percent.[24] The major sources of inaccuracy are biases in local counts for symptomatic data and the possibility that the estimated rates employed in the technique may be inaccurate. These potential problems suggest some subjective understanding of local conditions be applied to the selection of indicators. In general, the composite technique is to be recommended when accurate and disaggregated estimates are required.

Multiple Regression Techniques

The multiple regression approach to population estimation and projection is a powerful tool that may be used directly or as an adjunct to another technique. It is extremely flexible with regard to its data requirements, can readily be modified to meet specific local situations, and can, if necessary, be tied into a rather sophisticated body of statistical literature. (See, e.g., Theil;[25] Draper and Smith.[26])

In a regression analytic approach time-series or cross-sectional data are used to generate a predictive equation for the value of the dependent variable based on the values for the independent variables. An example of such an equation is:

$$(2.1) \qquad dY = b_0 + b_1X_1 + b_2X_2 + b_3dX_3 + b_4X_4 + b_5X_5$$

Where dY = change in the population size
          X_1 = change in the number of utility hookups
          X_2 = change in the number of registered voters
          X_3 = change in total school enrollment
          X_4 = number of births
          X_5 = number of deaths

The available data are used to statistically estimate the values of the parameters (bs) in the equation. Then values of the independent (X) variables for the points in time to be estimated are entered into the formula to produce an estimate of the dependent variable (Y).

As an example, it might be useful to estimate recent population changes in neighborhoods of the aforementioned small city. The city might be divided into ten subareas corresponding to administrative boundaries of relevance to the project and its effects. Data for the independent and dependent variables in Equation 2.1 could be collected for each subarea for the year in which the last actual population census was conducted, or if more than one census had been conducted in the recent past, data for several time points for each area might be obtained. If the analyst is confident that the factors determining population change are constant from subsection to subsection and over time, this time series of cross-section data may be pooled to estimate the equation by appropriate techniques (see Theil[25]). If a recent time series of population-change data does not exist, it may be possible to estimate the parameters using only the cross-section data. Given these estimates, and equation such as Equation 2.2 may result:

$$dY = 25 + 2.6X_1 + 1.7X_2 + 2.5X_3 + 0.7X_4 - 0.6X_5 \qquad (2.2)$$

(the actual values used for parameters here are entirely hypothetical). Data for the independent variables for periods to be estimated can be collected for each subsection and plugged into the equation to produce estimates of population change.

A wide number of alternative approaches may be employed, roughly paralleling the other techniques available for estimation and projection. The share of larger-area population to be prorated to a smaller area may be considered as dependent on a variety of characteristics (or ratios between characteristics) of both areas, and a regression may be applied to produce variable ratios for the actual population prorating. A time variable can be included in a regression on population size or rate of change of population to provide an extension of direct-trend extrapolation. Separate regression equations may be generated for cohorts disaggregated by age, sex, and race, following the composite method. In a technique developed by Eugene Ericksen[27, 28] sample data and symptomatic information are combined in a regression formulation to produce population estimates. In an approach to be considered in more detail in the Fourth section, regression analysis can be used to produce migration estimates which can then be included in a component analysis. A wide variety of other variations of this powerful technique are also possible.

Housing Unit and Related Methods

The housing-unit method and other techniques employing the same logic are similar to the composite and vital rates methods in that they employ sympto-

matic data to develop population estimates. They differ, however, in that
instead of keying to events, such as births and deaths, which are related to both
a rate and the size of the population effected by that rate, they focus on more or
less direct indicators of carrying capacity utilized, such as the number of housing units or utility hookups. The basic approach is to first develop some estimate of the change in the number of housing units since the last actual count of
the population. This may be done on the basis of building permits, aerial
photographs, utility hookup figures, tax records, and so on. This estimate is
corrected to allow for unoccupied units. Then the number of units occupied is
multiplied by the presumed number of individuals per unit which produces an
estimate of the change in population since the last actual count. In cases where
data is available it is possible to disaggregate these calculations by both housing
type and occupancy rate and thus produce a more accurate estimate.

These problems with such techniques are: first, they are subject to errors in
the techniques used to estimate number of units occupied and the average
number of occupants per unit; second, they make disaggregation of population
characteristics difficult; and finally, they invoke no causal model of population
change. They are in common usuage and so have been mentioned briefly, but
except in unusual circumstances, where high-quality housing census data is
available, they are not to be recommended as part of the impact assessment
process. It should be noted, however, that recent research on the use of satellite
data and high-altitude photographs has shown great promise in population
estimation, and developments in this area may greatly enhance the accuracy
and thus the utility of methods based on such data (see, e.g., Lindgren[29]).

The Component Method

The component method of projection and estimation is a true demographic
approach. By breaking the causes of population change into component elements, it allows maximal use of all available demographic information. The
basic rationale of the approach may be expressed via Equation 2.3:

$$Y_{t+1} = Y_t + B_{t \to t+1} - D_{t \to t+1} + M_{t \to t+1} \qquad (2.3)$$

where Y_t is the population at time t
Y_{t+1} is the population at time $t + 1$
$B_{t \to t+1}$ is the number of births from time t to time $t + 1$
$D_{t \to t+1}$ is the number of deaths from time t to time $t + 1$
$M_{t \to t+1}$ is the net number of migrants from time t to time $t + 1$

Such a formula estimates the population at time $t + 1$ from the initial population and the number of births, deaths, and migrations that have occurred over
the interval t to $t + 1$.

In actual practice, of course, the application of the component method is far more complex than is indicated by Equation 2.3. First, for accuracy and compositional refinement, a system of equations such as Equations 2.4, 2.5, and 2.6 is actually applied (a number of equations between 2.5 and 2.6 are deleted for simplicity):

$$Y_{t+1,0\text{-}4} = Y_{t,0\text{-}4} + B_{t \to t+1} - D_{t+1,0\text{-}4} + M_{t \to t+1,0\text{-}4} - A_{t \to t+1,0\text{-}4} \qquad (2.4)$$

$$Y_{t+1,5\text{-}9} = Y_{t,5\text{-}9} - D_{t \to t+1,5\text{-}9} + M_{t \to t+1,5\text{-}9} - A_{t \to t+1,5\text{-}9} + A_{t \to t+1,0\text{-}4} \qquad (2.5)$$

$$Y_{t+1,80+} = Y_{t,80+} - D_{t \to t+1,80+} + M_{t \to t+1,80+} + A_{t \to t+1,75\text{-}79} \qquad (2.6)$$

where $Y_{t,0\text{-}4}$ is the population aged 0–4 at time t

$Y_{t,5\text{-}9}$ is the population aged 5–9 at time t etc.

$B_{t \to t+1}$ is the number of births from time t to time $t + 1$

$D_{t \to t+1,0\text{-}4}$ is the number of deaths of individuals aged 0–4 in the interval $t \to t + 1$, etc.

$M_{t \to t+1,0\text{-}4}$ is the net number of migrants in the 0–4 age group in the interval $t \to t + 1$, etc.

$A_{t \to t+1,0\text{-}4}$ is the number of individuals aging from 4 to 5 in the interval from t to $t + 1$

Here the population is broken into age groups (cohorts), and each group is treated separately. Additional disaggregation by race and sex are often employed. Breakdowns by other population characteristics are possible but less common.

With a system such as Equations 2.4, 2.5, and 2.6, it is necessary to apply a data set and to develop a series of conventions regarding the use of the equations. If the component method is being used for population estimations, actual birth and death figures may be derived from health registration materials. Migration may be estimated from any number of sources. The number of children enrolled in school in excess of what would be expected, given the initial resident population, most commonly serves as a migration indicator (see the previous section on estimation by the composite method). When the component technique is applied to the problem of population projection, it is necessary to develop some assumptions regarding future birth, death, and migration rates. In most cases, mortality and fertility figures for the specific age, race, and sex groups involved in the analysis are gathered from national statistics. These may be directly applied to the local model or may be adjusted to take into consideration other compositional aspects of the population.

As an example of the use of the component method, let us consider again the rural community near a dam site. Component techniques could first be applied to estimate changes in the community population since the last actual count. It would be useful to disaggregate by age, since age structure may be undergoing substantial change, and by sex, to improve the precision with which mortality rates may be applied to the population. Substantial ethnic diversity may warrant additional disaggregation by race. The initial size of each cohort is obtained from the most recent actual count and is aged and subjected to mortality and fertility using data from birth and death registrations. Migration estimates may be developed by the techniques discussed in the fifth section or from school enrollment records, as mentioned in the discussion of composite estimation.

The use of the component method for projection requires careful attention to assumptions. Aging, fertility, mortality, and migration are applied to the disaggregated initial population of the town (possibly obtained by component estimation, to project the population into the future.) Even for an elementary case the computational rules that must be followed for consistency are rather complex. In a greatly simplified approach one might begin by applying fertility rates (age and race specific, and possibly adjusted to allow for local trends) to the reproductive female population to arrive at the number of births during the interval. These births are added to the appropriate sex and race-specific age 0–4 cohorts. Then mortality rates are applied to each cohort, and the projected number of deaths are subtracted out. Migration presents a further problem, estimates of the number of net migrants can be developed from the techniques outlined in the fifth section or by trend extrapolation (with the effects of a hypothetical project translated into migration trends via the techniques suggested in the second section). A convention must be developed as to whether migrants should be added to a given cohort before or after mortality and fertility rates are applied to that cohort. Mortality, fertility, and migration are obviously continuous and simultaneous processes, but computational considerations require the simplification of these events as if all births occurred at one point in time, all deaths at another, and all migrations at yet another. Error is, of course, introduced by these assumptions, and the analyst should be careful to note the possible effects of such error. For the small town under consideration the number of migrants may be sufficiently small or background data for migration models may be so slight that it is not possible to develop cohort-specific migration estimates. In such a situation total migration may be projected, and national or regional age-, sex-, and race-specific migration rates could be applied to disaggregate the initial figure.

In this case, it would be useful to develop several projections for comparative purposes, including one based on trend extrapolation of current migration, one assuming no net migration, and several projections based on differing estimates of project-related migration. If the natural increase component plays an important role, it would be advisable to incorporate sets of differing assumptions regarding fertility rates, based on U.S. Census Bureau projections, to allow for possible changes in natural increase.

Advantages of the Component Technique of Estimation of Population Change

The component technique is computationaly complex and requires a substantial data base for its application. However, it offers several advantages that recommend it for the impact assessment process. First, the final results of estimation and projection by this approach include not only raw population size estimates, but also projections of whichever aspects of the population were used for disaggregation. Thus final results may include age, sex, and ethnic detail not readily available from other methods. Second, by disaggregating the population causal influences may be taken into account, leading to more accurate estimates and projections than would otherwise be the case. A population with a large proportion of people in the 20–30 age group will tend to have a high birth rate; a population with many individuals over 65 will have a high death rate. By using the component technique the causes of population growth and decline are made explicit. Finally, and most important, the component approach specifically disaggregates migration from other causes of population change. After the effects of mortality and fertility are considered, one is left with an estimate of that component of population change that is most relevant to impact assessment. (But note that some migrants die and others have babies, thus contributing to natural increase after they arrive, so the analysis is somewhat more complicated than it may seem at face value.) In traditional applications of component forecasting migration estimates were based on trend extrapolation where a constant number of migrants or rate of migration was assumed. This approach is not satisfactory for impact assessment, except for comparative purposes. As was suggested in the preceeding example, it is possible to incorporate migration estimates into component projections, thus allowing the quantitative forecasting techniques of the fifth section to be directly integrated into the analysis. If it is not possible to utilize these methods, the component approach permits the use of qualitative high-, medium-, and low-migration forecasts, such as could be developed using the simple identification techniques outlined in the second section. Despite the disadvantages of the component technique, the explicit treatment of migration gives it great advantages over other simpler methods.

This section has attempted to provide an overview of commonly used methods of projection and estimation. Hopefully, a greater familiarity with the various methods available and the strength and weaknesses of each will lead to their more thoughtful use and analysis. In particular, the impact assessor will want to reserve for comparative purposes only techniques such as trend extrapolation which do not disaggregate either population characteristics or the sources of growth. More useful are the more complex techniques, particularly component analysis, that allow specific treatment of a disaggregated migration sector, the critical factor in demographic impacts of projects. Hopefully, the effective use of time sharing on full-scale and mini-computers and of programmable calculators will reduce computational burdens as the federal, state, and local data bases continue to improve. Ideally, future treatments of population change in impact assessment will utilize several estimation and projection techniques, and compare the assumptions and implications of each.

QUANTITATIVE APPROACHES TO IMPACT ASSESSMENT

Traditional approaches to population projection invoke rather simple treatments of migration. Since population movement is the central concern in demographic impact assessment, it is necessary to move beyond simple trend extrapolation approaches to detailed consideration of migration and mobility. This section examines some quantitative and semiquantitative methods that deserve further exploration as first steps in that direction. Before turning to those methods, however, it is useful to briefly review some present perspectives on population movement phenomona.

In so brief a space it is of course impossible to fully summarize current knowledge of a subject as complex as migration. However, some basic information is useful to anyone involved in impact assessment and should serve as an adequate introduction to the literature for those requiring a more detailed treatment.

Migration Research

Morrison[30] has noted that a considerable body of evidence suggests that population mobility processes are best analyzed by a two-stage model. The first stage deals with the question of who moves? and attempts to elucidate the characteristics of a pool of potential movers. The second stage allocates members of this pool of hypermobile individuals to destinations based on the site-specific characteristics of those destinations. This approach to mobility and migration analysis is a powerful tool for the impact analyst. The second stage of the model provides a framework for determining whether the project under consideration will increase or decrease site attractiveness and thus will encourage or discourage population growth. The first stage of the model provides the analyst with some information on the likely characteristics of in- and out-migrants and allows some consideration to the effects of the project on local population composition.

A number of studies have made it possible to develop a profile of the hypermobile individual. (See, e.g., Lowry;[31] Speare, Jr.;[32] Lansing and Mueller;[33]

Rossi.[34] For overviews of previous research and some new analyses, see Morrison.[30, 35, 36]) The results, such as those summarized in Tables 3, 4, and 5, are not surprising. As can be seen in Table 3, the self-employed tend to be more tied down, and among wage and salary earners, white-collar workers are the most likely to move substantial distances, but blue-collar workers are more likely to

Table 3   Annual Mobility of the Employed Civilian Male Population 14-Years Old and over, by Occupation, March 1969 through March 1970

| | Mobility Rate Per Hundred Population | | | |
| | Migration | | | |
Occupation[a]	Total	Intra-state	Inter-state	Local Mobility
Total employed males 14 and over	18.2	3.2	3.1	12.0
Major occupation group				
White-collar workers	18.6	3.8	4.1	10.8
Professional, technical, and kindred	21.5	4.4	5.2	11.8
Managers, officials, and proprietors	15.3	3.2	3.5	8.5
Clerical and kindred	18.5	3.0	2.8	12.6
Sales	20.4	4.5	4.1	11.8
Manual workers	19.0	2.9	2.7	13.5
Craftsmen, foremen, and kindred	17.0	2.8	2.3	11.9
Operatives and kindred	20.4	3.0	3.0	14.5
Laborers	21.0	2.9	3.0	15.1
Service workers	16.0	2.0	1.8	12.1
Farm workers	10.5	2.2	1.1	7.2
Farmers and farm managers	5.7	1.4	0.4	3.9
Farm laborers and farm foremen	19.2	3.7	2.3	13.2
Class or worker				
Wage and salary workers	19.3	3.4	3.3	12.6
Self-employed workers	10.0	1.6	1.4	7.1

SOURCE.   U.S. Bureau of the Census, *Current Population Reports,* Series P-20, No. 210, January 15, 1971, Tables 8 and 9.
[a] As of March 1970.
From Morrison[36], p. 12, Table 2.

change residences within a local area. Service workers are less likely to make either short- or long-distance moves than either blue- or white-color workers, though they are intermediate in local mobility. Table 4 shows information from the Lansing and Mueller study on reasons for moving, with economic factors clearly constituting the set of dominating motivations. The importance of economic factors seem to decrease with age and increase with education, as may be seen in Table 5. Further research[35,33] has also demonstrated that mobility is critically affected by mobility history; people who have already moved are more likely to move again than those who have never moved; those who have moved recently are more likely to move than the less recent or less frequent movers.

There emerges, as Morrison has suggested, a portrait of the extreme ends of the mover-stayer continuum. Movers and, therefore, both in- and out-migrants tend to be young, well-educated, white-collar workers who are concerned with economic opportunities and who are likely to have moved in the past and to move again in the future. This portrait could be quantified, and a probability of movement model developed from previous studies; for the purposes at hand, however, a general understanding of the characteristics of the mobile population should suffice.

Table 4   Reasons for Most Recent Move for Family Heads Moving During Past Five Years

Reasons	Percentage of Moves[a]
Purely economic reasons (no noneconomic reasons given)	58
Partly economic reasons (economic plus either family or community reasons or both)	14
Noneconomic reasons	23
No reason given	5
Total	100%
Number of moves	737

SOURCE.   Lansing and Mueller, see p. 38.
[a] Note that this distribution refers to the most recent moves of heads of families who moved in the last five years. It is based on all available data including the extra sample of moves from reinterviews with movers originally interviewed in other surveys. Less inclusive tabulations and tabulations based on all moves from 1950 to date of interview may be expected to lead to slightly different results.
From Morrison[36], p. 25, Table 11.

Table 5 Kinds of Economic Reasons for Moving by Occupation and Education—Percentage Distribution of Heads of Families Who Moved in the Last 5 Years[a]

| | | Kinds of Economic Reason | | | | | |
	Transfer, Reassignment	Unemployment: Moved to Find New, More, or Steadier Work	Higher Rate of Pay: Better Job	Other Economic Reasons	No Economic or Occupational Reasons Given	Total	Number of Cases
Occupation							
Professional, technical	23%	7	50	4	16	100%	108
Other white collar	41%	14	27	4	14	100%	102
Blue collar	13%	26	25	10	26	100%	179
Education							
Eight grades or less	9%	19	20	12	40	100%	78
High school	13%	21	24	13	29	100%	208
College	32%	7	36	7	18	100%	189
Age							
18–24	9%	33	26	11	21	100%	78
25–34	25%	11	37	8	19	100%	164
35–44	24%	11	31	9	25	100%	93
45–54	20%	13	30	12	25	100%	69
55–64	20%	20	8	13	39	100%	51
65 and over	0	3	3	13	81	100%	35
All	20%	15	29	10	26	100%	474

SOURCE. Lansing and Mueller, see Tables 18 and 19.

[a] Excludes moves in or out of armed forces and moves to and from ciollege. From Morrison[36], p. 27, Table 12.

The selection of destination is the second phase of the population movement model. The concern of the mover population with economic factors would lead one to suspect that economic factors are the critical lure to in-migration. Areas undergoing economic booms can be expected to grow in size, whereas those with less dynamic economies will decline. The available evidence[30, 35] suggests that the most appropriate formulation is one of economic pull, rather than of push. Any area will have a pool of potential out-migrants who will leave for economically attractive areas. Areas of economic growth will attract more than enough movers to compensate for out-migrants and experience net in-migration.

The preceding discussion focuses on long-distance moves of the type usually classified as migration. The characteristics of specific sites that attract short-distance movers are less well understood than those affecting the long-distance mover. The data that does exist is difficult to generalize and is probably specific to the region and characteristics of the population from which it was obtained. Nonetheless, a review of some conclusions of one study of site selection factors is useful to identify important variables. In 1965 interviews were conducted with 1720 occupants of residential subdivisions in the Akron, Ohio area to determine the factors that had been involved in site selection.[37] The following factors were deemed most important in the decision to purchase one homesite over another:

1. Quality of schools.
2. Appearance of house.
3. Size of house.
4. Cost of house.
5. Scenic qualities of site.
6. Tax rates.
7. Proximity to schools and churches.
8. Accessibility to highways.
9. Prestige of neighborhood.
10. Availability and cost of sewage and water treatment facilities.

Again, the available empirical research produces a common-sense picture: short-distance movers have a rather straightforward set of desired site characteristics, and an understanding of these can aid in assessing changes in the desirability of a given site. Hopefully, the future will see future microlevel research on factors influencing site selection among short-distance movers. An important step in this direction would be a better integration of housing market research data into the analyses of short-distance migration. Meanwhile, studies such as the aforementioned can provide some rule of thumb to the impact assessor concerned with short-distance movers.

Given the present level of understanding of migration, it is not surprising that no general and precise quantitative model exists that is suitable to impact assessment. There are, however, a few techniques which, although far from perfect, can provide some insight into the problems facing the impact assessor, and which are briefly reviewed here.

Modeling and Simulation of Migration

The most frequently used approach to migration forecasting is that of the regional analyst. (A classic overview of regional analysis may be found in Isard.[38]) The specific techniques employed differ from study to study, but the basic concept involved is the development of an analytical model that describes the relative attractiveness of specific sites in terms of economic and other attractiveness factors. A pool of migrants may be then allocated to regions based on their attractiveness or pull. Contemporary efforts along these lines usually employ dynamic computer adaptations of the analytical models that account for changes in site characteristics over time. Typically, an initial attractiveness factor is calculated for each site, and a portion of the migrant pool (or in some cases of the total population) is allocated based on these factors. Then the attractiveness for each site is recalculated based on changes in density, land use, and economic patterns. Movers are allocated on the basis of the new attractiveness figures, and the process is continued for as many iterations as the analyst wishes. Some models focus on aesthetic and related qualities,[39] others utilize economic, market, and locational considerations relative to housing demand,[40] whereas still others center on density limits such as zoning.[20]

Although such dynamic models and their analytic precursors are of some interest to the analyst, they are not without substantial difficulties. First, they are of necessity based on broad simplifications and often include a mix of empirical and a priori estimates of key parameters. It is difficult to see how a given model could simultaneously be general enough to be applicable outside of the region for which it was developed and still be sufficiently specific to be useful for the fine-grain analysis required for impact assessment. Second, computer models that are complex enough to allow altering assumptions (in particular, the project/no-project comparison) can be extremely expensive to develop, test, and run (though it should be noted that the small computers and programmable calculators now becoming available offer some interesting potential for future development of simulation models). Unless a model is already developed and operational, few impact studies can allocate sufficient resources or employ personnel to utilize such methods. Finally, even some of the most carefully developed and elaborate computer models have a mediocre track record at handling small-scale perturbations of the sort central to most impact assessment.

Despite these problems, computer models do offer some promise for the impact assessor. Simulations are expressly designed for conducting "paper" experiments with complex systems. This perspective of experimentation with alternative assumptions is central to impact assessment; the analyst needs to consider the effects of the project, possible mitigation measures, and the situation that might develop without the project. The use of simulation models requires careful thought about the interrelationships among variables and about the relative sensitivity of various elements within an overall system. Dynamic simulation models cannot as yet, and may never, provide the analyst with conclusive answers, but their development and use can help in providing a holistic and integrative analytical perspective on impact analysis by displaying a set of "might happens."

Regression Models

Another quantitative technique that in some circumstances can be applied to the prediction of migration is regression analysis. As was noted in the previous section on this topic, regression analysis may be directly applied to population (or migration) estimation. However, when the situation calls for projection, an immediate problem arises: values for the independent variables to be entered in the regression equation do not exist for future points in time. Two basic approaches may be used singly or in combination to circumvent this lack of future data points. One strategy is to employ lagged variables in the analysis. Thus, current in-migration is presumed to be caused by previous housing prices, levels of unemployment, quality of life indices, and so on. Although some lag in the effects of such variables is plausible, it is unlikely that such effects would be significant for more than about 5 years in the future, so the time horizon for projection is extremely limited. It should also be noted that the use of lagged variables in regression may lead to some statistical and computational complexities which the analyst should not ignore.[25]

An alternative approach would be to develop a regression equation based on past empirical evidence, using as independent predictor variables only quantities for which reasonable projections either already exist or may be developed. Thus migration at any point in time may be estimated as a function of trip time to an urban center, the price of housing, interest rates, national and regional population growth projections, and so on. The equations may be generated using available time series and cross-section data; future migration may be estimated by using projections for the independent variables in the equation. In using such a scheme it should be noted that precise future projections of predictor variables are not essential. It is often useful to employ limited independent variables with either a binary (yes-no) or limited (high-medium-low) level of measurement. In general, reducing a continuous measure (such as rate of uneployment) to a limited measure (such as high, medium, or low level of unemployment) involves a loss of information. However, the ability to develop "ball park" projections of future levels of predictor variables and to alter these projections based on differing assumptions about the project in question will often more than compensate for this information loss. The use of limited independent variables in regression analysis is common and is a technique that deserves further exploration in forecasting migration.

Delphi Surveys

Another approach to quantitative and semiquantitative migration for forecasting, that of the Delphi technique, has been noted by Morrison[15] (p. 50). Its justification lies in the fact that any forecasting technique involves the extensive use of considered judgement on the part of the analyst in selecting methodologies, conventions, data sets, and so on. The Delphi method makes explicit use of the judgemental elements that are implicit in other techniques. In essence, the Delphi technique combines the informed opinions of experts, allowing the individuals involved to move toward a concensus while staying relatively free from social pressure that might otherwise tend to bias results (for detailed expositions and critiques of the Delphi technique, see Pill;[41] Brown;[42] Helmer;[43] Duncan;[3] Ayres,[44] Chapter 8). The actual procedure involves the repeated interrogation of an "expert" panel on the subject area via questionnaires. First, the panel itself must be selected. In the present context a panel may contain a mix of local officials, knowledgeable individuals, and members of the effected community who have an intimate understanding of local conditions, of regional officials who presumably have a somewhat broader perspective, and of academic economists, regional scientists, and demographers, who can add an analytical perspective. Each member of the panel is given some basic background information on the area and project in question and a list of quantities or events to be forecast. Based on the background information and their own insights, they are then asked to suggest other topics for inclusion in the forecasting stage of the study. The investigator compiles a final list of events and quantities to be included in a questionnaire. Questions may ask for direct numerical responses (i.e., In what year will the population of area A reach size X? In 1990, what will the level of unemployment be in the area Y?), a simple agree or disagree (The population of area A will stabilize by 1990. The population of area B will be more than 50 percent blue-collar workers in 1980.) or may ask for a subjective probability rating of a given statement (What is the probability that 25 percent of the households in area A will receive Social Security benefits in 1980? High, medium, or low?). The questionnaires are completed by the panel and returned to the investigator, who then compiles means, medians, quartiles, and other analyses of the response to questions during the preceding round. This information along with selected quotations from any written or verbal justifications for their personal positions by the panelists become input data for the next round. The process is repeated as many times as the investigator desires, although most studies indicate that responses stabilize after three or four iterations. The final result of the study is a series of quantitative and semiquantitative projections and some subjective and objective data on the reasons for the projections and the degree of consensus behind them. Many past applications of the Delphi technique have been rather problematic. Too often, the authors have paid little heed to traditional methods of survey design, administration and analysis and have tended to consider their results uncritically (for a detailed review and criticism, see Sackman.[45]) The Delphi technique should not be considered a solution to forecasting problems; as a special-purpose survey research technique, however, it can be of great utility, particularly if employed early in the preparation of an EIR, where it could help the analyst identify many variables for consideration—aside from those exclusively concerned with population. With more methodological care, larger and more carefully defined panels of experts, and more cautious analysis, it has great potential for providing insight into social impact assessment problems and a wide variety of other forecasting and identification problems.

CONCLUSION

This chapter has attempted to outline various perspectives on the assessment of demographic impacts of various origins. The approach outlined in the second section should allow the analyst to identify potential impacts on population size, distribution, and composition, and to present such impacts in perspective. The third and fourth sections have considered data sources and traditional methodologies available for displaying such perspectives. Hopefully, careful attention to methods and the data they require will lead to a better understanding of the strenths and weaknesses of population analysis techniques, to a more thorough and thoughtful presentation of demographic information, and to the use of detailed, disaggregated, and comparative projections in project planning and impact assessment. Finally, the fifth section suggests some methodologies that may prove useful in forecasting migration. None of these methods is well developed here, but their further exploration by the reader should provide a great deal of insight into the effects of techno-environmental change on social systems.

There are no answers in this chapter, nor any robust methodologies. The state of the art in demography and in the social sciences in general does not permit quantitative forecasting with any high degree of accuracy. However, as Duncan has noted, the critical value of a forecasting effort lies in drawing attention to sensitive variables and key issues. This applies as much to attempts to foresee the social impacts of the construction of a dam as it does to attempts to model the state of the global economic system 25 years hence. If this chapter provides some first steps toward the better identification of demographic impacts and the development of a framework in which to consider them, it has been successful.

NOTES

1. Bogue, Donald J. *Principles of Demography* Wiley, New York, 1969.

2. Hollis, John and James McEvoy III, Demographic Effects of Water Development in Charles R. Goldman, James McEvoy III, and Peter J. Richerson, Eds. *Environmental Quality and Water Development* W. H. Freeman, San Francisco, 1973.

3. Duncan, Otis Dudley, Social Forecasting–The State of the Art *Public Interest* **17**, pp. 88–118, 1969.

4. Burdge, Rable, *Factors Influenceing Relocation in Response to Reservoir Development* Water Resources Institute, Lexington, Kentucky, 1970.

5. U.S.Bureau of the Census, *1970 Census User's Guide, Parts I and II*, Government Printing Office, Washington, D.C., 1970.

6. U.S.Bureau of the Census, *Current Population Reports: Population Estimates and Projections (Series P-25)*, Government Printing Office, Washington, D.C.,

7. U.S. Bureau of the Census, *Index to Census Bureau Methodological Research 1963–1971*, Government Printing Office, Washington, D.C., 1973.

8. U.S. Bureau of the Census, *The 1970 Census and You, A General Introduction to Census Data,* Government Printing Office, Washington, D.C., 1973.

9. U.S. Bureau of the Census, *Census Data for Community Action,* Government Printing Offices, Washington, D.C., 1972.

10. U.S. Bureau of the Census, *Current Population Reports: Federal-State Cooperative Programs for Population Estimates (Series P-26,)* Government Printing Office, Washington, D.C.,

11. U.S. Bureau of the Census, *Current Population Reports: (Special Censuses Series P-25)*, Government Printing Office, Washington, D.C.,

12. U.S. Bureau of the Census, *Directory of Federal Statistics for Local Areas: A Guide to Sources,* Government Printing Office, Washington, D.C., 1966.

13. U.S. Bureau of the Census, *Directory of Federal Statistics for States: A Guide to Sources,* Government Printing Office, Washington, D.C., 1967.

14. U.S. Bureau of the Census, *Directory of Federal Statistics, Non-Federal Statistics for State and Local Areas: A Guide to Sources,* Government Printing Office, Washington, D.C., 1969.

15. Morrison, Peter A., *Demographic Information for Cities* The Rand Corp., Santa Monica, 1971.

16. Morrison, Peter A., *Small Area Population Estimates for the City of St. Louis, 1960–1972, With a Method for Updating Them* The Rand Corp., Santa Monica, 1973.

17. Atchley, Robert C., *Population Projections and Estimates for Local Areas* Scripps Foundation for Research in Population Problems, Miami, Ohio, 1970.

18. Pittenger, Donald B. *Projecting State and Local Populations* Ballinger Publishing Co., Cambridge, Mass. 1976.

19. Shryock, Henry S., Jacob Siegel, and Associates, *The Materials and Methods of Demography* U.S. Bureau of the Census, Washington, D.C., 1971.

20. Greenberg, Michael R., Donald A. Krueckberg, and Richard Mautner, *Long-Range Population Projections for Minor Civil Divisions.* Center for Urban Policy Research, Rutgers University, New Brunswick, New Jersey, 1973.

21. Bogue, Donald J., A Technique for Making Extensive Population Estimates *J. Am. Stat. Assoc.* **45,** pp. 149–163.

22. U.S. Bureau of the Census, *Current Population Reports Series P-25,* No. 97, Government Printing Office, Washington, D.C., 1954.

23. Bogue, Donald J. and Beverly Duncan, A Composite Method for Estimating Postcensal Population of Small Areas by Age, Sex and Color *Vital Statistics-Special Reports,* Selected Studies **47,** 1959.

24. Zitter, Meyer, and Henry S. Shryock, Accuracy of Methods of Preparing Postcensal Estimates for State and Local Areas *Demography 1* pp. 227–241, 1964.

25. Theil, Henri, *Principles of Econometrics.* Wiley, New York, 1971.

26. Draper, N. R. and H. Smith, *Applied Regression Analysis,* Wiley, New York, 1966.

27. Ericksen, Eugene P., A Method for Combining Sample Survey Data and Symptomatic Indicators to Obtain Population Estimates for Local Areas *Demography* **10,** pp. 137–160, 1973.

28. Ericksen, Eugene P., A Regression Method for Estimating Population Changes of Local Areas *J. Am. Stat. Assoc.* **69,** 348, pp. 867–875, 1974.

29. Lindgren, David T., Dwelling Estimation from Color-Infrared Photography *Photogr. Eng.* pp. 373–377, April 1974.

30. Morrison, Peter A., *Theoretical Issues in the Design of Population Mobility Models* The Rand Corp. Santa Monica, 1969.

31. Lowry, R. Ira S., *Migration and Metropolitan Growth* Chandler San Francisco, 1966.

32. Speare, Alden, Jr., Home Ownership, Life Cycle Stage and Residential Mobility *Demography* **7,** pp, 449–458, 1970.

33. Lansing, John B. and Eva Mueller, *The Geographic Mobility of Labor* Survey Research Center, Institute for Social Research, Ann Arbor, Michigan, 1967.

34. Rossi, Peter A., *Why Families Move* Free Press, Glencoe, Illinois, 1955.

35. Morrison, Peter A., *The Propensity to Move* The Rand Corp., Santa Monica, 1971.

36. Morrison, Peter A., *Population Movements and the Shape of Urban Growth* The Rand Corp., Santa Monica, 1972.

37. Tri-County Regional Planning Commission, *Residential Subdivisions and Their Inhabitants* Tri-County Regional Planning Commission, Akron, Ohio, 1965.

38. Isard, Walter, *Methods of Regional Analysis* The M.I.T. Press, Cambridge, 1960.

39. Burby, Raymond J., III, *A Model for Simulating Residential Development in Reservoir Recreation Areas* Water Resources Research Institute, Raleigh, North Carolina, 1971.

40. Hamilton, H. R., S. E. Goldstone, J. W. Milliman, A. L. Pugh III, E. B. Roberts, and A. Zellner, *Systems Simulation for Regional Analysis* The M.I.T. Press, Cambridge, 1969.

41. Pill, J., The Delphi Method: Substance, Content, A Critique and an Annotated Bibliography *Socio-Economic Planning Sciences* **5,** pp. 55–71.

42. Brown, Bernice B., *Delphi Process: A Methodology for the Use of Elicited Opinion of Experts* The Rand Corp., Santa Monica, 1968.

43. Helmer, Olaf, *Social Technology* Basic Books, New York, 1966.

44. Ayres, Robert U., *Technological Forecasting and Long-Range Planning* McGraw-Hill Co., New York, 1969.

45. Sackman, H., *Delphi Assessment: Expert Opinion, Forecasting and Group Process* The Rand Corp., Santa Monica, 1974.

FOUR

The Assessment of
Land Use Impacts

THEODORE D. BERNS

LAND USE IMPACTS: A CONCEPTUAL FRAMEWORK

Virtually every dimension of the human environment, that is, our physical, psychological, social, and economic well-being is related in some manner to the utilization of land. Sociologists, demographers, and planners have long been interested in the relationships between land use and the size, distribution, and composition of human populations. The field of community-environmental health has been concerned with the physical and psychological effects of land use on human populations, such as impacts from crowding, substandard neighborhood conditions, and health and safety effects resulting from the proximity of incompatible land uses. Historians have traced the rise and fall of entire regions in terms of the impacts of particular types of land uses on the area.[1] The classic example of these impacts is, of course, the rapid development and equally rapid abandonment of the boom towns of the west in response to the discovery of gold and silver. Indeed, the ways in which land is used and misused can be seen to have such a pervasive influence on social systems that many of the topics dealt with in this book and grouped under the generic label of social impacts could fit comfortably within a treatise on land use.

For introductory purposes, it is useful to discuss briefly the relationships between effects on land use and other categories of social impacts generated by resource development projects. Perhaps the most basic concept with which a person attempting to assess the social impacts of a development project in the preparation of an environmental impact statement or report must be familiar is that *changes in land use are often both the cause and effect of impacts on other social variables*. This relationship is well illustrated by the types of social and economic effects that are often associated with the development or improvement of transportation facilities. The extension of highways or the improvement of existing routes may be immediately caused by increased traffic volumes stemming from regional economic and population growth which in turn may reflect changes in land use, such as the development of major industrial plants or large government facilities. Conversely, the highway project may be a direct cause of other significant social impacts such as the encouragement of land use conversion along transportation corridors with the attendant consequences of increased noise, aesthetic effects, and changes in land values[2] (Schott, Chapter 6). Although this example grossly oversimplifies the nature of the relationship between land use and other social variables, it serves to emphasize the need for a detailed and systematic examination of the effects of a proposed project on land use as part of the social impact assessment process.

Land Use Information in the Preparation of Impact Statements

Since this volume is primarily designed to be a useful tool for persons charged with the assessment of environmental impacts, including those effects on the human environment described as social impacts, a word of introduction concerning the utilization of this chapter in the preparation and review of impact statements or reports is in order. A comprehensive treatment of the role of land use in the human environment and of approaches and methods for analyzing changes in land use would fill many volumes. The present chapter, therefore, can do no more than provide a set of guidelines to be followed in dealing with the many problems of land use impact assessment.

The initial portion of the chapter is devoted to the development of a conceptual framework for the assessment of impacts on land use. Since there are, unfortunately, no formulas or equations that can be "plugged in" to data concerning a proposed project to identify specific land use impacts, this conceptual framework forms the basis of the approaches and methods which will be suggested later in the chapter. Although this introduction may appear overly simplistic to persons possessing a substantial background in land use studies, it serves a two-fold function. These introductory discussions emphasize that factors which affect the utilization of land must be examined from several perspectives to ensure a comprehensive identification and evaluation of potential impacts on land use. In addition, examples of ways in which land use impacts may affect other socioeconomic phenomena, which are discussed elsewhere in this book, are also presented. Finally, the discussions that follow illustrate several ways in which various categories of land use variables may be affected by resource development projects.

The presentation late in the chapter of approaches and methods for the existing, (preimpact) state of land use for the identification and evaluation of land use impacts must also be considered as a set of guidelines rather than as step-by-step instructions for land use impact assessment. When detailed quantitative methodologies are applicable, these are presented and examples of their utilization for impact assessment are provided. In other cases when potentially significant impacts on land use are not subject to such methodologies, approaches for describing and evaluating these land use effects are suggested and examples are again provided. In all cases emphasis in this chapter is placed on making the assessment of land use impacts useful to planners and other decision makers who must review proposed development projects and suggest mitigation measures or adapt existing area plans and policies to deal with anticipated environmental consequences of these projects.

As is often the case when a subject encompasses a diversity of interests, the concept of land use has evolved and expanded until there exists at present no clearly defined boundaries that distinguish land use from other social, economic, or environmental variables. In response to the involvement of a broad spectrum of academic disciplines including the fields of planning, economics, sociology, political science, law, and (most recently) ecology, the concept of land use has undergone a transformation away from a narrowly defined concern with the type of human activity that takes place on land toward a broad, multidimensional concept which attempts to deal with the entire range of human interrelationships with land.[3] To begin the development of a conceptual framework for the assessment of land use impacts, it is therefore necessary to distinguish those aspects or dimensions of land use that are essential to an assessment of a project's impacts on the human environment. As they are dealt with in this chapter they are: land use activities, improvements to land, land use economics, and land tenure and controls.[3]

Land Use Activity

The most familiar category of land use impacts involves changes in the type of human activity that takes place on a particular parcel of land. This type of impact is often referred to as the process of land use conversion and has received considerable attention. Economists and sociologists as well as urban and regional planners have long been involved in the study of forces that shape patterns of land use activity in both urban and rural areas. Also, ecologists and environmental planners have become concerned with examining conflicts between particular types of land use activity and the ecological capabilities of land.[4,5] In some areas, such as California, the encroachment of urban land use activities into areas of prime agricultural land has resulted in legislation that is designed to provide mechanisms for the mitigation or prevention of these impacts at the urban-rural fringe.[6]

In recent years, increased attention has been focused on the impacts of large-scale resource development projects on existing patterns of land use activity. Numerous studies have examined changes in land use associated with the development of large water resource projects. Also, considerable attention has been given to the role of transportation projects in shaping land use activity patterns.[2] From these and other analyses, it is apparent that impacts on land use activity attributable to development projects involve several distinct subcategories of changes in land use. A project may, for example, involve the addition of new types of land use activity to an area and the deletion of existing uses. On other parcels, a proposed use may be compatible with existing activities resulting in multiple land uses. Rangeland near a proposed reservoir, for example, may be utilized in one way by the rancher, in another by a hunter or hiker, and in addition, may be crossed by electrical distribution facilities or water distribution structures associated with the project, thereby serving yet another type of land use activity.

In addition to changes in the type of activities in a project area, the effect of a proposed development on the intensity of land use may be significant in that these changes will affect other social and environmental variables. For example, the value of certain types of recreational experiences such as hiking and camping may depend on maintaining a relatively low population density in a given area at a given time. On the other hand, the provision of adequate educational facilities or the maintenance of transportation routes and other services may require much greater densities to be practical. In regard to some types of use activity, intensity of use may be measured in terms of the number of persons per unit of area who are engaged in the activity, such as recreation area visitor days, whereas for other activity types relevant indicators may refer to the output of goods and services per unit of land, such as agricultural productivity per acre or volume of average daily traffic (ADT).

Impacts on the intensity of land use may be initiated in a variety of ways by a development project. In the case of agricultural uses, the natural productive qualities of land may be altered and increased by the provision of irrigation or drainage facilities that will result in increased levels of productivity. The intensity of commercial, residential, or recreational uses may be affected by the availability of services and utilities, such as improved access roads, sewers, or fire and police protection. Another group of variables that may influence land use intensity are commonly categorized as amenity factors. These may include aesthetically attractive natural or man-made views, the availability of nearby recreational opportunities, a pleasing climate, or the presence of unique historical or cultural areas. The demand for amenity-oriented second-home or commuter subdivision development, for example, is testimony to the significance of amenity variables in shaping demands for land use.[7]

It is important to note that in regard to most types of development projects there are likely to be two spatial levels or spheres of impacts on land use activity. A project may involve the immediate conversion of land to new types of activity or the intensification of activities at the project site, thereby causing impacts that are relatively obvious and susceptible to precise measurement. The second or macrosphere of impacts is likely to occur incrementally throughout the project area and will be considerably more difficult to link directly to the project. An irrigation program, for example, will involve the conversion of land for storage and distribution facilities (impacts on types of land use activity) and will increase agricultural productivity on land which is to be supplied with irrigation water (impacts on intensity of land use). Outside of the immediate project site, increases in productivity and changes in area cropping patterns may generate what economists have termed "stemming and induced" economic benefits in the form of demands for processing facilities and transportation services that will involve the conversion of land to commercial or industrial uses.[8] In addition to these impacts, increased employment opportunities in the area may stimulate demands for residential land use to meet housing needs. Table 1 presents a summary of land use changes that were found to have occurred in areas immediately adjacent to one reservoir development project over a 30-year period.

Table 1 Changes in Land Use Recorded Over a 30-Year Period Near a Large Reservoir (acres)

Type of Use	1938	1951	1960	1967	Total Change	
Agricultural	111,285	110,617	110,186	104,144	7141	(−)
Residential	310	941	1,388	7,191	6881	(+)
Commercial	18	39	53	127	109	(+)
Public	48	64	44	199	151	(+)
Water	5,535	5,535	5,535	5,535	0	
Total	117,196	117,196	117,196	117,196		

SOURCE. Preeble, Billy R., *Patterns of Land Use Change Around a Large Reservoir,* Water Resources Research Institute, University of Kentucky, Lexington, 1969.

Improvements to Land

In addition to changes in land use activity, project-generated effects on various types of improvements to land may be a source of significant impacts on the human environment. In general, improvements to land can be defined as any modifications that affect the utility of land for a particular human activity. This definition of improvement is clearly nonnormative in the sense that improvement does not imply any increase or decrease in absolute social or economic benefits that may be associated with the alteration of land. The improvement of land for a particular type of activity will often render the land less attractive or perhaps totally unsuitable for other activity types. For example, the widening of a highway represents an improvement to land, even though the project may necessitate the destruction of homes and businesses in the projected right of way.[3]

Although impacts on improvements to land will in most cases be very closely related to changes in land use activity patterns, it is important to distinguish these two categories of land use impacts, since each may have distinct consequences for other socioeconomic variables which influence the human environment. Concern over social impacts associated with improvements to land has perhaps been most visible in regard to the quality of residential, commercial, and recreational developments in urban and rural areas. The aesthetic effects of improvements to land, for example, represent a major environmental concern in any resource development project. The aesthetic impacts of a project may result either from the addition or removal of structural improvements or from alterations to existing vegetation or landforms. Several studies have considered aesthetic impacts of land use improvements and have coined the term "visual pollution" to describe this phenomena.[9, 10]

Aside from aesthetic effects, a number of other factors can be counted among the social impacts of improvements to land. The condition of residential or commercial development in terms of the general state of repair, the adequacy of insulation from weather and noise, and the provision of adequate privacy and sufficient floor space will have significant impacts on the physical and psychological well-being of persons who live or work in these developments.[11] The concept of substandardness in regard to urban development has attracted the attention of urban planners. One study, for example, has approached the issue of social impacts from improvements to land by identifying various "substandardness" criteria and by developing methods for evaluating the quality of residential and nonresidential improvements.[12,13]

Improvements to land may also have a substantial effect on the size and composition of both temporary and permanent populations within an area. The development of improved campgrounds and boating facilities at a reservoir area may generate substantial increases in visitor population and may attract very different types of visitors than if the area had been left in an undeveloped or wilderness state. Dietz, in the previous chapter, considered numerous factors of this type. Finally, the prices and rents associated with improvements to land can be expected to have effects on demographic variables. Demands for recreational amenities, for example, are affected by the costs associated with particular recreational uses.[14] In another context, planners and other urban decision makers have long been plagued by the problems involved in ensuring a sufficient supply of quality low to moderate cost housing in areas when amenity factors tend to encourage high-cost "exclusive" residential development.

Another type of social impact associated with improvements to land are impacts on historical and cultural values within the project area. In some cases, an existing structure or a prominent natural feature may be of great national or regional significance. In other situations, structures that would be removed or altered by a proposed project may be valued only by residents of the immediate area. Also important is the possibility that historical or cultural effects may be particularly severe for a specific ethnic or religious group. American Indian organizations, for example, have often objected to developments that would infringe on areas or structures of cultural or religious significance to their people.

A final example of social impacts that may be generated by improvements to land are the variety of growth-inducing effects which may flow from a project. The relationship between improvements such as sewers and the intensity (as well as the type) of land uses in surrounding areas has already been briefly mentioned. In California, for example, the federal Central Valley Project together with the state's California Water Project are excellent examples of the potential magnitude of growth-inducing impacts that may be attributable to improvements to land. It has been estimated that approximately 9 out of 10 residents of southern California presently depend on water furnished from the northern areas of the state by these two projects.[15, 16, 17]

Land Use Economics

The third major category of land use impacts involves the effect of development projects on the economics of land use. Perhaps the most significant determinant of the manner in which land is used, or misused, is the interplay of economic forces that together account for area prices, rents, and market activity. A large corporate-owned shopping center replaces a number of small independent businesses; a central urban area is allowed to decay into a slum; or potentially productive agricultural land lies fallow at the urban-rural fringe, all in response to a variety of market factors. Although a detailed treatment of land use economics is beyond the scope of the present chapter, it is important for later discussions to identify and briefly discuss several economic concepts that are basic to an assessment of land use impacts.

The concept of *land rent* as it is applied in land use economics involves more than the amount paid by the apartment dweller or business proprietor to a landowner. Land rent has been defined as ". . . the economic return that accrues or should accrue to land for its use in production"[18] (p. 157). The amount of land rent generated by a given parcel is, therefore, the surplus of revenues or economic returns that accrues to the landowner after all costs associated with the ownership of the parcel have been deducted. Thus land rent, for purposes of assessing the impacts of development projects, will be affected both by those features of a project that tend to generate increased levels of economic returns and by those features that affect the various costs of production for the parcel.

A closely related economic concept is the *use capacity* of land resources. This concept refers to ". . . the *relative ability* of a given unit of land resource to produce a surplus of returns and/or satisfactions above its cost of utilization"[18] (p. 13). Although land rent involves the actual amount of surplus economic revenues that accrue from a particular use activity on the land, use capacity involves all the factors which together determine the potential ability of the land to generate surplus revenues. One author has divided the factors which affect use capacity into those that are basically locational in nature, such as the location of a parcel with respect to sources of employment or materials, and those factors that are concerned with the quality of the land resource, such as the effect of irrigation or drainage on the fertility of the soil, the presence of necessary improvements, and aesthetic (amenity) considerations[18] (p. 63). As an illustration of the concept of use capacity, consider a parcel of rural land presently being utilized for low-intensity agricultural use such as grazing. The land rent generated by the parcel may be marginal, and the use capacity will be correspondingly limited, since the parcel possesses few qualities which would render it suitable for other, more profitable, types of use activity. The construction of a reservoir project near the location of the parcel may have an immediate effect on the use capacity of the land in that residential or commercial uses become possible. If sewers, water, and other services are extended into the area, the use capacity of the parcel is further enhanced until the point at which conversion to a new land use activity occurs, and the parcel begins to generate increased levels of land rent. The rate of change in use capacity as well as the magnitude of change in both use capacity and land rent will depend on demands for new use activities and on the many costs associated with land use conversion. Figure 4.1 illustrates the relationship between use capacity and land rent.

In the case of Parcel *A*, the land resource is suitable for an activity for which the total costs of production are low in relation to the returns which are generated for the owner. Land rent is, therefore, relatively high. For Parcel *B* the land is not suitable for the same use activity. The use here entails production costs which are a much greater percentage of the total revenues generated by the parcel, and land rent is consequently reduced. By the time condition *C* is reached, the land may not be suited for any use activity that will generate a surplus of revenues over total production cost. This is the no-rent margin beyond which an owner could not profitably use the land resource.

When a given area of land may be potentially suitable for several types of use activity, land use economists speak of the "highest and best use" of land. As a general rule it could be expected that landowners would always opt for the use activity which would generate the highest level of land rent. However, factors such as the risk involved in land development, the amount of development capital that will be required, and the time lag involved in the conversion of the land may have a substantial influence on land use decisions[19, 20] (Chapter 7). In addition to these factors, studies in rural areas have indicated that a variety of other socioeconomic variables concerning the owners of land may play a significant role in landowner-developer decisions.[21, 22] The concept of highest and best use is important in the assessment of land use impacts. Planners and environmentalists have often pointed to the fact that conflicts may arise between choices over uses which may represent the highest and best for the individual parcel owner but which may also involve social costs that make the use objectionable to the remainder of the community. A current example of this conflict is the increasing desire of communities to preserve open space versus the desire of landowners to cash in on the market for intensive residential or commercial uses.

The final concept concerning land use economics that is important for an assessment of land use impacts involves the *intensity* of land use. Economists deal with the intensity of use in terms of the "intensive and extensive margins of land use"[18] (pp. 150–153). The *intensive margin* of land use refers to the factors of production such as labor and raw materials that a parcel of land can

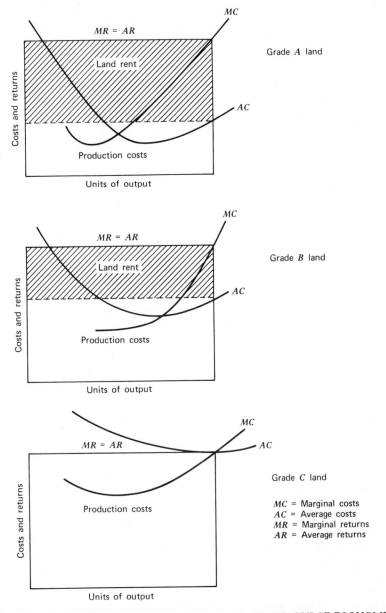

Figure 4.1 Use capacity and land rent. Raleigh Barlowe, LAND RESOURCE ECONOMICS: *The Economics of Real Property,* 2nd. ed., © 1972, p. 161. Reprinted by permission of Prentice-Hall, Inc., Englewood Cliffs, New Jersey.

utilize. This margin is reached when the parcel has absorbed all possible units of production costs while still generating a surplus of marginal returns over marginal costs. For example, a parcel of agricultural land may be able to absorb X dollars of inputs such as seed or labor and generate revenues at a level where marginal costs just equal marginal returns. If irrigation water is supplied to the parcel, it may become possible to absorb $X + Y$ dollars of input, thereby resulting in increased intensity of land use and an increase in land rent for the parcel owner.

The *extensive margin* of land use has been described as ". . . the no-rent margin at which land under optimum conditions will barely yield enough to cover the costs of production"[18] (p. 152). For example, as a result of adverse soil conditions and climate, a parcel of rural land may be barely able to generate a surplus of returns over costs if it is devoted to the production of field crops. If prices or costs change, these crops may become entirely unprofitable. At this point the extensive margin has been reached, and the owner must shift his use of the parcel, perhaps to grazing or pasture crops, so that the land will be able to generate surplus returns. Therefore, as land approaches the extensive margin for an existing type of use, land use conversion becomes more likely, since owners will have little, if anything, to lose from the discontinuance of their present land use activity. Figure 4.2 illustrates the intensive and extensive margins of land use.

In Figure 4.2 the owner of parcel A finds that he can utilize 14 units of input (capital and labor) on his land before marginal costs (MC) just equal marginal returns (MR). At this point, the addition of one more unit of input (one additional unit of marginal cost) would result in a net decrease in total land rent. Parcel B, on the other hand, has the economic capacity to absorb only 10 units of input before the point is reached at which $MC = MR$. Note that the total amount of land rent has decreased. Parcel C represents the extensive margin of land use on the parcel. Five units of input are required to utilize the parcel for the prevailing use activity At this point, MC just equals MR, and average costs just equal average returns; therefore, Parcel C is at the break-even point or the no-rent, extensive margin of land use for this particular land use activity. In general, the impacts of development projects on the economics of land use may be analyzed in terms of their effect on the use capacity of land and on the intensive and extensive margins of land use. The nature of these effects is considered in somewhat greater detail in the latter part of this chapter in a discussion of methods and approaches for the assessment of land use impacts.

The Economics of Land Use and Other Social Impacts

Now that a few basic economic concepts concerning land use have been identified, it is useful to briefly consider some of the relationships between impacts on land use economics and other categories of socioeconomic impacts.

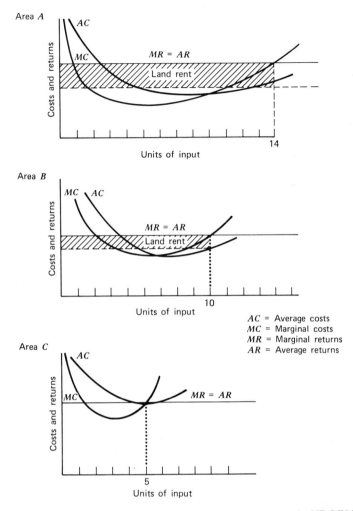

Figure 4.2 Intensive and extensive margins of land use. Raleigh Barlowe, LAND RESOURCES ECONOMICS: *The Economics of Real Property,* 2nd. ed., © 1972, pp. 151, 152. Reprinted by permission of Prentice-Hall, Inc., Englewood Cliffs, New Jersey.

It has already been suggested that a direct relationship exists between the timing, rate, and magnitude of land use conversion and various economic factors affecting land use.[19,7,18] An area, for example, in which the use capacity (and land rents) are relatively low and where many parcels are at or near the extensive margin of land use for present activities may be a target for rapid conversion by land speculators if a proposed development project presents the likelihood of future demands for more profitable types of land-use activity. The example of the premature subdivision of land that often occurs near large-scale recreational developments is an excellent illustration of this effect. Agricultural land may be withdrawn from production and lie idle in empty subdivisions for years as a result of the promotion of speculators and investors hoping for quick resale profits.

For example, studies of one rural area near a reservoir that had been proposed for development by the Bureau of Reclamation and the U.S. Army Corps of Engineers have indicated that agricultural land was being subdivided and sold to speculators as early as 1960. Out of a total of almost 400 lots in one of several subdivision projects, only 22 structural improvements had been started by January 1, 1973 for a buildout rate of approximately 5.5 percent in 13 years. Moreover, because of economic and environmental conditions, it is unlikely that the proposed reservoir will ever be constructed.[23] It is important to note here that this sort of premature land use conversion may have significant aesthetic and ecological impacts if, as in this case, trees are felled, roads are gouged out, and signs or utility structures are allowed to scar open-space area.

Prices and rents charged by landowners will affect the composition and size of both temporary and permanent populations. When supplies of suitable land are limited and demands for particular types of use activities are high, per-unit or per-acre values may be pushed up beyond the reach of lower income groups. When attempts are made to provide low to moderate cost housing in areas with rising raw land values, the cost of raw land becomes an ever increasing percentage of the total unit price.[19] This effect may result in pressures for smaller lot sizes with correspondingly increased densities (perhaps to the point at which excessive crowding occurs) and in trends toward lower cost (and often lower quality) improvements to the land in an attempt to keep total unit costs down. Conversely, when prices and rents that can be charged by landowners decline as a result of loss of area employment or other effects on land use, demands for residential or commercial uses may be forced toward the extensive margin. In this situation, owners will be unable or will have little incentive to adequately maintain their properties in an effort to minimize costs. The result for the area may be substantially increased vacancy rates and the deterioration of improvements toward slum conditions. This sort of impact on land use economics has been particularly noticeable in many urban centers where core areas of the central city have been affected by the shift of population to surburban areas and by the development of peripheral shopping centers that compete with central business districts. Dietz discusses these matters in more detail in Chapter 3.

Land Tenure and Land Use Controls

The final concept of land use that must be considered as part of the impact assessment process involves land tenure and land use controls. Although previous discussions have suggested that land use patterns and changes in these patterns can be analyzed in terms of various economic concepts, it is clear that a plethora of other socioeconomic factors associated with ownership of land play a substantial role in land use decisions. Studies have examined the relationships among social and economic characteristics of landowners and the impact of these characteristics on land use decisions.[21, 22, 24] For example, an owner who is faced with potential changes in the use capacity of his land that would entail the conversion to a new type of activity faces three options. He may choose to develop the property himself and thereby assume all risks of development in the hope of increased land rents. On the other hand, if the owner is either unable or unwilling to engage in the development of the parcel, he may sell all or part of his interest in the property, thereby exchanging the possibility of future profits for more certain present benefits. In the third option, the owner may choose not to develop the parcel at all. This may occur because the risks that are perceived are too great, because there is a desire to hold the land for sale at some later date when market prices may be more favorable, or simply because there is a desire to retain the property in its present state because of the personal attitudes and preferences of the landowner. Among the socioeconomic variables that can be expected to influence these decisions are the age of the landowner, the length of ownership of the land, the ability of the owner to raise development capital, and the costs which would be incurred in land use conversion.[21, 22, 24]

In addition to the role of the landowner in land use decisions, a number of public and private land use controls may have a significant effect on the type and intensity of land use. Public controls over land use can be divided into those that regulate the type and intensity of use activity which is allowed on a particular parcel and those that control improvements which exist on the land.[25] The first category includes both prohibitory land use control mechanisms such as the zoning power and more positive forms of land use control such as preferential taxation schemes that seek to encourage socially desireable patterns of land use. In the latter category of land use controls are a variety of statutes and or ordinances designed to protect public health and safety from substandard structural improvements. Included here are county or municipal building codes, architectural review committees in local governments, and statutes governing public and private nuisances.

An often overlooked type of land use controls includes the various covenants, conditions, and restrictions which may be attached to a parcel of land by the owner at the time the land is sold for development. As one commentator has pointed out, the imposition of public controls on land use has traditionally raised cries of "unjust taking" of "private property" and will no doubt continue to raise the ire of property owners. However, purchasers of land have long been willing to accept restrictions on the use of their property which are imposed by way of conditions or restrictions in deeds and which go far beyond the level of control that would be tolerated if imposed by local or state government.[25] The most common example of these privately imposed controls on land use are the restrictions that are often associated with the ownership of land in large residential subdivisions. These restrictions may extend to such matters as the color which can be used on the home, the pets which the owner is allowed to keep, the type and placement of shrubbery which is permitted, and the frequency with which the owner must mow his lawn. In addition to these restrictive covenants, owners may be forced to belong and pay assessments to a homeowners' association that is charged with the maintenance of public areas in the subdivision.

A development project may affect land tenure and land use controls in a variety of ways. Immediate effects of the project may include the purchase of property rights in the area including entire parcels and easement rights for project purposes, such as roadways or sewer and water lines. The magnitude of these impacts on patterns of area land ownership may range from minimal effects to the purchase of numerous parcels and the corresponding displacement of many area residents. Table 2 presents an example of the impacts of one reservoir project on land tenure. In addition, Burdge and Dietz (chapters 7 and

Table 2 Land Requirements for the Construction and Operation of a Water-Resources Development Project

Project Feature	Land Requirements (acres)			
	Private Land Fee Title	Easement	Public Land	Total
Construction of dams and reservoirs	10,220	—	2310	12,530
Conveyance and distribution facilities	724	—	27	751
Recreational facilities	4,480	—	1610	6,090
Fish and wildlife enhancement	1,932	420	1315	3,667
Total	17,356	420	5262	23,038

ADDITIONAL IMPACTS ON AREA PROPERTY RIGHTS

1. Infringement of grazing leases	4234 acres
2. Infringement of timber harvesting rights	1448 acres
3. Possible infringement on mining claims	225 claims

SOURCE. A Report on the Feasibility of Water Supply Development—Consumnes River Division, Central Valley Project, California. U.S. Bureau of Reclamation, Sacramento, California, 1968.

3) consider various impacts associated with displacements of population in further detail.

The effect of a development project on land use planning within the project area is particularly important in an assessment of land use impacts. At present, there exists a tremendous variation in the level of planning expertise exercised at state and local levels. In many areas planning consists of little more than an arbitrarily drawn zoning map, possibly prepared many years ago, which bears little relationship to actual land use conditions. In other areas, and particularly in urban areas, comprehensive, long-range general plans have been developed to control and guide development.

Project impacts on land use planning may include the issuance of a variance or special use permit if the project conflicts with existing regulations. Perhaps the most severe impacts on land use controls will be likely to stem from rapid increases in demand for land use and the corresponding land use conversion that may be produced by the project. These impacts are likely to be severe when the project area does not possess a comprehensive land use plan. Planning staffs in such areas may not be able to cope with the rapid pace of development that can (and often does) result in undesirable patterns of land use such as strip development, aesthetically unattractive structures, or "sprawl" development which, once established, renders effective land use planning extremely difficult.

APPROACHES AND METHODS FOR THE ASSESSMENT OF LAND USE IMPACTS

Assessment Methodology

The preceding discussions have attempted to outline a conceptual framework that can be used in considering potential impacts of resource development projects on land use. The balance of the present chapter deals with approaches and methods for the actual assessment of land use impacts. At the outset it is important to note that the development of methodologies for the identification and evaluation of land use impacts remains in its infancy. Numerous texts, articles, and reports have dealt with relatively narrow problems concerning the identification and measurement of impacts on the human environment.[21,22,24,26,12,13,27,28,29,30] However, until recently there existed no single work that attempted to address the full range of methodological problems which are involved in land use impact assessment. In November, 1974 the Urban Institute's Land Use Center published a report by Schaenman and Muller entitled, *Measuring Impacts of Land Development: An Initial Approach.*[30] This work, in the words of the authors, "sets forth measures and procedures for assessing the impact of land development on economic, environmental, aesthetic, public and private service, housing, and social concerns" (p. 1). Although the Urban Institute report, as its title suggests, is a preliminary effort, it provides an outline for the development and utilization of land use impact measures and presents examples of methods and procedures for the collection and analysis of data that can be readily utilized for the assessment of impacts on the four categories of land use variables described in the first part of this chapter. In addition to reviewing the work of Schaenman and Muller, the remainder of the present chapter suggests other approaches for the identification and evaluation of land use impacts.

Stages in Land Use Impact Assessment

The assessment of land use impacts may be viewed as a 3-stage process. The initial stage involves an analysis of the existing state of land use within the area identified as being potentially affected by a proposed project. All four categories of land use variables must be examined, and summaries or profiles of area land use patterns must be prepared and displayed. This stage of the assessment process should be of considerable value to planners and decision-makers by continually calling attention to changes in area land use patterns and by providing data that can be utilized in the review of local and regional plans. Moreover, the assessment of existing land use conditions may reveal impacts that have been caused by past development projects. This information may in turn aid in the forecasting of effects from future developments.

The second stage in land use impact assessment calls for the identification of all possible impacts on land use. It should be emphasized that this stage of impact assessment is not particularly concerned with either the specific nature or magnitude of the effects of a project on land use. Rather, the purpose of this stage is to ensure a systematic and comprehensive review of all features of a proposed project in regard to all possible types of land use impacts.

The third and final stage in the assessment process entails an evaluation of the nature and probable magnitude of land use impacts. This process will utilize data concerning the features of the project and the existing stage of land use to assess the site-specific impacts of a project. For some types of land use impacts, considerable precision will be possible. For example, an industrial park or subdivision will convert a given number of acres to a new use activity. Similarly, an irrigation program can be expected to increase the intensity of agricultural land use by an identifiable amount. For other impacts, somewhat less precision will be possible. An industrial park that produces new employment opportunities can be expected to also create demands for residential, commercial, and recreational land uses. However, the precise number of new dwelling units that will be required in the project area as a result of the project may depend on prevailing vacancy and employment rates, the types of employment opportunities which will be created, and the number of persons who will migrate into the area as a result of these opportunities. The amount and rate of new commercial or recreational development that may occur from an increase in residential land use is even less susceptible to measurement. As discussed later in the chapter, it should be noted that a lack of precise measurement does not necessarily detract from the utility of the land use impact analysis.

Assessment of the Existing State of Land Use

To begin an assessment of the existing stage of land use, the initial task is to define the boundaries of the area likely to be affected by a proposed project. Unfortunately, no reliable criteria exist that can be used to determine the scope of land use effects from a particular project. In approaching this problem, two suggestions are useful. Since many types of data concerning land use are collected and analyzed for areas defined by political subdivision boundaries, these units will often be most convenient for purposes of defining the project area. Second, it should be stressed that the boundaries of the study area should be kept open, since once the effects of a project become apparent, these boundaries may need to be revised and additional land use data may need to be collected.

The description of land use within the project area will typically involve the utilization of both primary and secondary data sources. Primary data involves the on-site collection of information concerning land use and includes a variety of field survey methodologies. Secondary land use data sources include all types of statistics, surveys, and other analyses of existing land use conditions that have been compiled by both public and private sources.

Data concerning land use is available from a wide range of sources and may be obtained at levels of detail ranging from national statistics to information regarding a particular facet of land use within a local area. Perhaps the most comprehensive treatment to date concerning the types of land use data that are available and the sources of these data has been compiled by Marion Clawson under the sponsorship of Resources for the Future, Inc.[3] The reader is encouraged to refer to this book to supplement the summary of suggested data sources provided in the following discussions.

At the national level, data involving many aspects of land use are collected by the U.S. Bureau of the Census. The bureau collects data concerning virtually every major type of land use activity, and in addition, census divisions dealing with business, agriculture, industry, and housing collect large amounts of data on improvements to land. Aside from the Bureau of the Census, many other federal agencies regularly collect land use data. For example, the Department of Agriculture (USDA) through the Soil Conservation Service surveys agricultural lands and classifies rural areas by soil type and other indicators of agricultural productivity. The U.S. Forest Service conducts surveys and inventories of forest lands in the United States and provides many types of data for these areas. Finally, through its Economic Research Service the department provides data concerning the economics of land use in rural areas[3] (App. C, D, E, F).

Although land use data collected by federal agencies will often be useful, these data in many cases may have been collected at a level of aggregation that is too large to provide the detailed descriptions necessary in the preparation of an environmental impact statement or report. Fortunately, state, regional, and local governments, as well as private organizations, are also rich sources of data concerning land use. Local government planning offices should be able to provide information concerning all aspects of area land use within their jurisdictions. City or county building inspectors may be a source of data on improvements to land. In addition, local health departments should be able to provide data describing the presence or absence of substandard residential, commercial, and recreational conditions. Finally, the local assessor's office and real estate associations are sources of data on land tenure, prices, rents, and market activity within the study area.

For particular land use variables, secondary data sources may either be unavailable or of limited utility for the project area. In these cases secondary data sources must be supplemented by the on-site collection of information to adequately describe the existing state of area land use. The collection of data on land use activities will probably involve the utilization of a classification and coding system as part of a land use survey of the area. Many classification-coding systems have been developed by federal, state, and local agencies. One such system that has received widespread use since its introduction in 1964 is the Federal Standard Land Use Coding Manual developed by the Urban Renewal Administrattion and the Bureau of Public Roads.[3] This system of classifying land use activities is based on the classification of economic activity contained in the Federal Standard Industrial Classification (SIC). The Standard Land Use Coding Manual involves a field survey of area land use activities that are recorded on field listing forms including the location and a description of the activity for each parcel. Each parcel is then assigned a one- to four-digit classification number and, in some cases, one or more auxiliary code numbers that refer to a standardized land use activity category. Once land in the project area has been surveyed and coded, it is then possible to prepare tabular summaries, charts, graphs, and map displays of the existing state of land use activity within the project area.[3,31,32]

The description of the existing state of improvements to land may also necessitate the use of on-site survey methods if these data have not been compiled by local governments. Some of these surveys have been termed structural and environmental quality surveys and have been utilized by planners to identify conditions of blight in urban areas and to develop urban renewal plans, redevelopment programs, or other area rehabilitation policies.[31, 32] Standards for use in reviewing the condition of improvements to land are typically established by local building and health departments for various types of development. When such standards have not been set, other public and private organizations have established recommended criteria for neighborhood environmental quality.[11]

A variety of survey methodologies have been applied by planners to assess the condition of improvements to land. Most of these methods involve on-site inspection of existing development and the application of an appraisal "scoring system" to evaluate area conditions in terms of predefined substandardness criteria.[12, 13] Some of these survey techniques also have attempted to evaluate both the present condition of structures and the external effects of these structures on surrounding parcels.[12, 13, 31, 32] The *external* effects of improvements to land may be defined as those factors that affect the suitability or desirability of surrounding parcels for particular types of human activity. For example, the operation of a cement plant may impose substantial external effects on the surrounding countryside in the form of discharges of smoke and particulate matter that may have serious adverse effects on health and aesthetics within the affected area. Since external effects of improvement to land often represent a major source of impact on the human environment, any feature of a proposed project that would exacerbate or mitigate these phenomena must be fully discussed, and a comprehensive assessment of the types and magnitude of external effects that exist in the project area must be conducted. Aerial photographs may be particularly useful. Table 3 illustrates the variety of external effects that may be associated with existing improvements to land.

Once one or more land use survey techniques have been applied, the resulting data must be summarized for presentation to decision makers. Wherever possible, map overlay techniques should be used to adequately display the location of various types, intensities, conditions, and external effects of improvements to land within the project area.[4, 33]

Another aspect of area land use that will often require the collection of primary data is the condition of the visual environment. Attempts to assess aesthetic impacts of development projects have been plagued by a lack of methods for portraying objectively the existing aesthetic environment. Recently, increased attention has been focused on the need for such descriptive methodologies.[30] One such quantitative method for evaluating the visual environment has been applied to an area at Lake Tahoe as part of the regional planning program in that area.[9, 10] This methodology involves the division of the study area into measured sections and the on-site recording and coding of

Table 3 External Effects Associated with Improvements to Land

SOURCE	NUISANCE OR HAZARD								
	Night Glare	Noise and Vibration	Objectionable Odors	Fire and Explosion	Smoke or Dust	Vermin, Rodents and Insects	Traffic Accidents	Hazards to Morals and the Public Peace	Pollution of Land or Water
TRANSPORTATION									
Railroads............	★	★	...	...	★	...	★	...	...
Airplanes...........	...	★	...	★	...	...	★	...	...
Street traffic........	★	★	★	...	...	...	★	...	...
INDUSTRY									
Metal products (extraction, processing).........	★	★	★	...	★	...	a	...	★
Heavy machinery (manufacturing).........	★	★	...	...	★	...	a	...	★
Light machinery (manufacturing).........	★	★	...	...	...	...	a	...	...
Transportation (storage, servicing, repair).......	★	★	★	★	...	...	a	...	...
Stone, clay and glass products (extraction and processing).........	...	★	...	...	★	...	...	...	★
Building construction materials (manufacturing, storage)............	...	★	...	★	...	...	a	...	...
Petroleum and coal products (extraction, processing, storage, servicing).......	★	★	★	★	★	...	...	...	★

Forest products and paper (processing, manufacturing and storage)

Chemical and related products (manufacturing, processing, storage)

Textiles, leather and furs (processing, manufacturing, storage and repair)

Foods (processing, manufacturing, storage, servicing)

COMMERCE

Warehouses

Retail stores of various types

Poorly maintained food stores

Bars and taverns

Night clubs

Poolrooms, etc.

Houses of prostitution

Gambling places

Sports arenas and other large-scale commercial amusements

a Additional traffic loads and hazards may result from the presence of industry, commerce, warehousing and large-scale entertainment in built-up areas. For that reason they should be considered sources of potential traffic accidents, although the actual accidents are caused by street or railroad traffic servicing the establishments.

SOURCE	NUISANCE OR HAZARD								
	Night Glare	Noise and Vibration	Objection- able Odors	Fire and Explosion	Smoke or Dust	Vermin, Rodents and Insects	Traffic Accidents	Hazards to Morals and the Public Peace	Pollution of Land or Water
MISCELLANEOUS									
Refuse dumps		★	★			★			
Junk yards		★				★			
Storage of miscellaneous waste products						★			
Sewage disposal plants			★						★
Garbage disposal plants			★		★				
Improper waste disposal from off-site structures									★
Dilapidated abandoned structures						★			
Vacant lots in insanitary condition					★	★			
Open land, unplanted (such as unsurfaced playgrounds and playfields and plowed unplanted farm land)					★				
Farms, especially dairy and animal husbandry			★			★			

all visible artificial and natural objects within each section. Coding procedures were developed to express recorded visual obstructions in a quantitative format on field coding sheets for computer processing. From these field coding forms, summaries were prepared for each area section including variables such as

- The total amount of blocked footage from the road expressed in linear feet;
- The total amount of open space expressed in linear feet;
- The total footage of power line in the section;
- The total number of objects recorded in the section;
- The primary land use type (activity) expressed to the 2-digit level of the Federal Standard Land Use Code;
- The secondary land use type;
- The total view potential of the unit.

Admittedly, the development of such methodologies is far from complete. However, selective applications of such methods together with the extensive use of photography can be utilized to develop a profile of the existing visual environment and to identify aspects of area aesthetics that may be particularly susceptible to changes caused by the proposed project.

Once data concerning land use within the project area have been collected from both secondary and primary sources, these data must be assembled and used to construct various profiles of the existing state of land use. The particular land use factors that have been emphasized in the collection of data will, of course, vary considerably depending on the nature of the proposed project and the particular project area. The discussions that follow are intended only to illustrate the types of descriptive data summaries which will need to be prepared. It should be noted that in addition to data concerning the existing (preimpact) state of land use, it will often be desirable to describe past trends in land use patterns. Many sources of land use information provide data series that can be used to construct trends for particular aspects of land use. For example, it will often be desirable to identify trends in both the rate and types of new construction in an area as well as trends in vacancy rates or land prices and rents if the proposed project is expected to result in a substantial in-migration of persons into the project area.

In regard to land use activity patterns, the impact analysis must provide a summary presentation of the types and amounts of each type of activity within the area. Tabular summaries may be used together with map overlay techniques to identify the location of various activity types in relation to the proposed project site. It will often be desirable to describe certain types of use activity in greater detail than others. For example, a project that anticipates a substantial in-migration of new residents may require detailed descriptions of the amount and location of vacant land which is suitable for residential and commercial development. The intensity of use should also be presented both in tabular and map overlay form. Obviously, the measurement of data of this kind is also useful in the analysis of other impacts, particularly those discussed by Dietz and Dickinson and Blackmarr in this book.

The presentation of data concerning improvements to land within the project area must include variables such as the number and relative frequency of improvements classified as to the type of activity with which they are associated. Also included here should be a summary presentation of a structural and environmental quality survey if these data are available for the project area. Areas with particular blight problems must be identified.

Another important aspect of area land use that must be displayed within the impact assessment report includes data concerning the types, location, and conditions of avaiable essential services, such as sewers, water, fire and police protection, and municipal recreation areas. Again, map overlays should be provided to relate the location of these services to data concerning other land use variables and to the proposed project site. Finally, the results of any aesthetic survey of the project area should be included in the description of land use improvements. If a quantitative assessment of area aesthetics has been conducted, summaries of these data should be presented including photographic displays that will orient the project reviewer to the area and the existing status of the area's visual environment. Significant views or visual areas that would be directly affected by the proposed project should be given particular attention within the impact statement or report.

Profiles of prevailing land prices, rents, and market activity must be developed and presented in a summary of the economics of land use for the project area. For example, it will be desirable to present the amount of housing available at various price ranges. Other variables for which data will be required include the availability and prices for vacant land suitable for various use activities. For both rural and urban areas it will be necessary to identify locations where the existing use is near or at marginal levels of productivity, since these areas may become prime targets for land use conversion. In the presentation of data concerning land use economics, significant trends in prices, rents, and market activity should also be displayed.

A discussion of the existing state of land tenure and land use controls should contain both quantitative and qualitative analyses of these aspects of area land use. In regard to land tenure, the impact report will require a summary of land ownership patterns including data on the number of owners and the size of parcels for land that will be affected by the project. The quantitative evaluation of land use controls will include a set of maps presenting the amount and location of land zoned for various use activities and intensities of use. It will be desirable to distinguish between vacant and developed areas on this map. Existing general and specific land use plans should be reviewed to determine the proportion or mix of uses provided under each plan and the size of area population forecast by the plans. The qualitative evaluation of area land use planning involves an examination of the forecasts and assumptions on which present plans are based.[31,32] This review must consider what sort of population projections were used in the formulation of existing plans and should determine whether these projections remain sound. Also, any economic studies that have been conducted should be consulted to determine whether area growth is meeting or exceeding the rates forecast in existing land use plans. This issue is discussed in some detail by Dickinson and Blackmarr in Chapter 5.

Immediately following the collection of data concerning the existing state of land use and before the development of data summaries or profiles, all land use information must be carefully reviewed and an attempt made to identify or "red flag" those aspects of area land use that are of particular concern within the project area. These aspects of land use may be variables that are either peculiar to the project area or that differ significantly from state or regional norms. Examples of this type of condition might be an unusually high area vacancy rate for residential and commercial parcels or extremely inflated prices and rents with a corresponding shortage of available low to moderate cost housing. Other examples include essential municipal services such as sewers, water, fire, and police protection, or schools that have either reached or are rapidly nearing capacities. In regard to these problem aspects of area land use, it will be desirable to include a separate discussion for each variable of any present or planned mitigation measures. All features of the proposed project must then be carefully examined for possible impacts on these critical aspects of area land use.

Identification of Land Use Impacts

Following the assessment of the existing state of land use conditions within the project area, the next major stage in the impact assessment process is the identification of all possible land use impacts. It is possible to identify three phases in the identification of land use impacts. First, impact measures must be defined for each of the four categories of land use variables described in the first part of this chapter. Next, all significant features of a proposed development project must be identified. Finally, the impact measures and project features must be arranged in an organizational framework that will facilitate a systematic and comprehensive review of possible effects on land use.

IMPACT MEASURES

Schaenman and Muller have presented an approach for developing a set of impact measures for use in the identification of land use impacts as well as other effects.[30] Briefly summarized, this approach involves the identification of community objectives in regard to land use and the definition of appropriate measures for the attainment of these objectives. For example, in regard to improvements to land, one objective might be the prevention of physical deterioration of commercial and residential structures and the maintenance of an overall aesthetic environment that is pleasing to the community. Appropriate impact measures in terms of this objective might include: (1) the number and percentage of structures that are classified as substandard or in need of external repairs; (2) the number and percentage of dwellings of various ages, sizes, and architectural styles; and (3) the number and magnitude of various external effects of improvements to land such as glare, odors, smoke, dust and noise within the project area.

It is, of course, not possible to specify a set of land use objectives or impact measures that would be desirable for every community. Local decision makers should develop lists of such objectives and measures for each of the four categories of land use variables that, in their judgment, best reflect the needs and goals of their communities.[30] For purposes of illustration, Tables 4 and 5 present lists of community objectives and impact measures for a broad range of social and economic impacts.

PROJECT FEATURES

Once all relevant community objectives and impact measures have been listed, the next stage in the impact identification process involves the identification of all features of a proposed project that could possibly have an effect on land use. It will often be necessary to divide the features of a proposed project into temporal and spatial dimensions. For example, a project involving a substantial amount of construction activity may be divided into those features that will occur during the planning and authorization stages (preconstruction), features that will become significant during the construction of the project, features that will not occur until after the completion of the project (operational stage), and finally, those features that may not become apparent until long after the project has become operational. The division of project features into spatial dimensiohs will identify those features that will be experienced at the project site, those that will occur in areas immediately surrounding the project location and those that can be expected to occur at a considerable distance from the project area. Table 6 illustrates the temporal and spatial categorization of features for a hypothetical development project. The precise manner in which a proposed project should be divided into a temporal and spatial display of project features will, of course, depend on the nature and size of the proposed development and on the particular circumstances of the project area. However, care should be taken to avoid lumping too many distinct aspects of a project into a single category since this may result in the failure to identify potentially significant land use impacts.

ORGANIZATION AND DISPLAY

The final task before attempting to identify possible impacts on land use requires the arrangement of relevant impact measures and project features into an organizational framework that will allow decision makers to conduct a systematic and comprehensive review of the proposed development. Before discussing possible organizational formats, it is important to point out that any impact measures or land use variables which were "red flagged" during the assessment process must be clearly identified. This will allow impact reviewers to focus their attention on features of a proposed development that could affect particularly significant aspects of land use within the project area. For example, if the assessment of the existing state of land use has revealed a shortage of low- and moderate-income housing, all impact measures that reflect on this variable should be identified. Then, if it appears that any features of a proposed development could affect demands for or supplies of low- and moderate-cost housing, this potential impact can immediately be brought to the attention of impact reviewers.

The organization of information for the assessment of environmental impacts has received considerable attention.[26,29] Two methodologies that received widespread utilization are impact checklists and various sorts of matrices that portray impact measures and project features in a two-dimensional display format. Impact checklists have been used extensively by state and local governments as a method for conducting a preliminary review of proposed projects to determine whether a more detailed impact assessment should be required. Most checklists consist simply of a series of questions that constitute rough impact measures for all relevant environmental variables. The features of a proposed project are reviewed in terms of these questions, and a decision is made concerning whether the project could possibly have significant environmental impacts. Figure 4.3 presents an example of a typical impact checklist.

The impact checklist may be a useful device for assisting decision makers in making the threshold determination concerning whether a project merits a more extensive and time-consuming impact assessment. However, this approach is considerably less useful in obtaining a comprehensive identification of all possible land use impacts. In the case of most development projects, the number of project features and impact measures will be so large that it would be extremely difficult to examine every feature of the project in terms of all impact measures. It is, therefore, unlikely that checklists can be used for more than very small, uncomplicated projects.

A more useful organizational tool for the identification of potential land use

Table 4   Community Objectives for Regulating Land Development

I.   **Local Economy:**

To keep the local government fiscally solvent without excessive taxes; to maintain a high level of stable employment and to reduce unemployment and under-employment in the community; to maintain prosperity; and to enable citizens in the community to achieve levels of personal income and wealth consistent with a decent standard of living (1-4).

II.   **Natural Environment:**

To minimize pollution, protect wildlife and ecologically important features, preserve the natural environment, and conserve scarce resources (5-12).

III.   **Aesthetic and Cultural Values:**

To protect and improve the physical and cultural attractiveness of the community (5-10, 13-16).

IV.   **Public and Private Services:**

- *Health and Safety.* To minimize illness, injury, death rates, and property loss or damage (5-7, 17-24, 35-36, 39).

- *Recreation.* To provide a variety of accessible and enjoyable recreational facilities and programs in the community (6, 8, 25-27).

- *Education.* To provide quality education at all levels for all people in the community; to provide as diverse educational experiences as the community requires; and to assure the convenience and pleasantness of attending school (16, 28-30).

- *Local Transportation.* To provide access to an adequate choice of community services, facilities, and employment in a safe, quick, and convenient manner; and to move goods efficiently (31-36).

- *Shopping.* To promote the adequacy, variety, convenience and pleasantness of shopping for people in the community (37-38).

V. Housing and Social Conditions:

- *Housing.* To increase the opportunity for all citizens to obtain satisfactory housing at prices they can afford (39-40, 46-48).

- *Social Concerns and Community Morale.* To promote friendliness, psychological well-being, and good community morale while protecting individual's privacy and ability to regulate their interpersonal contacts (41-48).

- *Fairness to All Groups.* To apply each objective with equity to all within the community (1-48, reported by clientele group).

NOTES: 1. This set of objectives is illustrative. Each community should determine goals consistent with the desires and values of its citizens.

2. The numbers in parentheses following each objective correspond to the impact measures in Exhibit 1 which help describe whether a development will contribute to the objective.

3. The order of the objectives implies no ranking of priorities.

137

Table 5 Measures for Evaluating the Impacts of Land Developments

Impact Area[1]	Measure		
I. *Local Economy*			
Public Fiscal Balance	1. Net change in government fiscal flow (revenues less operating expenditures and annualized capital expenditures).		proves or lessens the over neighborhood attracti ness, pleasantness, a uniqueness.[4]
Employment	2. Number of new long-term and short-term jobs provided.	Landmarks	16. Rarity and perceived imp tance of cultural. histo or scientific landmarks to lost or made inaccessible.
	3. Change in numbers and percent employed, unemployed, and underemployed.	**IV. *Public and Private Services***	
		Drinking Water	17. Change in rate of wa shortage incidents.
Wealth	4. Change in land values.		18. Change in indexes of dri ing water quality and safe
II. *Natural Environment*[2]		Hospital Care	19. Change in number of c zens who are beyond
Air	5. Change in level of air pollutants and number of people at risk or bothered by air pollution.		minutes travel time from hospital emergency ro (using such time as community considers sonable).
Water	6. Change in level of water pollutants, change in tolerable types of use, and number of persons affected, for each body of water.		20. Change in average num of days of waiting time hospital admittance for el tive surgery.
Noise	7. Change in noise and vibration levels. and number of people bothered by excessive noise and vibration.	Crime Control	21. Change in rate of crimes existing community or r development (or expert ing of change in hazard).
Greenery and Open Space	8. Amount and percent change in greenery and open space.		22. Change in percent of pec feeling a lack of secu from crime.
Wildlife and Vegetation	9. Number and types of endangered or rare species that will be threatened.	Fire Protection	23. Change in fire incide rates.
	10. Change in abundance and diversity of wildlife and vegetation in the development and community.		24. Change in rating of spread and rescue haza
Scarce Resource Consumption	11. Change in frequency, duration, and magnitude of shortages of critically scarce resources. and the number of persons affected.	Recreation[5]	25. Change in the number people within—or beyonc reasonable distance (x m or y minutes) from rec tional facilities. by type facility.
Natural Disasters	12. Change in number of people and value of property endangered by flooding. earthquakes, landslides. mudslides. and other natural disasters.		26. Change in usage as a perc of capacity; waiting tin number of people tur away; facility space resident; and citizen perc tions of crowdedness recreational facilities.
III. *Aesthetics and Cultural Values*[3]			27. Change in perceived pl antness of recreational perience.[8]
Views	13. Number of people whose views are blocked, degraded, or improved.	Education[6]	28. Change in number of dents within x minutes v or y minutes ride f school. by type of sch
Attractiveness	14. Visual attractiveness of the development as rated by citizens and "experts."		29. Number and percent students having to sw
	15. Percent of citizens who think the development im-		

schools or busing status (from walking to busing or vice versa).

30. Change in crowdedness "breakpoints" (such as need for added shifts) or indicators (such as student-teacher ratios); student. teacher, and parent perceptions of crowdedness and pleasantness of schooling.

Local Transportation[7] 31. Change in vehicular travel times between selected origins and destinations.

32. Change in duration and severity of congestion.

33. Change in likelihood of finding a satisfactory parking space within x distance from destination or resident.

34. Change in numbers and percent of residents with access to public transit within x feet of their residences; and numbers and percent of employees who can get within x distance of work location by public transit.

35. Change in the rate of traffic accidents (or expert rating of change in hazard presented).

36. Number and percent of citizens perceiving a change in neighborhood traffic hazard; and change in pedestrian usage of streets, sidewalks. and other outdoor space.[8]

Shopping 37. Change in number of stores and services, by type, available within x distance of y people.

38. Change in the percent of people generally satisfied with local shopping conditions (access, variety, crowdedness).[8]

V. Housing and Social Conditions

Housing Adequacy 39. Change in number and percent of housing units that are substandard, and change in number and percent of people living in such units.

40. Change in number and percent of housing units by type (price or rent range, zoning category, owner-occupied and rental. etc.) relative to demand or to number of families in various income classes in the community.

People Displaced 41. Number of residents. or workers. displaced by development—and by whether they are satisfied with having to move.

Population Mix 42. Change in the population distribution by age, income, religion, racial or ethnic group, occupational class. and household type.

Crowdedness 43. Change in percent of people who perceive their neighborhood as too crowded.[8]

Sociability-Friendliness 44. Change in frequency of visits to friends among people in the existing neighborhood, and frequency of visits between people in the existing neighborhood and the new development.

45. Change in percent of people perceiving the neighborhood as friendly.[8]

Privacy 46. Number and percent of people with change in "visual" or "auditory" privacy.

47. Number and percent of people perceiving a loss of privacy.[8]

Overall Contentment with Neighborhood 48. Change in percent of people who perceive their community as a good place to live.[8]

Fairness to All Groups — The above measures should be considered with respect to specific clientele groups or population segments that are affected to reflect the quality of fairness in new developments.

NOTES:
These impact areas correspond to community objectives for regulating land development (see Exhibit 2).
In some situations, a measure of the change in the microclimate near a development should be added to the list.
Measures 5 through 10 also reflect aspects of aesthetics. See text for discussion of overlapping of objectives and interrelation of measures.
Some may find a new development physically attractive (Measure 14), but prefer the current appearance of the neighborhood for its "character," image, relation to personal identity, and so forth.
Changes in the use of informal recreational facilities such as streets, sidewalks, and open space should be included.
No satisfactory measure of development impacts on the quality of education received has been found.
Impacts of land use changes on accessibility by foot are reflected in part in measures for recreation (25), schools (28), and shopping (37).
Measures dealing with citizen perceptions are much harder to estimate quantitatively for proposed developments than for past developments. However, bounds or ranges may be estimated in some situations, and in all they should be considered at least qualitatively.

Reprinted by permission from *Measuring Impacts of Land Development,* Philip S. Schaenman and Thomas Muller, 1974, Washington, D.C.: The Urban Institute.

Table 6 Hypothetical Development Project Features

Project Features	Temporal			Spatial		
	Primary Impacts occurring within 3 yrs	3–10 yrs	10 yrs +	Impacts on site of construction	Project area	Remote Locations
Planning and feasibility studies	*			*		
Land acquisition	*	*		*	*	
Necessary government permits or licenses secured	*	*		*	*	*
Contracts let (water service contracts, etc.)	*	*		*	*	*
Initial site clearance grading preliminary construction activities	*			*		
Construction of major project features (dams and distribution facilities)	*	*		*		
Filling of reservoir		*		*		
Generation of electrical power		*	*	*	*	*
Recreational facilities completed		*	*	*	*	*
Supply of irrigation water		*	*	*	*	*
Supply of municipal-industrial water		*	*	*	*	*

impacts is the impact matrix. The matrix is essentially a two-dimensional checklist in which all relevant impact measures are arranged in a row at the side of the matrix and all project features are arrayed along the top of the matrix.[28] With all information arranged in this framework, it is possible for reviewers to systematically consider each feature of a proposed project in terms of possible effects on each impact measure. Figure 4.4 presents an abbreviated, hypothetical impact identification matrix.

For example, looking at the matrix in Figure 4.4, a reviewer might perceive that the construction of major project features, which will involve the influx of laborers, may have an effect on the availability of low- and moderate-cost housing in the area. In addition, if housing supplies become strained, the construction phase of the project may result in an increase in the number of persons residing in substandard or marginal quality housing within the project area. Since both of these impact measures have been identified as representing existing area problems, decision makers and reviewers should be alerted, and a careful evaluation should be conducted to determine the nature and probable magnitude of these impacts. In utilizing the impact identification matrix, attention should also be given to the temporal and spatial aspects of project features. (see p. 125). If it is believed, for example, that the construction of major project features could cause potentially serious impacts, it will be important to consider whether these impacts can be expected to continue over a long period of time and whether they will be confined to the immediate project area.

IMPACT IDENTIFICATION

Unfortunately, it is not possible to list every conceivable manner in which impacts on land use variables may be produced by all types of development projects. The approach that is suggested in the Urban Institute's recent report provides at least a guide for persons charged with the assessment of land use impacts.[30] In addition, it was possible in the development of a conceptual framework (in the first part of this chapter) to identify a number of ways in which each of the four categories of land use variables might be affected by resource development projects. Consider, for example, a proposed processing facility for agricultural products. In regard to possible impacts on land use activity variables, it is possible to identify several ways in which impacts could be produced. These would include: (1) the direct and immediate conversion of land for the construction of project features; (2) the generation of new or increased demands for particular land use activities such as demands resulting from "stemming" and "induced" economic benefits (see p. 118) or from the in-migration of persons in response to new employment opportunities; (3) effects on the development potential of surrounding parcels caused by the extension of municipal services into the area or by a change in zoning to accomodate the

	Yes	No
I. Characteristics of the natural environment		
Does the project site involve a unique landform or biological area, such as beaches, sand dunes, marshes, tidelands, or San Francisco Bay?	—	—
A. Land (topography, soils, geology)		
Will the project involve construction on slopes of forty percent or greater?	—	—
Is the project to be located in an area of soil instability (subsidence, landslide, or severe erosion)?	—	—
Is the project site located on or adjacent to a known earthquake fault?	—	—
B. Water		
Is the proposed project located within a floodplain?	—	—
Does the proposed project involve a natural drainage channel or streambed?	—	—
C. Biota		
Are there any rare or endangered species of plant life in the project area?	—	—
Will any mature trees be removed or relocated?	—	—
Is the project site adjacent to, or does it include, a habitat, food source, water source, nesting place, or breeding place for a rare or endangered wildlife species?	—	—
Could the project significantly affect fish, wildlife, reptiles, or plant life?	—	—
Is the project located inside or within 200 feet of a fish or wildlife refuge or reserve?	—	—
D. Potential alteration of natural features		
Will the proposed project result in the removal of a natural resource for commercial purposes (including rock, sand, gravel, oil, trees, or minerals)?	—	—
Will the project involve grading in excess of 300 cubic yards?	—	—
II. Pollution (air, water, noise, land)		
Will the project create dust, fumes, smoke, or odors?	—	—
Will the project involve the burning of any material, including brush, trees, and construction materials?	—	—
Is the project expected to result in the generation of noise levels in excess of that currently existing in the area?	—	—
Will the project involve the application, use, or disposal of potentially hazardous materials, including pesticides, herbicides, other toxic substances, or radioactive material?	—	—
III. Applicable pollution controls and standards		
Will the proposed project require a permit or other approval from any of the following agencies?	—	—
State Water Resources Control Board	—	—
Regional Water Quality Control Board	—	—
State Department of Public Health	—	—
Bay Area Air Pollution Control District	—	—
San Francisco Bay Conservation and Development Commission	—	—
Metropolitan Transportation Commission	—	—
U.S. Environmental Protection Agency	—	—
County Airport Land-Use Commission	—	—
Does the project require variance from established environmental standards (e.g., air quality, noise, water quality)?	—	—

Figure 4.3 Environmental impact checklist.

IV.   Impact on infrastructure

A.   Circulation

Is the project expected to cause noticeable increase in pedestrian traffic or a change in pedestrian patterns?   —   —

Will the project result in noticeable changes in vehicular traffic patterns or volumes (including bicycles)?   —   —

Will the proposed project involve the use of off-the-road vehicles of any kind (such as trail bikes)?   —   —

E.   Water supply and sewage disposal

Will the project entail the acquisition of water from wells or surface sources for commercial and/or nondomestic use?   —   —

Will septic tanks be utilized for sewage disposal?   —   —

C.   Demand for service from special districts and/or municipalities or county

Will the project require the extension of existing public utility lines?   —   —

Will the proposed project require public services from an agency, district, or public utility that is currently operating at or near capacity?   —   —

V.   Social effect

Is the project apt to result in the congregating of more than 50 people on a regular basis?   —   —

Will the project result in the introduction of activities not currently found within the community?   —   —

VI.   Miscellaneous

Will the project employ equipment that could interfere with existing communication and/or defense systems?   —   —

Is the project located within the flight path or noise impact area of an airport?   —   —

VII.   Land use

Is the proposed project expected to result in other changes in land use, either on or off the project site?   —   —

Could the project serve to encourage development of presently undeveloped areas, or increases in development intensity of already developed areas (examples include the introduction of new or expanded public utilities, new industry, commercial facilities, or recreation activities)?   —   —

Does the project involve the construction of more than twenty dwelling units?   —   —

Is the project adjacent to or within 500 feet of an existing public facility or site for same?   —   —

Does the project require variance from adopted community plans, policies, or goals?   —   —

Does the project involve lands currently protected under the Williamson Act or an open space easement?   —   —

VIII.   Visual impact

Is the site for the proposed project adjacent to a designated scenic highway or within a scenic corridor?   —   —

Will the project obstruct scenic views from existing residential areas, public lands, or public roads?   —   —

Figure 4.3   (Continued)

143

Does the project involve the construction of buildings or structures in
excess of 3 stories or thirty-six feet in height?   —   —

IX.   Sociocultural impact
Will the project require the relocation of people or business in order to
clear the construction site?   —   —
Does the project site involve a known historical or archeological site?   —   —

SOURCE.   Dickert, Thomas G., with Domeny, Katherine R. Eds. *Environmental
Impact Assessment: Guidelines and Commentary,* University Extension, University of
California, Berkeley, 1974.

Figure 4.3   (Continued)

project; and (4) a variety of external effects that could have a preclusive or
restrictive effect on particular types of land use activities.

The following summary presents in outline form suggestions concerning
possible ways in which impacts on land use variables may occur. It should be
emphasized that this summary is not intended to be a comprehensive checklist
of possible land use impacts. Rather, it is intended only to illustrate the types of
social and economic factors that should be considered by reviewers in applying
an impact identification matrix or other methodology for the identification of
land use impacts.

SOME EXAMPLES OF IMPACTS FOR FOUR CATEGORIES OF LAND USE
VARIABLES: A SUMMARY

Land Use Activities

Direct conversion of land to new or multiple use activities: Both additions and
deletions of activities should be considered. These impacts may occur as a result
of the construction of project features or as a consequence of necessary project-
associated facilities (such as utility lines and roads).

Significant Evaluative Criteria: (a) the amount of land involved in the
conversion, (b) the number and types of use activities added or deleted, (c) the
significance of these changes in terms of area land use patterns as a whole (e.g.,
a measure of the amount of land of a particular use activity that would be
converted by a project in relation to the present total amount of land of that use
activity expressed as a ratio (amount converted/area total), (d) the location of
areas to be converted in relation to the project location and to other significant
area land use features.

*Alterations of land forms, availability of services, accessibility, and other fac-
tors affecting the intensity of area land use*: These impacts may occur either as
direct or indirect results of a development project. For example, the availability

of water for irrigation or electricity may present opportunities for more intensive land use, whereas the development of freeways that reroute traffic flows may drastically affect the intensity of commercial land uses along older highway corridors.

Significant Evaluative Criteria: (a) the amount of land that could be affected by the project, (b) the location of these impacts, (c) estimates of the number of persons and/or parcels that would be affected in terms of changes in the intensity of land use, (d) measures of the potential magnitude of increases and/or decreases in intensity of land use (e.g., estimated reductions in traffic volumes or sales, and effects on vacancy rates, etc.).

Generation of demands for particular land use activities: Included here are stemming and induced effects of a project on demands for land use, such as demands for residential development that could be expected to accompany the development of a large industrial park or a large water resource development project. These impacts may be viewed as indirect only in the sense that they are often not considered by developers of large-scale projects and, until recently, received little attention from city councils, county supervisors, and other groups charged with the review and approval of development projects.

Significant Evaluative Criteria: (a) indicators of the potential magnitude of demands for various types of land use such as the amount of in-migration that is anticipated to flow from the proposed project (see Dietz, Chapter 3) or estimates of economic opportunities which the project may create (e.g., markets for agricultural processing and transportation service resulting from changes in cropping patterns caused by an irrigation project), (b) assessments of presently existing area capacities and trends such as present vacancy and new construction rates and present capacities of municipal services, highways, and so on (see Dickinson and Blackmarr, Chapter 5).

External factors that may affect present and potential land use activities and intensities: Included here are the various external effects that might be associated with the construction and operation of a development project such as smoke, dust, glare, odors, or noise (see Table 3). These external factors may merely reduce the amenity value of an area for particular types of land use activities or may cause serious threats to health and safety, such as the creation of serious traffic hazards in presently existing residential areas.

Significant Evaluative Criteria: (a) estimates concerning the possible magnitude of these external effects such as decibels of noise, amounts of particulate matter to be emmitted, and other external effects (see Table 3), (b) estimates of the amount of land that might be affected by these external effects, (c) the number, types, intensities, and locations of existing land use activities that might be affected by these factors, (d) the nature and magnitude of any presently existing external effects that might be mitigated or eliminated by the proposed project.

Project features / Impact measures

Project features (columns):
1. Planning-feasibility studies
2. Land acquisition
3. Permits-licenses obtained
4. Contracts let water, labor and so on
5. Initial site clearing grading, etc.
6. Preliminary construction activity
7. Construction of major project features
8. Filling of reservoir
9. Generation of electrical power
10. Recreation facilities completed
11. Irrigation water supplied
12. Municipal-industrial water supplied

Impact measures (rows):

1. Change in number of persons within a reasonable distance (x miles or y min) from recreational areas

2. Amount and percent of greenery and open space

3. Net change in amount of land devoted to various use activities
   - Agricultural
   - Recreational
   - Commercial
   - Industrial
   - Residential

Improvements to land

1. Changes in noise, glare, odors and dust in terms of magnitude of effect and number of persons to be exposed

2. Addition of new structures by number, type, size.

3. Deletion of existing improvements by number, type, size, etc.

4. Change in number and percent of housing units that are substandard
   - Low income
   - Moderate income

5. Number of persons whose views are blocked, de—
   graded, or improved.
6. Effects on cultural, historic, or scientific landmarks.

Land use economics

1. Change in number and percent of housing units
   that are available at various prices and rents

   Low income
   Moderate income

2. Changes in land values for all types of land use
   activities

   Agricultural
   Recreational
   Commercial
   Residential

Land tenure and land use controls

1. Changes in land ownership patterns.

2. Consolidation of parcels.

3. Subdivision of parcels.

4. Change in number and percent of resident and
   nonresident owners.

5. Change in amount and percent of land zoned for
   various use activities.

   Agricultural
   Recreational
   Commercial
   Residential

Figure 4.4 Impact identification matrix for land use impacts.

147

Improvements to Land

Quantitative factors relating to improvements to land: Quantitative factors include the number of improvements that might be made to (or on) the land as a direct or indirect result of the proposed project. Also included here is a consideration of the rate at which these improvements are expected to occur. For example, an irrigation program may involve the construction of water distribution facilities (direct impacts) that will lead to new cropping patterns requiring activities such as grading, leveling, drainage facilities, and possibly the utilization of chemicals such as fertilizers by agricultural landowners (indirect impacts).

Significant Evaluative Criteria: (a) measurements of the number of improvements of various types that may occur, (b) the amount of land that might be affected by such improvements, (c) the significance of the amount of land that might be involved in relation to area totals for various types of use activity.

Qualitative factors relating to improvements: These factors involve the nature of improvements associated with a proposed project and include the addition or deletion of improvements made on land as well as changes in natural land forms and vegetation as a result of the project.

Significant Evaluative Criteria: (a) technical (descriptive) specifications concerning all improvements that are to be made to or on the land, (b) descriptions of land use activities that will be either enhanced or restricted by these improvements, (c) discussion of the aesthetic significance of these improvements including the use of photography and/or quantitative methodologies.

Land Use Economics

Factors that may affect market prices of land: These are factors that are associated with a proposed project which may result in the appreciation or depreciation of land prices.

Significant Evaluative Criteria: (a) the purchase price of land acquired for the development of the proposed project as compared to other sales of similar land in the project area, (b) possible indicators of the potential appreciation or depreciation in market prices that may be caused by land use conversion associated with the project (e.g., one indicator might be the difference between the market price for raw agricultural lands and the price for residential subdivision land considering all development costs), (c) possible indicators of the effects on market prices caused by project-generated impacts on the intensity of land use (e.g., the difference in market prices for agricultural lands that are suitable for various cropping patterns).

Factors that may affect the costs associated with land use activities: These factors include the effects of a project on various costs of production that are necessary for various land use activities. An example is the impacts on farm budgets that are typically calculated as part of the feasibility study for a proposed irrigation program. Dickinson and Blackmarr (Chapter 5) deal with effects of projects on costs for essential municipal services. Perhaps the most important consideration in regard to the economic impact of a proposed development will be the effect of project-generated costs on the prices and rents that are charged for various land use activities. For example, if a project will involve residential development, either directly or indirectly, it will be important to estimate the probable prices and rents that will be charged for various types of dwelling units.

Significant Evaluative Criteria: (a) estimates concerning the nature and amount of changes in the costs of production for various land use activities, (b) estimates concerning the amount and location of area land that might be affected by changes in costs of production, (c) estimates of prices and rents that would be charged for various land use activities which would be affected by the proposed project (e.g., it may be necessary to compare the per-unit prices that are projected by the developer of a proposed subdivision with present area profiles of housing costs to determine whether the project would meet housing needs of specific socioeconomic groups).

Land Tenure and Land Use Controls

Factors affecting area land ownership: These factors include all project features that may affect property rights, such as the purchase of parcels and the purchase of various easements and mining claims. Another significant factor may be the effects of a project on the economies of scale for particular land use activities. For example, an irrigation project may encourage new cropping patterns that can be operated most efficiently at a scale which is larger or smaller than prevailing patterns of land ownership.

Significant Evaluative Criteria: (a) estimates of the number of fee and nonfee rights that may be affected by the development of the project and estimates of the number of owners who would be affected (particularly by any eminent domain proceedings), (b) the location of these purchases in the project area, (c) estimates concerning the effects of economies of scale on existing ownership patterns. (Benefit/cost analysis and other methods might be used to examine the effects of economies of scale on land ownership.)

Factors affecting area land use controls: All possible impacts of the proposed project on both present and future land use controls should be discussed. These impacts may include the possible consequences of external effects produced by the project on present and future zoning, the effect of the project's impact on population, the economic impacts of development on planning base studies, and the effect of impacts on transportation.

Significant Evaluative Criteria: (a) estimates of the nature, magnitude, and location of possible external effects that could result from the project in relation to present land use plans, (b) consideration of the magnitude of demands for various land use activities that may be expected to result from the proposed project in relation to present land use controls (e.g., it may be desirable to compare projected demands for residential land use with the amount and location of vacant land that is presently zoned for residential development), (c) descriptions of the effect of present land use controls on the project, that is, whether variances or special use permits will be required, descriptions of the review stages through which the project must pass to gain approval by federal, state, and local governments, and discussions of all statutes and ordinances such as building codes or subdivision regulations which apply to the proposed project.

Evaluation of Land Use Impacts

EVALUATIVE METHODOLOGIES

The most difficult problem encountered in the assessment of land use impacts involves the evaluation of their nature and magnitude once they have been identified. As noted previously, the degree to which quantitative measurement of land use impacts will be possible will vary considerably both within and between projects. This shortcoming in the present state of the art in predictive or projective methodologies has hampered persons charged with the assessment of impacts on the human environment. Unfortunately, the lack of precise methods for the quantification of impacts has tended to result in a retreat from the problems of impact evaluation rather than in attempts to provide decision makers with the best available means of weighing the effects of a proposed project. In the absence of predictive methodologies, the person charged with the assessment of land use impacts is often left to rely on "professional judgment and intuitive reasoning" as the only available tools for the evaluation of impacts[34] (p. 135).

The foregoing discussion is both an introduction and an important caveat in regard to the problems of evaluating land use impacts. Persons charged with the evaluation of impacts must focus their efforts on two goals. For those impacts that are susceptible to quantitative measurement, evaluation should indicate the nature, estimated magnitude, and probable location of these impacts. In addition to the actual estimation of impacts, the evaluation should identify and discuss all methods that were employed, the precision and reliability of these methods, and the types and sources of data that were utilized. When no precise quantitative methods are applicable, impacts on land use should, notwithstanding this limitation, be fully discussed in terms of the anticipated site-specific nature of these impacts, that is, with reference to the existing state of land use. Such discussions must include, where possible, the opinions and observations of the evaluator concerning the nature and magnitude of impacts and must clearly indicate all assumptions and data that support these opinions and observations. As long as opinions, observations, assumptions, and approximations are supported to the extent possible by the appropriate scientific data, the evaluation of land use impacts will be valuable to planners, the public, and decision makers who must review the impact evaluation as part of their consideration of a proposed project.

As one example of the utilization of personal observations and opinions in the assessment of environmental impacts, an approach that has been suggested by Luna B. Leopold would have the evaluator assign two numbers from a 1–10 scale to each impact that has been identified in the impact identification matrix.[29] One of these numbers would represent the evaluator's assessment of the relative importance of that impact within the particular project area. The remaining number would represent the relative magnitude of the impact. These numerical evaluations are supported to the extent possible in the evaluation report by data concerning the project and the existing state. Once all impacts have been scaled in this manner, the completed evaluation matrix serves as a useful summary-display of potential impacts that decision makers can use for ready reference in their review of a proposed project. Although this sort of impact scaling approach is certainly less desirable than a detailed, quantitative evaluation of each land use impact, it at least has the merit of providing decision makers with the best available evaluation of anticipated impacts. Table 7 illustrates the use of this methodology for the display of land use impacts.

As one example of the sort of observations and commentary that should accompany this sort of impact-scaling summary, consider the values that have been assigned in Table 7 to the possible effects of the project on residential land use. The 9 value might indicate that in the opinion of the evaluator residential land use is an important variable in the particular project area. This observation might be supported with data concerning the availability, nature, condition, and prices of housing that presently exist in the area. In the case of high- and medium-density residential land use, the creation of new job opportunities (and consequently, new residential demands) is not expected to seriously affect these types of residential uses. This observation might be supported with data indicating a substantial availability of this type of housing or by data indicating that such housing would probably not be desired by the residents which the project is expected to draw. On the other hand, the 8 value assigned for low (single family) dwelling units indicates that the project is expected to have a serious impact on this variable. This observation might be supported by data indicating a present shortage of single family homes with attendent high market prices or by data concerning past and present construction rates in relation to projected demands for new homes which the project is anticipated to produce.

Land use planners, economists, sociologists, and other specialists concerned

Table 7 Hypothetical Impact Matric (Partial) Land Use Activities

| Project Features | Activities Affected by Proposed Project | | | | | | |
| | Residential | | | Commercial | | Recreational | |
	High Density	Medium Density	Low Density	Retail Sales	Other	Outdoor	Indoor
Creation of jobs for 250 persons	9/4	9/4	9/8	7/9	2/2	9/2	9/8
Construction of improved access roads to be dedicated to county	9/5	9/5	9/5	7/1	2/1	9/3	9/1
Creation of markets for manu-facturing and processing supplies	9/3	9/3	9/3	7/4	7/9	9/1	9/1
Generation of odors, noise, dust	9/9	9/9	9/3	7/1	7/1	9/9	9/5
Increase in traffic (ADT) on several roads	9/9	9/9	9/9	7/8	7/8	9/9	9/5

Scale: Least 1/1 ←— Importance of Impact —→ Greatest 9/9
            Magnitude of Impact

with the forces that shape land use patterns have developed a variety of predictive methodologies which either directly or indirectly attempt to forecast changes in land use within regions. Although these methods are useful for purposes of obtaining general, areawide forecasts over substantial periods of time, they are of limited utility in the assessment of specific land use impacts from particular development projects.[31, 32, 27]

Economic base theory, as one example of these methodologies, is an approach that attempts to explain regional growth patterns in terms of changes in so-called basic and nonbasic activities in the region. Basic industries are defined as those activities that produce goods and services within the area which are then exported beyond the borders of the region. Base theory postulates that these basic activities ". . . not only provide the means of payment for raw materials, food, and manufactured products which the region cannot produce itself, but also support the 'service' activities, which are principally local in productive scope and market areas"[27] (p. 190).

Using data on total basic and nonbasic employment within a region, a regional employment multiplier can be calculated that describes the ratio of basic to nonbasic employment in the area. Once this multiplier is calculated, it is then theoretically possible to project changes in nonbasic employment that can be expected to result from a known change in basic employment within the region. By providing a projection of changes in employment, economic base theory may provide at least a rough indicator of a project's impacts on demands for various types of land use activity. The calculation of the regional multiplier for employment may be particularly useful to planners and decision-makers in situations where a proposed project is expected to create a substantial number of new jobs or to generate dramatic shifts in the types of economic activities within the project area.

Although projective methodologies such as economic base theory, input-output analysis, and a variety of computer modeling and simulation techniques may be potentially valuable for particular projects and project areas, these methods have the common flaw of requiring levels of data, time, expertise, and expense that are seldom available for the assessment of land use impacts of specific development projects.

EVALUATION OF LAND USE IMPACTS FOR SPECIFIC DEVELOPMENT PROJECTS: ONE APPROACH

Aside from the problems inherent in using wholly qualitative approaches for the evaluation of land use impacts, it is significant to note that, in many cases, qualitative judgments can be combined with quantitative assessments concerning the probable nature and magnitude of impacts. For example, many types of potential impacts on land use can often be described in terms of the probable effects of a project on the existing capacities of area land use variables and on past and present trends in land use. As an illustration, assume that Community Y presently contains 50 vacant dwelling units of various types, conditions, and prices. In addition, assume that trends in new residential construction (esti- mated from time series data from local building departments) indicate that approximately 75 new units per year will be constructed if such trends continue. The capacity of Community Y to absorb demands for residential land use activity can, therefore, be expressed as approximately 125 dwelling units over the next 1-year period.

Project A will involve the creation of 500 new jobs over a 1-year period in Community Y. Assuming for purposes of illustration that 400 of these jobs will entail the in-migration of approximately 1200 persons and that new workers cannot feasibly commute from other communities, a demand for approximately 400 dwelling units can be expected. When compared to existing capacities and trends in residential land use, a deficiency of 275 dwelling units is apparent. This impact on residential land use activity may then be expressed either in terms of the total number of additional dwellings that will be required or in terms of the probable impact on the rate of new construction in the project area. Effects on regional population and transportation are also likely as Schott and Dietz point out in chapters 3 and 6. This example is, of course, greatly oversimplified. In reality, the evaluation of impacts on residential land use would involve consideration of such factors as the possibility of commuting from surrounding areas, the amount and price of suitable vacant land for residential development, and other factors that may affect the supply of housing in the project area.

Somewhat less precision will be possible in evaluating the impacts of Project A on nonresidential land use activities. However, these effects may also be dis- cussed in terms of existing land use capacities and trends. The amount of recreational land use within the project area may, for example, be described in terms of the number of acres (or square feet or other unit) per given unit of population (e.g., acres/1000 persons). If the impact of the project on area population is known (see Chapter 3), then the impact of the project on recrea- tional land use may be described in terms of the additional land that would be necessary to maintain existing area/population ratios or in terms of the change in these ratios if no additional recreation areas are created. Neighborhood quality standards for adequate community recreational opportunities may be consulted in the evaluation of these impacts to compare projected area ratios to established standards.[11]

Similar approaches involving the estimation of the effects of a project on existing land use ratios can be applied to commercial land use activities. Table 8 illustrates an evaluation of anticipated impacts on residential, recreational, and commercial land use activities from a hypothetical development project. It

Table 8 Evaluating the Possible Impacts of a Development Project on Area Land Use Patterns

A. *Community Playground Space*

Assume that a neighborhood has a present population of approximately 1000 persons (275 families). Assume further that neighborhood quality standards for adequate playground facilities are as follows

2.75 acres
2.75 acres/1000 population
435 square feet/family

Present conditions are somewhat inadequate in providing the following space/population ratios

1.75 acres
1.75 acres/1000 population
277 square feet/family

If a development project is projected to result in an in-migration of up to 100 new families (364 persons), area conditions would be as follows assuming no increase in playground space

1.75 acres
1.28 acres/1000 population
202 square feet/family

Therefore, to meet recommended standards an increase of 1.99 acres would be necessary, whereas an additional .63 acres would be required to maintain present ratios of playground space to population.

B. *Neighborhood Parks*

Neighborhood population presently is 1000 persons (275 families). Recommended neighborhood standards are

1.50 acres of park space
1.50 acres/1000 population
238 square feet/family

Present area conditions are

1.35 acres
1.35 acres/1000 population
214 square feet/family

Table 8 (Continued)

If a development project could result in an in-migration of 100 new families (364 persons), area conditions would be (assuming no additional park space)

1.35 acres
99 acres/1000 population
157 square feet/family

Therefore, to meet recommended standards an increase of .70 acres of park space would be required, whereas an additional .49 acres would be necessary to maintain presently existing space/population ratios.

C. *Neighborhood Shopping*

Neighborhood population presently is 1000 persons (275 families). Recommended neighborhood standards for shopping facilities are

.80 acres
.80 acres/1000 population
125 square feet/family

Present area conditions are

.60 acres
.60 acres/1000 population
95.04 square feet/family

Assuming a projected in-migration of 100 families (364 persons), area conditions would be (assuming no additional shopping area)

.60 acres
.44 acres/1000 population
69.70 square feet/family

Therefore, to meet recommended standards an increase of .48 acres of shopping facilities would be necessary, whereas an additional .22 acres of space would be required to maintain presently existing ratios.

SOURCE FOR NEIGHBORHOOD QUALITY STANDARDS. American Public Health Association (APHA), *Planning the Neighborhood: Standards for Healthful Housing,* Public Administration Service, Chicago, 1960.

is important to emphasize that the preceding approach is merely intended to provide one example of how decision makers can be provided with useful information to relate the projected effects of a development project to area land use conditions and needs. Since many possible standards of neighborhood or community quality could be devised, the preceding example using ratios of various types and/or intensities of land use to area population represents only one possible approach to the problem of evaluating possible impacts of development projects on the mix of land uses within an area.

Impacts on the economics of area land use may also be evaluated in terms of anticipated changes in the use capacity of land affected by a proposed project. For example, if the project will entail a rezoning of surrounding property, the impact on use capacity may be partially described by the difference in prevailing market prices between land zoned at the projected new classification and the land under presently existing zoning. Similarly, if services such as sewers, water, or improved access to roads are to be extended into the area, the difference between prices for raw, unimproved land and existing subdivision land in the project area may provide one indicator of the effects of such improvements on land prices and rents.

If a project can be expected to have a very widespread and substantial effect on the development potential of area land, the use of analogy may be desirable when other areas can be found that have experienced similar types of impacts on land use. The use of analogy is not limited to effects on land use economics and has been suggested as a potentially useful approach for dealing with many types of environmental impacts. Two examples of situations in which analogy may be useful are large-scale transportation projects and water resource developments. In the case of a proposed reservoir development, for example, prevailing patterns of land use activity and prices and rents in areas near similar reservoirs in the same geographic region may provide indicators of potential impacts on land use within the project area. The use of analogy may be particularly valuable when undesirable land use patterns or other sorts of land use problems that can be attributed to similar projects can be identified in other areas. The nature of these problems and explanations of these conditions can be brought to the attention of decision makers in the impact evaluation together with suggestions for avoiding or mitigating these potentially adverse effects on land within the proposed project area. Of course, in any situation in which analogy is utilized, the sources for all assumptions, estimates, and observations must be clearly identified, and all similarities and differences between the study area and analogous areas must be fully discussed.

Finally, impacts on land tenure and land use controls may also be evaluated in both qualitative and quantitative terms. Immediate impacts on land tenure will include the purchase of all types of property rights for the construction and operation of the project. Indirect effects on land tenure will generally stem from economic forces set in motion by the proposed project. An irrigation project, for example, that anticipates a radical shift in area cropping patterns may produce economies (or diseconomies) of scale which will encourage the combination of small parcels or the division of large tracts of rangeland into smaller, more intensive farm units. In regard to these indirect effects on land ownership, it will often be possible only to estimate the amount of land, number of parcels, and number of ownerships that might be affected by the project. Data concerning development costs involved in the conversion of land to new activity types will be useful in estimating the probability and magnitude of effects on land tenure, that is, the probable number of owners who will sell rather than develop their parcels. If, for example, agricultural land is likely to become a target for conversion to residential and commercial uses, the projected per-acre or per-unit development costs can be estimated.[19] These costs may then be evaluated in terms of the present availability of capital to present landowners and the likelihood that these owners will choose to personally incur these costs to develop their parcels.[21, 22, 24]

Possible impacts on existing land use controls will be at best speculative. Perhaps the most useful information that can be presented to decision makers concerning land use controls will be an evaluation of the adequacy of present land use controls in light of projected demands for land use conversion which are expected to flow from a proposed project. For example, if the area lacks an adequate body of subdivision regulations or building codes or comprehensive, long-range general plans for area development, these inadequacies must be discussed in terms of the development pressures that are likely to occur in the area. Decision makers must be informed through the environmental impact analysis that if adequate planning and land use control mechanisms are not adopted before development pressures are allowed to intensify, patterns of development that are undesirable to the community will be almost impossible to prevent, and effective land use planning will be rendered extremely difficult. The slipshod patterns of urban growth which scar many otherwise beautiful recreational areas are testimony to this phenomenon.[9, 10]

SUMMARY AND CONCLUSION

It is important to reemphasize the goals and purposes of the present chapter. All the ways in which development projects may affect the utilization of land cannot be discussed in a single chapter. The purpose of the preceding discussions has been to suggest that the person charged with assessing the socioeconomic impacts of projects on the human environment can approach the effects of a project on land use in a systematic and comprehensive manner to identify and, to the extent possible, evaluate significant land use impacts. It has been pointed out that one of the most valuable benefits of conducting a land use impact analysis will be the presentation of information concerning the existing state of land use to planners and other decision makers. This information will permit decision makers to review and consider a proposed project with a more realistic and informed perspective than if only technical data concerning the features of the project were available. The continuing input of land use data should also be useful to planners and others in reviewing and continually upgrading land use plans and policies to deal with the effects of increased development. Finally, area conditions that pose present or potential problems for the physical, social, and economic well-being of the area and its inhabitants can be discovered and hopefully remedied by decision-makers through the process of impact review and project design.

A substantial portion of the chapter has been devoted to a discussion of the concept of land use impacts and to the relationship between various aspects of land use and other features of the human environment. It is hoped that this somewhat detailed treatment of the concept of land use impacts together with the more general discussion of various approaches and methods for the identification and evaluation of land use effects will provide a basis of information and ideas for persons charged with the assessment of the social, economic, and ecological impacts of resource development projects. It is hoped that planners, resource specialists, government officials, and others involved in the review of proposed development projects will build on the concepts, methods, and approaches that have been outlined and suggested here to formulate specific checklists, matricies, and other quantitative and nonquantitative methodologies for their particular needs and circumstances.

In addition to persons charged with the actual preparation of environmental impact assessments, the chapter should be valuable as a handbook or checklist for persons who must review these impact documents. By separating the concept of land use into four categories of land use variables and by suggesting ways in which these variables may be affected by development projects, the preceding discussions should aid decision makers in discovering inadequacies and omissions in impact analyses. Moreover, the presentation of methods and approaches for assessing the existing state of land use and for the identification and evaluation of land use impacts should assist reviewers in making specific suggestions and comments for the improvement of impact statements and reports that are found to be inadequate.

This book as a whole comes at a time in which concern with land use problems is rapidly increasing. These concerns have generated many new experiments in land use planning and other forms of land resource management that observers have described as a "quiet revolution in land use control."[35] [36] There can be little doubt that the enactment of a national land use policy act, such as the one which narrowly missed passage in 1974, will lend still greater impetus to the concern over the forces that shape land use throughout the nation. These developments make it clear that an analysis of what have been described in this chapter as land use impacts should form an integral part of attempts to assess the effects of resource development projects on the human environment.

NOTES

1. Jackson, W. Turrentine, and Donald Pisani, *From Resort Area to Urban Recreation Center: Themes in the Development of Lake Tahoe,* I.G.A., University of California, Davis, 1973.

2. U.S. Department of Transportation, *Economic and Social Effects of Highways,* Washington, D.C., 1972.

3. Clawson, Marion and Charles L. Stewart, *Land Use Information; A Critical Survey of U.S. Statistics Including Possibilities for Greater Uniformity,* Johns Hopkins Press, Baltimore, 1965.

4. McHarg, Ian, *Design with Nature,* Doubleday, New York, 1969.

5. Pepper, James E., *An Approach to Environmental Impact Evaluation of Land Use Plans and Policies: The Tahoe Basin Planning Information System,* University of California, Berkeley, 1972.

6. California Government Code, sections 51200 et seq., *California Land Conservation Act of 1965, the Williamson Act.*

7. Weiss, Shirley F., John E. Smith, Edward J. Kaiser, and Kenneth B. Kenney, *Residential Developer Decisions: A Focused View of the Urban Growth Process,* Center for Urban and Regional Studies, University of North Carolina, Chapel Hill, 1966.

8. Eckstein, Otto, *Water Resource Development: The Economics of Project Evaluation,* Harvard University, Cambridge, 1958.

9. McEvoy, James, III, and Sharon Williams, *Quantitative Assessment of Visual Obstructions of Scenic Roads, A Method for the Digital Representation of the Obstruction and Scenic Degradation Present in the Lake Tahoe Basin,* Tahoe Research Group, Davis, California, 1970.

10. McEvoy, James, III and Sharon Williams, *Visual Pollution In the Lake Tahoe Basin,* I.G.A., University of California, Davis, 1971.

11. APHA (American Public Health Association), *Planning the Neighborhood, Standards for Healthful Housing,* Public Administration Service, Chicago, 1960.

12. Guttenberg, Albert Z., *New Directions in Land Use Classification,* American Society of Planning Officials (ASPO), Chicago, 1965.

13. Guttenberg, Albert Z., *The Social Evaluation of Non-residential Land Use: Substandardness Criteria,* University of Illinois, Urbana, 1967.

14. Clawson, Marion, and Jack L. Knetsch, *Economics of Outdoor Recreation,* Johns Hopkins Press, Baltimore, 1966.

15. Hollis, John and James McEvoy III. Demographic Effects of Water Development in *Environmental Quality and Water Development,* C. R. Goldman, J. McEvoy III and P. Richerson, Eds., W. H. Freeman, San Francisco, 1973.

16. Seckler, David, Ed., *California Water, A Study In Resource Management,* University of California, Berkeley, 1971.

17. Berkman, Richard L. and W. Kip Viscusi, *Damming the West: Ralph Nader's Study Group Report on the Bureau of Reclamation,* Grossman, New York, 1973.

18. Barlowe, Raleigh, *Land Resource Economics, The Economics of Real Property,* (second ed.) Prentice-Hall, Englewood, N.J., 1972.

19. Schmid, A. Allan, *Converting Land From Rural to Urban Uses,* Johns Hopkins Press, Baltimore, 1968.

20. Clawson, Marion, *Suburban Land Conversion in the United States: An Economic and Governmental Process,* Johns Hopkins Press, Baltimore, 1971.

21. Burby, Raymond J. III, and Shirley F. Weiss, *Public Policy and Shoreline Landowner Behavior,* North Carolina State University, Water Resources Research Institute, Raleigh, 1970.

22. Burby, Raymond J. III, *Household Decision Processes In the Purchase and Use of Reservoir Recreation Land,* University of North Carolina, Water Resources Research Institute, Chapel Hill, 1971.

23. Vine, E. L., *Residential Development In Reservoir Recreation Areas,* unpublished paper University of California, Davis, 1973.

24. Burby, Raymond J. III, *Lake Oriented Subdivision in North Carolina: Decision Factors and Policy Implications for Urban Growth Patterns,* University of North Carolina, Water Resources Research Institute, Chapel Hill, 1971.

25. Delafons, John, *Land Use Controls in The United States* (second ed.), The M.I.T. Press, Cambridge, 1969.

26. Dickert, Thomas G., Methods for Environmental Impact Assessment: A Comparison in *Environmental Impact Assessment: Guidelines and Commentary,* T. Dickert, and K. Domeny, Eds., University Extension, Berkeley, 1974.

27. Isard, Walter, *Methods of Regional Analysis,* The M.I.T. Press, Cambridge, 1960.

28. Leopold, Luna B., Frank E. Clarke, Bruce B. Hanshaw, and James R. Balsey, *Geological Survey Circular 645, A Procedure for Evaluating Environmental Impact,* U.S. Dept. of Interior, Washington, D.C., 1971.

29. Leopold, Luna B., The Use of Data in Environmental Impact Assessment, in *Environmental Impact Assessment: Guidelines and Commentary,* T. Dickert and K. Domeny, Eds., University Extension, Berkeley, 1974.

30. Schaenman, Phillip S. and Thomas Muller, *Measuring Impacts of Land Development: An Initial Approach,* The Urban Institute, Washington, D.C., 1974.

31. Chapin, F. Stuart, *Urban Land Use Planning* (second ed.), University of Illinois Press, Urbana, 1965.

32. ICMA (International City Managers Association), *Principles and Practises of Urban Planning,* Washington, D.C., 1968.

33. Harvard University, Graduate School of Design, *Three Approaches to Environmental Resource Analysis,* Conservation Foundation, 1967.

34. Dickert, Thomas G. and Katherine R. Domeny, Eds., *Environmental Impact Assessment: Guidelines and Commentary,* University Extension, Berkeley, 1974.

35. Bosselman, Fred and David Callies, *The Quiet Revolution In Land Use Control,* CEQ, Washington, D.C. 1971.

36. McAllister, Donald M., Ed., *Environment: A New Focus for Land Use Planning,* N.S.F./ RANN, Washington D.C., 1973.

FIVE

Evaluation of Private and Public Economic Impacts Caused by Developments

THOMAS E. DICKINSON

JAMES R. BLACKMARR

INSTITUTIONAL IMPACTS

In recent years a substantial number of local jurisdictions have become concerned about the fiscal impacts of proposed projects. There has developed increasing skepticism of cost-benefit analyses that have sometimes shown highly inflated local benefits resulting from a proposed project. This is predicated on experience which indicates that the benefits may be relatively short-lived, whereas the attendent costs are more long lasting. There are numerous examples of this, ranging from the Alaskan Pipeline or the Oroville Dam to the location of a tire factory in Hanford, California. The purported immediate beneficial impacts of these projects were to provide increased employment opportunities. In the cases of the pipeline and the dam, unemployed people were drawn to the area by the lure of high-paying jobs. In reality there were no jobs to be had, or the jobs available required high-skilled people. Unable to obtain construction jobs, these people often went on welfare or were forced to be content with temporary unskilled jobs; unfortunately, many found themselves trapped in the area.[1] The attraction of an excess of new people is only one of many possible impacts.[2] The Oroville Dam (California) case is typical of many one-shot projects; new stores opened or expanded, schools became crowded, and more demands were made on city and county governments. All too soon, the euphoria of the new prosperity was gone. The completion of dam construction left unemployment levels higher than before, empty store fronts replacing bustling business, and mushrooming lines at the welfare offices.[3]

The Hanford tire factory indicates another set of unforeseen impacts. The location of the plant was actively courted by the local city officials. The unemployment rate in the area was high, and it was estimated that the new factory would offer a substantial number of jobs. The first problem arose when it became apparent that most of the local unemployed persons who were skilled were overqualified for the newly created unskilled jobs. The new industry did have beneficial effects on the surrounding areas. The unemployment rate for many cities dropped as unskilled workers moved in to take the new jobs. With them came increased public protection and welfare costs. An analysis done by the city, after the fact, revealed that the new plant had not lowered unemployment or the tax rate.[4]

WHAT ARE THE REAL COSTS AND BENEFITS OF COMMUNITY GROWTH?

Local resistance to unplanned growth, and sometimes to any growth, abounds. It has been sardonically called the "gang plank syndrome—climb aboard and pull up the gang plank." That emotional response is not necessarily good or bad, but it is not enough. Planners and elected officials as well as citizens badly need more facts about the real costs and benefits of city, county, or regional growth. At least four different questions may be involved in any argument over community growth. First, does the new development pattern require more in service costs than the tax revenue it produces? Second, what are the job levels (skilled or unskilled), wages, sales, and profits generated by the development? Third, what are the environmental impacts—loss of open space, overloading of sewerage treatment plants, destruction of vistas, or impacts on native flora and fauna? Finally, what are the noneconomic social impacts? For example, will there be congestion or traffic problems, double sessions in schools, or a disruption of existing ethnic communities created by growth or alterations of the physical environment of communities or regions?

This chapter devotes itself to essentially the first two questions regarding community growth. It attempts to lay out some of the theoretical and practical issues involved in developing information to help answer those questions. Then it examines some examples where such methodology has been employed—the kinds of results obtained and the application of impact assessment processes.

The impact analyst must look at several critical issues in trying to assess the fiscal and economic impacts of a project on the local region, city, or county. These issues are (1) What is the current level of unemployment? (2) What is the skill level of those people who are unemployed? (3) Is there an excess capacity in the public services sector (i.e., are the schools, fire, police, sewerage facilities operating at capacity, below capacity, or above capacity)? (4) What are the demographic characteristics (such as the age structure) of the population in the impacted area? (5) What is the probability of new migration into the area? (6) Finally, how long will the initial economic or other stimulus remain, and once that stimulus is gone, will there be something to continue to provide new income at the same level that the original project did? As Dietz points out in Chapter 3, a knowledge of many of these issues or variables is also essential in forecasting or analyzing demographic or population changes that may occur in a region or area affected by a particular project.

There are basically three techniques that have been used and seem appropriate to use in an investigation of economic impacts on local governments and communities which result from public works projects and private development of significant size/scale. One is cost-revenue analysis which deals with government impacts. The other two, which principally address private sector impacts, are economic base studies and input-output analysis.

COST-REVENUE ANALYSIS

Cost-revenue studies, in general, are limited to consideration of the fiscal costs and benefits of a proposal accruing to particular government units. The major question is what will the city, county, or service district have to provide in the way of services, and what kinds of revenues can they expect to obtain from a particular development or set of developments. The direct fiscal impact on local governments of public works projects such as freeway construction, purchase of private lands for public parks, or the development of large, multipurpose reservoir systems is sometimes limited primarily to the removal of real estate from the local government property tax rolls. Reductions in property tax revenues can be severe. In the case of the Bureau of Reclamation's construction of Trinity Dam during the mid 1950s in Trinity County, California, critical revenue losses were anticipated. The federal government holds 85 percent of the county's land area in national forests. The Bureau's Trinity River Project took much land which in private ownership was generating property tax revenues for the county. As a result of local concern, the funding legislation for the project provided that payment be made to Trinity County throughout the construction and operation of the project in lieu of the tax revenues that would have accrued.[5] The amount was established according to county property tax rates and the value of land and improvements at the time the bureau purchased the property. Such revenue losses result directly from these projects, although the local governments are likely to achieve some savings in service costs at the same time. Development of such projects may include additional service requirements such as the building and maintainenance of access roads to new freeways or the development of public recreation and sanitation facilities at new reservoirs. These direct costs are obviously attributable to project development.

The generation of indirect costs and revenues stemming from public projects should also be considered. When projects are situated away from metropolitan areas, construction crews and their families may reside temporarily in local permanent housing or in mobile home facilities. Children of these workers may increase local education expenditures. Other public service costs may increase as well. The rerouting of highways may diminish or destroy the trading potential of local commercial businesses, such as gas stations, restaurants, and motels, which cater to highway travelers. Net revenue losses can result when these establishments are forced to relocate or go out of business. The fiscal impacts may include increased welfare expenditures as well as property and sales tax revenue losses. On the other hand, new freeway interchanges may stimulate the development of commercial facilities with attendant public service costs and revenues. If such a highway relocation occurs within the jurisdiction of a single local government such as an isolated town in a rural area overall costs may be balanced or even outweighed by revenues. If the highway project relocates the route outside the town entirely, the town may experience large fiscal losses, and the county government may receive fiscal benefits. To evaluate the kinds of impacts mentioned in these illustrative examples, the whole chain of events likely to be triggered by the project under consideration must be anticipated and the relevant cost and revenue data sought. Such indirect fiscal effects are more difficult to forecast than direct impacts such as changes in property tax revenues resulting from project-related changes in land use. The past experience at similar project sites should be investigated by the analyst to increase the validity of these estimates of activities likely to be induced by the projects under study.

Development projects undertaken by the private economic sector will incur similar costs and revenues. Various commercial, industrial, or residential developments will require the full range of public services and will generate a wide variety of tax and other revenues that will accrue to local governments. Attributing service costs to specific development activities is often difficult, and allocation is sometimes highly arbitrary. A single family residential subdivision will result in increased school costs as well as a wide variety of utility, property protection, and other service costs. The subdivision will directly yield revenues consisting largely of property taxes. However, such a subdivision will not be developed in isolation from other economic activity. Unless it is of the recreational second-home type in a rural setting or all its employed residents commute to jobs out of the local area, it is likely to be accompanied by a net increase in local employment and commercial or industrial business activity. These businesses will yield property tax revenues but will also require increases in public services.

The new residents will make local retail purchases that bring sales tax revenues to the local government. Whether to attribute increased sales tax revenues, for example, to the new residential subdivision or to the retail businesses themselves is not an easy matter to determine. Conventional cost-revenue analyses usually try to consider individual residential, commercial, or industrial developments in isolation without considering indirect effects or associated economic activity (causal relationships are difficult or impossible to establish. Did the jobs or business potential exist prior to the resident work force?). For this reason a fairly detailed methodology generally is developed to attempt to allocate the expected expenditures and expected revenue to the particular land use activity (or set of activities) being analyzed. The results that are generated from these studies depend in no small measure on the assumptions used to make the allocation. For the most part we consider here the conventional approaches to fiscal impact analysis.

Some cost-revenue studies attempt to calculate the total costs and revenues stemming from different classes of land use (such as single family residential, retail commercial, etc.) within a jurisdiction on a per-acre or per-parcel average basis. Other fiscal studies attempt to identify the costs and revenues that can be anticipated from specific proposed development. Techniques for both approaches are very similar. The first is an attempt to allocate all costs and revenues among all lands in the local jurisdiction. The second approach is site specific and may not have to consider all types of revenues or services costs. Both types require assumptions about the sources or incidence of costs and revenues.

Allocation of Expenditures

One scheme of distributing service costs is to allocate some costs directly to land regardless of type of use. In this category are included: capital costs of roads and utilities not borne by the private developer, administrative overhead, planning, and a certain amount of road maintenance costs. Berns discusses the various origins of these costs in detail in Chapter 4. A second category is those social service costs attributable directly to people. A final category includes those costs for services with both people- and property-oriented characteristics.

Usually, only a small fraction of local government expenditures can be charged directly to the land itself. Capital improvements such as streets, sidewalks, and water and sewer mains fall into this particular category. The initial costs of these kinds of capital improvements can often be assigned to individual parcels of property as they are directly served by these improvements. Costs may be attributed to these lands on the basis of the number of factors such as length of street frontage and lot size. Obviously, some part of fire protection and police services are intended to protect property rather than people. Therefore, an allocation technique that places these costs in the third category would be realistic. Police activities can be analyzed in terms of "beat" patrols and calls for assistance enabling some costs to be allocated to land uses.[6] In a like manner, the activities of the fire department can be allocated to accounts for various land use types based on the frequency of calls for this type of protection.

Allocation of such services as health, welfare, sanitation, and public education provides a much more thorny problem. These kinds of expenditures are usually referred to either as services to people or services of community-wide benefit.[7] It has been argued that the cost of these functions cannot logically be charged back to the specific pieces of property. The costs are, however, very real and cannot be ignored in any cost-revenue analysis. People-oriented services usually represent a majority of the expenditures in the combined budgets of local governmental agencies, cities, counties, school districts and other special-purpose districts (see Table 1). Costs of services to people have been allocated in a series of ways to the different land uses in various cost revenue analyses.[8] These procedures include:

1. Allocating costs on a per capita basis to residential land use classes according to average densities.

2. Allocating costs according to average assessed valuation, acreage, or other characteristics of real property classes.

Table 1 Total Local Government Direct Expenditures by Functions (in millions) 1971-1972[a]

Item		Amount of Expenditure
Total		$104,822
Education		47,734
Local schools	45,168	
Institutions of higher education	2,566	
Public welfare		8,822
Health and hospitals		6,858
Hospitals	5,390	
Health	1,468	
Highways		2,747
Police protection		5,077
Sewerage		3,164
Housing and urban renewal		2,747
Local fire protection		2,577
General control		2,495
Local parks and recreation		2,323
Interest on general debt		2,185
Sanitation, other than sewerage		1,565
Financial administration		1,258
Other and unallocable		4,885

[a] From Government Finances in 1971-1972, U.S. Bureau of the Census GF 72 No. 5, p. 23, December 1973.

3. Assigning costs to land uses on the basis of the opinions of department personnel about which land use activities are responsible for what proportion of the program costs.

4. Using performance budgeting to attempt to determine the actual incidence of costs of services.

No matter what the allocative mechanism, the analyst needs to discover the pertinent data sources. Performance budgeting requires monitoring and data collection for all the relevant departments, but it may yield significantly different results from the other methods. One study calculated police protection costs for an entire subdivision at $7000 by means of performance budgeting, at $19,000 on the basis of the fraction of the city's assessed valuation accounted for by the subdivision, and at $22,440 on the basis of a police administrator's estimate. Studies that have been done in as comprehensive a manner as this required anywhere from 1- to 3-man-years time.[9] The problem is that most departments do not keep records from which costs can be allocated to specific parcels, neighborhoods, or land use types. In addition, the records of different departments may utilize widely varying methods of accounting. In reality, it is unlikely that detailed performance budgeting can be used except in those cases where a municipality is interested in obtaining the data for themselves to be used in the broader planning context. For the analyst who is faced with trying to assess the impacts of a proposed project such as a dam, a transportation network, or a new sewerage plant, it is likely that he will find it more advantageous to follow the approach of assessing costs and benefits by a shortcut method such as using assessed valuation as the basis for cost allocation or assigning average per capita expenditures for people-oriented services to residential land uses.

The sources of data absolutely essential in any of the shortcut methods are: city and county budgets, school district budgets, and budgets of special districts. The special districts' budgets are normally incorporated in the consolidated county budget, and occasionally, even school budgets are included in that document. Other sources of valuable information are the county agricultural extension office, if one should consider allocating costs and revenues to agricultural lands.

Public education costs often represent the biggest local government expenditure, and because education is a "service of community-wide benefit," the allocation of locally borne costs of education have been the principal point of contention among cost-revenue analysts or at least the focus of debate about allocating costs of services to people. Not surprisingly, many people advocate allocating the entire cost of education to residential land uses, since this is the direct source of the pupils. However, without a labor force or clientele, industrial or commercial land uses would not locate in a city or county. A work force or a consumer population is necessarily associated with educational expenditures for its children. The proponents of this view argue that it is misleading to attribute all educational expenditures to the existence of residential property unless, of course, this is the only land use class represented in the jurisdiction. When all costs of services to people are allocated to residential land uses, typically, these residential properties are shown not to "pay their way;" that is, they incur more in service costs than they generate in local government revenues. With such allocation procedures, only the most expensive housing or residences with few bedrooms (unsuitable for families with several school-age children) are apt to yield net revenues. It is not surprising that many of the advocates of allocating education and other people-related service costs to all land uses, rather than exclusively to residential land use, seem to be spokesmen for real estate, construction, and other development-oriented industries or else critics of the exclusionary effect of large residential lot-size requirements and other so-called "fiscal zoning."

We suggest that no general deficit land use categories are likely to emerge in cost-revenue studies unless services of community-wide benefit are assigned to a particular land use (i.e., residential).[10] The majority of suburban cost-revenue studies have done so and indicate that most residential developments are deficit-producing uses of land. Mace and Wicker[11] introduce the allocation procedure for their comparative cost-revenue study of hypothetical residential development in three contrasting fiscal settings by stating:

This analysis departs significantly from the more common approach by charging to the hypothetical subdivision only a portion of people generated service costs following the line of reasoning that services to people are of general benefit essential to nonresidential development. Most informed observers will concede the validity of charging some of these costs to business and other uses. Reasonably subject to question however, is the precise formula herein adopted to determine how much to charge the respective users.

The formula they use is to allocate the costs of "people services according to the proportion of total assessed valuation attributable to two land use categories, residential or nonresidential." If 65 percent of the tax base is residential property, then 65 percent of the public education costs are charged to residential property.

Is the allocation of costs of services of community-wide benefit by assessed valuation more justified than the allocation of these costs only to residential land uses? The method is based on the premise that the assessed value of land reflects the intensity of the land use and hence the relative importance of that use to the whole community compared to other land uses. The cost of services benefitting the whole community is then allocated to each land use category according to its relative economic importance.

There is no question that most commercial, industrial, residential, or agricultural uses of land are interdependent and unlikely to persist in isolation. If the region-wide average land use mix could be assumed to accompany any local development activity, it would not matter to which classes of land various costs were allocated, for it could be expected that any change in service costs would be balanced by a generally proportional increase in revenues. However, the fact is that local government property-taxing jurisdictions and their boundaries do not recognize this land use interdependence. In almost any region one cannot expect to find a homogeneous distribution of cost-generating and revenue-producing sources. Although recognizing that property tax and other fiscal resource inequities exist between local jurisdictions, in studies of fiscal impacts the analyst must treat the real costs which are caused by development. One could arbitrarily allocate costs in a manner that is closely related to the pattern of revenue allocations so that no classes of land use would show any significant surpluses or deficits, but this procedure is the absurd extreme. An update of the

Stockton/San Joaquin county analysis in Mace and Wicker's study allocates all education costs to residential land. The author argues that although an allocation by assessed value would be more in line with "welfare economics," the real question is whether residential land pays "its own way" with respect to government finances.[12]

Our consideration here is not whether the new subdivision bears its fair share of additional expenditures, but whether it pays its own way. . . . Our concern here is . . . whether or not the existence of the new subdivision will increase taxes for the current population.

Neither approach is right or wrong; however, they are both incomplete in the sense that they do not consider the fiscal effects of all the activities associated with resdental developments (as will be explained subsequently).

Revenue Allocations

Revenues of local government pose comparable allocation problems. Taxes for property are simple enough to allocate, since they are generated by specific parcels of land and are the result of the tax rate levied and the value placed on them by the assessor. Average or mean per-acre property tax revenues can thus be calculated for each land use class being considered. Other taxes and nontax revenues can be as difficult to allocate to particular land uses as are the costs of services to people. In states such as California, with a general sales tax, a portion of that revenue is returned to local governments from whose jurisdictions they were collected. Many cost-revenue studies have allocated this part of local revenues to retail-commercial land uses; others have allocated a large portion of sales tax revenues to residential land uses. The argument is, in the first case, that it is impossible to know what proportion of the sales tax is generated indigenously and what portion is generated by people from outside the jurisdiction. It can also be reasonably argued that if retail businesses were located outside the jurisdiction in question, the purchases by local residents would be made elsewhere and would generate no local sales tax revenue. However, when retail businesses are located within the jurisdiction, at least a part, and usually a majority, of the sales tax revenues are attributable to purchases by residents of that locality and can, therefore, be allocated to its residential land use classes rather than to retail commercial lands.

Sensitivity of Assumptions in Cost-Revenue Studies

Any allocation scheme developed under a need for costs or revenues is subject to the contention that the procedures used are arbitrary and that some other procedure may be entirely as logical. Alternative allocation procedures may completely change the findings of the cost-revenue study in terms of which land use classes show fiscal surpluses and which show deficits and even the magnitude of those surpluses or deficits. We contrast such methods subsequently.

To illustrate the sensitivity of cost-revenue findings to alternative allocations of service costs to people, Mace and Wicker's data for Stockton/San Joaquin County, California, Greensboro/Guilford County, North Carolina, and South Brunswick/Woodbridge, New Jersey are shown in Table 2 under two sets of assumptions:

1. All education, welfare, and recreation costs are allocated on a per capita basis entirely to residential land.

2. Partial education, welfare, and recreational costs are allocated to residential land according to the (relevant jurisdiction-wide) residential contribution to the tax rolls.

Mace and Wicker, in expenditure allocation, use a shortcut approximation approach rather than detailed performance budgeting. Their method of cost allocation is stated as follows:

While the process is complicated, it is possible to relate most "service to property" costs to new development such as the subdivisions herein hypothesized. To do this accurately, however, is an arduous and time-consuming task beyond the time and budget limitations of this study. . . . Precise cost measurement for this research would have required detailed sub-studies, involving field investigations in each community, of the various governmental activities and how they are performed. Fortunately, precise cost figures are not here required. Relatively realistic estimates or approximations, similarly derived, of service costs in the several communities studied are adequate to the intercommunity comparisons basic to this research.

. . . to estimate additional public health, welfare, and recreation costs generated by the new people moving into the study communities and settling in the hypothetical subdivisions, the short-cut device of employing community-wide averages is substituted for detailed analysis. It is reasonable to assume that the various locally financed activities performed under these broad categorical headings are provided for and . . . benefit every local resident. On the basis of this reasoning, total local costs are divided equally among all residents to obtain unit (per capita) generated costs.[13]

The costs of services to property are assigned in a variety of ways.[14] Fire protection, garbage collection, and waste disposal costs are allocated by assessed value. Water supply and sewerage are considered to be self-financing. Police costs attributable to residential property for Stockton and Greensboro were estimated by local personnel, whereas police costs for the other localities were allocated by assessed value. An average street maintenance cost was calculated and applied to the new street mileage in the hypothetical subdivisions. Finally,

Table 2 Net Revenues from Residential Development under Alternative Allocation of Costs of Services to People[a]

Variable	California		New Jersey		North Carolina	
	San Joaquin	Stockton	South Brunswick	Woodbridge	Guildord County	Greensboro
Household size (average)	3.3	3.1	3.6	3.7	3.3	3.3
Pupils per dwelling unit						
K–12	.95	.95	.97	.8	.7	.7
Junior college	.06	.06	n.a.	n.a.	n.a.	n.a.
Household income	$8,400	$8,400	$10,900	$10,900	$8,500	$8,500
Price of housing unit	$17,500	$17,500	$20,000	$20,000	$17,000	$17,500
Per pupil expenditure						
K–12	$515.52	$515.52	$726.40	$542.09	$426.63	$457.94
Junior college	$916.09	$916.09	n.a.	n.a.	n.a.	n.a.
% of Education costs borne locally						
K–12	43%	43%	86%	85%	32%	40%
Junior college	58%	58%	n.a.	n.a.	n.a.	n.a.
Residential property valuation as % of total valuation	65%	65%	49%	67%	46%	64%
Net revenues per ½-acre dwelling unit with 100% allocation to residential[b]	($81.47)	($112.08)	(158.49)	($188.14)	($81.19)	($22.02)
Net revenues per ½-acre dwelling unit with allocation according to assessed valuation[b]	$62.65	$46.44	$164.67	($52.55)	$134.91	$75.21

[a] Based on study by Mace and Wicker, *Do Single Family Homes Pay Their Own Way?* Urban Land Institute Research Monograph 15, Washington D.C., 1968.
[b] Negative values are shown by ( ).

administration and all other costs were allocated according to assessed valuation.

The results of recalculating the Mace and Wicker cost-revenue study are shown in the last two rows of Table 2. Mace and Wicker found that revenues exceeded costs by substantial margins when total annual revenues from the hypothetical subdivisions were compared with all continuing annual costs charged to the subdivisions.[15] However, when all costs of services to people were allocated completely to residential land, the results were completely opposite. The substantial net revenues became equally substantial net deficits for all but the North Carolina communities.

No matter what allocative formulas are used, this study provides valuable insight into the effect on local finances and on cost-revenue study results of different levels of nonlocal support for education and other local expenditures. The study also highlights the effect of the variation in the level of services provided. Greensboro and Guilford County, North Carolina, which spend the least on noneducational services and receive the greatest proportion of nonlocal support for education, show positive net revenues even when people-oriented costs are allocated 100 percent to residential land. The California and New Jersey communities spend more for noneducational services and receive relatively less federal and state grants for education which results in the greater sensitivity.

It was impossible to develop alternative formulations for revenues, because Mace and Wicker identified only state aid, local property tax revenues, and all other local revenues.[16] It was difficult to determine how revenues other than property taxes were allocated. It is likely that they have been allocated in a manner that enhances the fiscal position of residential land (e.g., most or all sales tax receipts have probably been credited to residential land).

Another Fiscal Impact Study—Santa Cruz, California

A recent study of the coastal and upland areas northwest of Santa Cruz, California provides examples of allocation schemes for estimating both revenues and service costs generated by hypothetical residential development. However, the study uses the shortcut method of community-wide averages and assessed value contributions of different land uses (Table 3).

Residences are 70% of the assessed value in the county and 57% of the assessed value in the city: Therefore, revenues or expenditures which were deemed proportional to the value of property were multiplied by 70% (county) or 57% (city) to get the appropriate share for residences. If the revenues or expenditures were judged to be more people or residence oriented, a higher percentage was used.[17]

Following this reasoning, they allocated over 80 percent of sales tax revenues to residential land. The authors show, using these procedures, that residential

Table 3 Percentages of Revenues and Expenditures Attributed to Residences of the City and County of Santa Cruz and Used in Making Per Capita Calculations

Revenues	Percentage Attributed to Residences
City of Santa Cruz[a, b]	
Local taxes and assessments	
Sales and use taxes	80
Transient occupancy tax	0
Cigarette tax	80
Lifeguard services	100
Franchise tax	0
Licenses and permits	
Business licenses	0
Dog licenses	100
Building inspection permits	57
Fines and forfeits	
Vehicle code fines	90
Other court fines	80
Animal shelter fees and services	100
Library fines	100
Interest on investments	57
Real Property rental	57
Revenues from other agencies	
State alcoholic beverage license	80
State motor vehicle in-lieu tax	90
State gasoline tax	70
State trailer coach fees	100
Revenue from other agencies ⎱ E.E.A. program ⎰	57
Charges for current services	
Planning fees / Engineering fees	57
Weed abatement charges	
Parking meter collections—beach	100
Park use fees	100
Recreation fees	100
Library fees	100
All other recurring revenues	57
Nonrecurring revenue	57
Intracity service activities	57

Expenditures	*Percentage Attributed to Residences*
General government	57
Public safety	
Police	75

Table 3 (Continued)

Fire	57
Inspections	57
Traffic engineering	57
Parking meters	75
Off-street parking (including debt service)	75
Flood control	57
Animal control	100
Weed control	57
Civil defense	100
Streets and highways	
Street maintenance	57
Parks and recreation	100
Library	100
Airport	70
Special assessment debt service	57
Capital improvements	
Gas tax street improvements	70
General capital improvements	57
Municipal bond improvement construction	57
Storm drain construction	57
Intracity service activities	57

County of Santa Cruz[a, c]

Revenues	*Percentage Attributed to Residences*
Taxes	
Sales and use taxes	85
Franchises	0
Other taxes	70
Licenses and permits	
Animal license	100
Business	0
Construction permits	70
Road privileges and permits	70
Zoning permits	70
Other licenses and permits	70
Fines, forfeits, and penalties	90
From use of money and property	70
Other revenue	70

Table 3   (Continued)

Expenditures	*Percentage Attributed to Residences*
General	70
Finance	70
Counsel	70
Personnel	70
Elections	100
Communications, property management and plant acquisition	70
Promotion	0
Other general	70
Public protection: judicial, police protection, and detention and correction	80
Fire protection	70
Protective inspection	0
Other protection	70
Road construction and maintenance	70
Health and sanitation	90
Public assistance	100
Agricultural education	0
Recreation and cultural services	100
Debt service	70
Public services	30

[a] The categories are taken from the Annual Financial Report of the City of Santa Cruz as they appeared 1971–1972.

[b] Residences comprise 57% of the assessed value in the City of Santa Cruz; from Wallace et al., *A Framework for Analyzing Public Service Costs and Revenues Associated with Land Use Alternatives,* University of California Agricultural Extension, June 1973 (mimeographed).

[c] Residences comprise 70% of the assessed value in the county of Santa Cruz. From Wallace, L. T., et al.

development of the coastal agricultural lands may yield net revenues when annexed by the city of Santa Cruz, assuming that houses average $35,000 in value (exclusive of their half-acre lots) and that household size and number of pupils per household approximate county- and city-wide averages. No attempt was made to project new commercial or industrial development that might accompany this development of about 18,000 new residents. Again, sales tax revenues calculated are city-wide or county-wide per capita averages. Whether new facilities are developed, the increment in retail sales that would accompany such development would surely result in an increase in assessed value of the area's commercial property. The increased property taxes that such appreciation would generate are not considered by the authors.

Suggestion of Resolution of Allocation Assumptions

A simple (but also simplistic) solution to resolve the arbitrary allocation dispute that can dramatically effect the outcome of cost-revenue analysis would be to employ two contrasting allocation procedures and report both sets of results. The calculations would be easy enough for the analyst to do, and the rationale for each method could be presented along with the cost-revenue summary tables. Then the public and decision makers could evaluate the meaning of each set of results. If two alternative allocative formulas are used, they should be structured to emphasize their differing effects on the results. Two that have been suggested are

1. The residential growth as a burden formulation:
(a) Cost of services to people allocated entirely to residential lands.
(b) Sales tax revenues allocated entirely to retail commercial lands.
(c) Other revenue and cost allocations are generally attributed, as far as possible, to residential growth.

2. The interdependent community formulation:
(a) Costs of service to people allocated according to land class by assessed value.
(b) Estimated fraction of sales tax revenue due to purchases by residents allocated to residential sector.
(c) Other cost and revenue allocations, when debatable, are treated as consistant with this approach.

For communities that are primarily bedroom suburbs, the two approaches should produce results which are very similar. In a more economically balanced community the results should differ substantially. As is apparent, those alternative allocation procedures do not alter the actual fiscal impacts of project development. They merely display the effects of varying assumptions for decision makers to consider.

Toward Better Cost-Revenue Studies

BETTER SPECIFICATION OF LAND CLASSES

The value of cost-revenue studies to local governments in projecting fiscal impacts of proposed developments is enhanced or diminished according to the precision with which the land classes are detailed and their fiscal characteristics calculated. Far too often, the classes that are analyzed are highly aggregated and the contemplated new development is outlined very imprecisely to save the analyst time and effort, and, therefore, the results are less usable for accurate projection of the fiscal impact of real development projects than would be data for more narrowly defined land use categories and precise patterns of development. City-wide average fiscal characteristics for single family homes are likely to be poor estimates of the fiscal impacts of a certain new single family housing tract, particularly if the characteristics of the planned new homes and their probable occupants are only vaguely known. The more detail with which the proposed development projects are specified and the costs and revenues for comparable existing developments are calculated, the greater will be the accuracy of the final analysis.

MARGINAL VERSUS AVERAGE COSTING

Critics of cost-revenue studies argue that the marginal cost rather than the average cost of service provision should be used. They point out that using community-wide averages as a shortcut is apt to distort the true fiscal picture, and in evaluating the specific impact of a new shopping center or neighborhood, they may not accurately reflect the costs or revenues at the margin.[18] This can occur because of existing excess capacity (in schools, sewerage plants, or other public facilities), because main utility lines have long since been extended to or beyond the site of the development, because of indivisibility of providing services (such as fire stations), or because the development is not similar to existing developments. Therefore, the marginal costs may be lower than, the same as, or higher than the average costs.

Marginal calculations also are an appropriate, if more difficult, way of determining revenues. Property tax receipts are estimated by specifying the likely assessed valuation of the real estate contemplated in the development. The property tax rate is then used to find the revenues which the development, so-valued, yields. The estimation of sales tax revenues is more difficult. Applying community-wide per capita sales tax revenues to a new residential neighborhood according to projected population is not valid. Some studies adjust the community-wide sales tax revenue figures according to the relation between the projected incomes of the new residents (established by the likely ratio of housing prices and income) and the average income in the community. Though this is something of an improvement, it is still a crude estimator. Forecasts must be made of the likely shopping patterns of the new residents in an attempt to estimate how much they will boost retail sales within the local jurisdiction. In addition to possible income differences, new residents may for several years exhibit substantially different spending patterns than the average household in the community while they furnish their homes, landscape their yards, and so on. New retail commercial developments may likewise generate increased sales tax revenues by attracting shoppers from outside the jurisdiction or conversely, by reducing the purchases that residents had been making outside the community. However, it is quite possible that they will reduce the revenues from other businesses located within the jurisdiction. Therefore, one should estimate the net sales tax revenue.

ESTIMATING ALL ANTICIPATABLE FISCAL IMPACTS

The most realistic approach to fiscal impact estimation requires the analyst to predict the full range of economic activities that will stem from or develop in conjunction with a specific public or private project. Techniques for determining these associated activities are not well developed, so educated guesses based on a thorough appraisal of existing local economic conditions are required. Several alternative scenarios of what might happen can be specified. If the project under consideration is a residential subdivision in a suburban bedroom community, there may be little net increase in local employment (other than temporary construction jobs) associated with project development, assuming new resident employees commute elsewhere to jobs. The increase in population may increase the trade of existing local businesses or form the basis (or part of the basis) for new businesses to locate in the suburb. Increased demand for various services may result in some additional jobs. If, on the other hand, new residents moving into the subdivision are apt to be employed locally, a large net increase in local industrial or commercial business activity can be anticipated. Local government service costs and property tax and other revenues are necessarily associated with the new business activity as well as the residential subdivision. The residential and associated commercial and industrial development occurring in the city or county can be viewed as a package,* none of whose components will occur without the others except in the very short run. (These economic activity components may be spread throughout a number of government jurisdictions. This is especially likely to occur in a metropolitan setting. Assumptions must be made about the spatial location or distribution of these activities.) As a result, with this approach there are no problems of allocating costs and revenues to particular land uses. Net changes in costs and revenues are ascribed to the package of changes in economic activities. Such an approach is well adapted for combination with input-output analysis (see below) for predicting the economic activities in the private sector that will accompany the particular development or proposed projects.

* Approach suggested by George Goldman.

Although the state of the art in cost-revenue analysis is not very advanced, this comprehensive approach should be attempted, because information about local public finances is an important input to the evaluation of the impacts of any project. However, the approach thus far has looked only at the effects on government and not on the private sector.

ECONOMIC BASE STUDIES[19]

The argument has been made that cost revenue studies are incomplete, because they only look at the public fiscal impacts of a project and not at the private sector impacts on the local economy. Furthermore, because of the static nature of the cost-revenue studies even if marginal cost-pricing is used, there is no allowance for synergistic effects that can occur because of the new project. Conceivably, this could be the case if the area under consideration for a project has a relatively high level of unemployment and the project can utilize the available labor. Under these circumstances it is possible that the cost-revenue calculation might overestimate the negative effects. Therefore, it seems valuable to look at not only the public cost-revenue effects, but also the private effects by the use of either an economic base model or an input-output model.

The economic base model is essentially a simplified input-output model. It consists of two sectors or categories: one labeled basic activity and the other classified as local activity. These models are used as a method of specifying the source and interrelationships of the income flows for a community or region.[20] Basic activities, also known as the export sector, are those that result in income being transferred into the area. Included are activities such as national manufacturing firms that have the majority of their sales to residents other than those in the area under consideration. The other parts of the economy (local activities) are the enterprises and undertakings that provide services primarily to the local residents or market.

The underlying assumption for distinguishing between the two sectors is that growth of a region depends on the goods and services produced locally but sold beyond its border. Production in the basic sector provides a means of paying for goods and services that cannot be produced within the region as well as supporting the service activities which are primarily local in scope.

In the 1930s Homer Hoyt developed the idea of a "basic service ratio." This was the first time that any attempt had been made to measure quantitatively the basic and service components of a region's economy. Hoyt's ratio describes either (1) the ratio between total employment in a region's basic or export activity and total employment in its service or local activity; or (2) the ratio between the increase in employment in a region's basic sector and the increase in its service sector. From the basic service ratio a regional employment multiplier is easy enough to calculate: it is simply the total (or increase in) employment in both basic and services activities divided by the total (or increase in) basic employment.

Development of the Regional Multiplier

The regional multiplier is sensitive to the base used to calculate the basic service ratio. A hypothetical example is shown in Table 4 to illustrate this situation. It is assumed that total basic employment in 1960 is 10,000 and in 1970 is 20,000. Further, it is assumed that total service employment is 27,000 in 1960 and 45,000 in 1970. With this information it is possible to calculate the basic service ratio based on 1960 total employment, 1970 total employment, or the change in employment 1960–1970. The accompanying regional employment multipliers are the ratio of total employment to basic employment (or the change in total employment to the change in basic employment) which is simply unity plus the basic service ratio. The choice of base to use depends on the purpose of the study. However, as Isard says, "that method based on change in employment is generally considered to yield the most relevant results."[21]

There have been many uses of the employment multiplier concept for projection purposes. Some analysts have made estimates of further increases in employment in the basic sector for a region and by using the employment multipliers are able to estimate changes in total employment. They then calculate potential future populations by using an employment-to-population ratio.[22] Obviously, techniques such as these would be very useful to the agency(s) responsible for preparing EIRs when the action under consideration could reasonably be expected to alter the employment multiplier.

Table 4   Basic-Service Ratios and Multipliers—A Hypothetical Example[a]

Basis	Basic-Service Ratio	Regional Employment Multiplier
Total employment—1960	$\frac{10,000}{27,000} = 1 : 2.7$	3.7
Total employment—1970	$\frac{20,000}{45,000} = 1 : 2.75$	3.25
Increase in employment 1960–1970	$\frac{10,000}{18,000} = 1 : 1.18$	2.8

[a] Assume that total basic employment in 1960 is 10,000 and in 1970 is 20,000. Also assume that total service employment is 27,000 in 1960 and 45,000 in 1970.

Case Example—Stockton and San Joaquin County

One attempt to utilize the economic base approach was undertaken by Baxter, McDonald, and Smart for Stockton and San Joaquin County.[23] The purpose of the study is stated to be the demonstration of various methodologies. As in our theoretical example, employment in the export sector is estimated first. Here the authors used time series data for the major export industries of the county from 1960–1970. They also reported employment data for these industries for the United States, the San Francisco Bay region, and the San Joaquin Valley. With additional data, the county's employment as a percent of each level's employment can be calculated. Given an estimate of total United States employment for 1980 and 1990 in the various export sectors, the authors estimate the county's employment for that sector in 1980 and 1990. The estimates for all export sectors are summed providing estimated employment in those sectors of 50,600 in 1980 and 62,600 in 1990. Using the county's export employment multiplier (2.25) developed in the manner described earlier, the report estimates a total employment of 127,900 in 1980 and 144,000 in 1990.

The shortcoming of this economic base study is that only future employment and population trends are projected. There is no analysis of specific development impacts. No matter what use is made of economic base models, there are some substantial limitations in their use. The problems are both technical and theoretical.

Technical Problems of Economic Base Models

A major technical problem is the selection of the unit of measurement. Most economic base models have used employment, the number of jobs, as the unit. In part, this may be due to the fact that employment figures are the easiest ones to obtain relative to any other measure. Further, employment breakdown by industry and occupation are considered significant economic variables with which policy makers and planners are likely to be concerned. There are, however, some inherent problems with using gross employment figures. First, there is little or no recognition of differences in wage rates among industries. Also, it is very difficult to indicate a differential change in expansion within any given industry as one shifts from less skilled workers for example to more skilled workers within the industry. Further, employment data does not reflect expansionary effects that may result for a period of time from changes in productivity rates. One example is, of course, in agriculture which has had a net decrease in employment but has actually had an expansionary effect due to the increase in productivity.

One means of overcoming these problems is to use total payrolls as the measurement unit. Some studies have actually used payroll figures as a weighting factor or a check on conclusions obtained from employment information. Using payroll data, however, has its own drawbacks, because it provides no direct measure of the actual number of jobholders. An additional problem arises from changing wage rates and price levels; it may eliminate the possibility of interperiod comparisons.

Another major problem is the inability of employment and payroll data to capture unearned income by transfer payments which in some sectors and regions is a substantial economic consideration. Therefore, it seems necessary to include income data as well as employment data in the calculation of the multiplier.

A significant problem is the identification of basic and service components. There have been several allocative mechanisms that have been developed. One which has been used allocates to the export sector all agriculture, forestry, fishing, mining, manufacturing, some transportation and activities of federal and state government, and a portion of public administration. Construction, other transportation, wholesale and retail trade, finance, insurance and real estate services, and other portions of public administration are normally considered to comprise the local sector. Any arbitrary allocation such as this is bound to result in some errors. However, for the analyst without the time or resources to do a complete study, this is perhaps a reasonable rule of thumb.

The final basic issue is what is the base area? In terms of collecting the relevant data, the analyst should choose a region such that he or she can get access to information from secondary sources. This almost immediately precludes looking at anything smaller than a county or an SMSA. In reality, most studies have been done at larger regional levels up to and including the state.

Theoretical Questions Concerning Economic Base Studies as Social Impact Analysis Tools

Although the technical questions about economic base studies and regional employment multipliers are important, there are questions of a more basic nature. General agreement can be reached that a careful economic base study contributes to the understanding of a region's economic components. However, the major reason for discussing the concept here is not for its descriptive or static nature but rather its dynamic and predictive value.

Any attempt to utilize a multiplier to estimate the results of future changes in basic activity is an attempt to predict. This prediction is based on existing data and is subject to errors based on changes in any of a number of social, economic, or technical conditions. In many cases it is difficult to estimate even crudely the influences of these variables, let alone to do it precisely. One of the most easy changes to identify is a shift in productivity that allows for the support of more service-type activities. See Dietz' discussions of population projection problems in Chapter 3.

Along with the productivity changes, there will be changes in other locational factors that will certainly affect the region. The region can become either more specialized or more self-sufficient; the latter is particularly likely in an expansionary economy. As an economy grows, more of the goods and services that were formally bought outside the region can now be produced within the region. The net result is that employment in the export sector as a percentage of the total employment begins to drop. Further, improved transportation will conceivably lead to greater specialization and regional interdependence that could have exactly the opposite effect. In any case, the basic service ratio will almost certainly shift over time.

Beside the fact that the economic composition of a region is unlikely to change in a manner similar to what happened in the past, there is another reason why a multiplier based on a basic-service ratio at any one point in time is apt to be inaccurate. The reason is that the volume of service activity associated with a change in the basic sector is not instantaneous. A means of alleviating this problem is to calculate the basic-service ratio over time, as was shown in Table 4. Preferably, the time period chosen should have as few of the complicating factors discussed previously as possible.

The final and perhaps largest question about using economic base models is that because of the high level of aggregation in the sectors, the analyst is left with an average figure. Industry A may use large quantities of locally provided goods and services, whereas Industry B may not. Therefore, secondary effects caused by increases of specific industries within the basic sector are likely to be substantially different.

It should be apparent from the preceding discussion that a regional employment multiplier derived from a basic service ratio of an economic base study is of limited usefulness and value. It can provide a reasonable statistical description of an economy, but the analyst should be cautious about using it for purposes of prediction. No matter what, the analyst should supplement economic base studies by other techniques. One means of overcoming some of the shortcomings of this approach is to use input-output analysis.

INPUT-OUTPUT ANALYSIS[24]

An input-output model provides a higher level of understanding of private economic impacts of a proposed project and is more relevant in dealing with questions of growth-inducing impacts than is an economic base study. The input-output matrix indicates how one portion of the economy is related to the other. The method allows investigation of the economic effects, albeit only the private effects of alternative resource uses. Therefore, the analyst can explore what occurs with various levels of projects including no project and trace the effects through the entire economy.

This methodology provides two things to the decision process. First is an economic description of the region, county, or SMSA, in the form of a dollar flow table. Second is an analysis of changes in the economy produced by a change in any one sector. This information is normally summarized in a matrix of direct and indirect requirements.

Development of Input-Output Sectors

An input-output model disaggregates the basic service sectors of the economic base study. A major question is How disaggregated a model is necessary to achieve the results desired? A trade-off exists between a degree of additional accuracy and the cost to build and run the more detailed model. Isard points out that using a more detailed model increases the numbers and types of hypotheses and models that can be tested. However, such detail does involve additional costs (which do not fall in a linear fashion with declining regional size) and the investigator must weigh the gains against these costs.[25]

A second important question is What is the objective of the study? If the purpose is to investigate the impacts of shifts of land from agriculture to other uses, such as Berns describes earlier, a majority of the model sectors will probably be agricultural with other economic enterprises being incorporated into highly aggregated sectors. Examples of this type of model are those by Goldman et al. that have been developed for at least ten California counties. The questions laid out for each of the studies were the following: what might be the total economic effect on the county of different resource development policies, what would be the effect of changes in taxation, land use, and zoning; what economic changes would occur if residential construction replaced agricultural land; and how much should the county encourage industrial development?[26]

In contrast to the studies described previously, the analyst may see the purpose of the study to be the examination, for example, of the effects of shifts from light to heavy industry. In this case it is likely that the model constructed would handle all the agriculture in one sector or have a sector for every manufacturing industry. Isard and others have developed numerous studies that are constructed in this manner. These have been primarily for major metropolitan areas such as Philadelphia,[27] and include his study on Alternative Recreational Complex Development in the Plymouth, Massachusetts Bay Area.[28] Of 196 sectors in the Philadelphia study, only six were for agriculture and 131 for various types of manufacturing. It would be highly unusual if the EIR analyst were able to command the resources to develop and use an input-output study that is much larger than 25–30 sectors, simply in terms of data collection and value of results with respect to the costs of collecting and running the model.

The Dollar Flow Table

The dollar flow table, depicted in Table 5, is simply a recording of all sales and purchases made by different parts or sectors of the economy for a time period, usually 1 year. In reading the table, the sales of the sector are read across the sector's row and the purchases of the sector are read down the sector's column. For example, sales by agriculture to services were $1,385,000 in 1965 as denoted by the intersection of the agriculture row and the services column. Every economic transaction taking place during the time period is included in the dollar flow table as a sale by one sector and a purchase by another sector. All calculations used in an input-output analysis are dependent on the dollar flow table.

The dollar flow table is constructed by dividing the economy into separate sectors, so that every economic activity in the area fits into only one sector. The question arises as to what happens to a business or enterprise that is engaged in several economic activities. For the sake of consistency, all the activity of an enterprise is allocated to that sector which comprises the majority of the business activity.

Development of Technical Coefficients

From the dollar flow table one is able to estimate the technical coefficient. This is simply each sector's cost as a proportion of sales (see Table 6). These coefficients are derived directly from the dollar flow table by dividing the expenditures in each sector's column by the total sales in that column. As an example, in Table 5 the services sector spent $1,385,000 in the agricultural sector, $4,832,000 in the industrial sector, and had total sales of $103,503,000. The technical coefficients then are $1,385/103,503 = .0134 and $4,832/103,503 = .0417. The technical coefficients are arranged in a table in a manner similar to the figures that show on the dollar flow table. Therefore, in each column of the dollar flow table are the expenditures of that sector, and in each column of the technical coefficients matrix are the proportion or the percentages of expenditures of each of the sectors. Technical coefficients do not contain any information about the total dollar volume of the sector. The technical coefficient matrix, however, does indicate for each sector how a typical sales dollar is divided among other sectors for input costs.

Table of Direct and Indirect Requirements

From the technical coefficient matrix one is able to develop a matrix of direct and indirect requirements that is the basis of the multipliers and the end result in which the analyst is interested (for illustration, see Table 7). This matrix

Table 5 Dollar Flow Table—Napa County, 1965 ($000's)[a]

Sector	Agriculture	Industry	Trade	Services	Households	Total External and government	Total Sales
Agriculture	2,688	8,343	—	1,385	—	12,283	24,699
Industry	2,131	1,811	806	4,832	1,399	68,917	79,896
Trade	1,889	1,565	1,973	4,550	33,895	6,417	50,289
Services	1,741	4,092	1,571	6,576	61,944	27,579	103,503
Households	6,213	27,377	22,564	36,098	1,887	100,337	194,476
Total external and government	10,037	26,708	23,375	50,062	95,351	5,861	
Total production	24,699	79,896	50,289	103,503	194,476		

[a] From Goldman, G., *Explanation and Applications of County Input-Output Models*. Cooperative Extension, University of California, Berkeley, p. 32, 1-08 March 1973.

Table 6 Matrix of Technical Coefficients–Napa County, 1965[a]

Sector	Agriculture	Industry	Trade	Services	Households
Agriculture	.1088	.1044	—	.0134	—
Industry	.0863	.0227	.0160	.0467	.0072
Trade	.0765	.0196	.0392	.0440	.1743
Services	.0705	.0512	.0312	.0635	.3185
Households	.2515	.3427	.4487	.3488	.0097
Total external	.4064	.4594	.4648	.4837	.4903
Total production	1.0000	1.0000	1.0000	1.0000	1.0000

[a] From Goldman, G. see Note 34, p. 33.

estimates the change in economic activity caused in each sector by a change of $1.00 of economic activity in any one of the sectors.

The major reason for constructing the input-output model is to be able to estimate the economic impact of different economic and resource changes in the geographic area under consideration. It is generally accepted that a change in one sector of the economy will have effects on other sectors of the economy. In Table 7, summing down a column of the matrix of direct and indirect requirements provides the total effect for an expenditure of $1.00, which can be translated as the multiplier. This multiplier indicates the total amount of economic activity that is generated by an increase in sales of $1.00 for that specific sector. It is composed of three parts: the initial expenditure, the first round effects, and the second round effects. The table then indicates that there will be some effect from a sector purchasing goods and services from the other sectors. This provides a first-round economic effect. Now as these sectors go ahead and purchase additional goods and services, we get secondary economic effects.

Table 7 Matrix of Direct and Indirect Requirements, Condensed Sectors, Napa County, 1965[a]

Sector	Agriculture	Industry	Retail	Services	Househoulds
Agriculture	1.1404	0.1273	0.0082	0.0272	0.0111
Industry	0.1210	1.0533	0.0369	0.0696	0.0365
Retail	0.2000	0.1440	1.1693	0.1612	0.2587
Services	0.2758	0.2603	0.2578	1.2661	0.4545
Households	0.5193	0.5537	0.6354	0.5500	1.3025
Total	2.2565	2.1385	2.1076	2.0741	2.0634

[a] From Goldman, see Note 34, p. 34.

There will be numerous rounds, each one smaller than the last as a result of the fact that some purchases are made from firms outside the region.

An excellent example is expenditures by tourists. Sales to tourists are an export from a county as much as are products produced within the county and sold outside. Let us assume that a tourist spends a night at a motel. The owner of the motel receives payment for the night of lodging and pays a part of it to his employees. He also pays himself for his labor and a return on his investment. In addition to the facilities and labor needed, there is maintenance and repairs, services of accountants, utility bills, laundry services, and other business services required. Some of these goods and services are provided by firms and people in the local region, and some are from outside. Those payments to local concerns provide additional economic activity to the region, whereas expenditures outside the region have no further local effect. Now the firms from whom the motel owner bought goods and services also make expenditures, some inside the region and some outside. The process continues until finally a round is reached where there is no further economic activity. Several questions concerning the inflation of these local benefits by agencies to "sell" the local population on a proposed project have been raised by numerous critics.

Data Gathering

Each of the sectors defined by the analyst will require information on total sales and on the expenditure pattern (i.e., the percentage of each dollar of expenditure which goes to each of the other sectors—the technical coefficient). The sources of the information are rather diverse, and the means by which the analyst can obtain the data is varied. If the project warrants it, it is always possible to engage in primary data collection in the form of surveys. An excellent explanation of the survey technique utilized can be found in Isard and Langford.[29] However, in most cases the analyst will find it advantageous to use secondary data sources.

Sales data for agricultural sectors is generally available from County Agricultural Commissioner's reports or reports put out by the State Department of Agriculture. Such information is often available from Enterprise Data Sheets which are put out by the County Agricultural Extension Service also. Data for most of the manufacturing industries can be obtained in a very straightforward and simple manner. The analyst first determines the employment in the sector under consideration; this data is generally available from the State Department of Employment. Then he can multiply the level of employment by the gross value of output per worker from the 1969 Census of Manufacturers.[30] This value becomes the total sales for the industry. In some cases information is available on a county basis and in such cases the analyst can simply multiply the employment in the sector by the gross output per worker for the county.

In most cases expenditure data is simply taken from existing models, the assumption being that the industries under consideration show the same level of technology that exists in the country as a whole. Therefore, the coefficients developed in the national model[31] are often used. It is also possible to take coefficients from other existing models,[32] although, in general, if the analyst checks carefully into state, regional, and subregional models they will find that originally those coefficients were taken from the national model anyway. The exception to that, of course, is when extensive surveys have been undertaken in the building of the other models. In such cases it is conceivable that the coefficients may be different.

Use of Input-Output Models

Suppose 100 acres of apricot orchard are sold to a subdivider. The planned subdivision will have 200 homes with an average of 4 people per house. The average family income is assumed to be $10,000, all of which is earned in jobs outside the region. The permanent initial economic change is then $2,000,000 ($10,000 × 200) in personal income. For simplicity, the increase in construction sales resulting from building the 200 homes is not considered, because it does not involve the same kind of permanent change in economic flows.

There would be a decrease in economic activity by removing the land from apricot production. Let us assume that the average sales per acre is $150. This would imply a reduction of $15,000 in apricot sales.

The input-output model can be used to estimate the changes in dollar flows caused by: (1) the increase of $2,000,000 in personal income and (2) the reduction of $15,000 in apricot sales. To evaluate the effect of an increase of $2,000,000 in personal income, the coefficients in the household column of the matrix of direct and indirect requirements are each multiplied by $2,000,000 to get the total change in sales in the county in each of the sectors. For simplification we use the coefficients from Table 7, although in reality we would want a more disaggregated analysis. The results are shown in Table 8.

The initial economic change of $2,000,000 per year in personal income in the region can be considered as the initial increase in total sales of the household sectors. There is also a $1,019,400 increase in sales due to in-region purchases by the families receiving the initial $200,000,000. There is also a $1,107,200 increase in sales caused by the increase in economic activity produced by the initial economic effect. All in all, there is an estimated increase of $4,126,600 of total sales in the region.

The effect of the decrease of $15,000 in apricot production can be explained in the same manner. Again for simplicity, we use the coefficients from column 1 of our sample matrix of direct and indirect requirements (Table 7). Each coefficient is multiplied by $15,000 to get the total reduction in the region. Table 9 presents these results.

Table 8 Increase in Local Annual Sales Due to an Increase of $2,000,000 in Personal Income

Sector	Coefficient from Column 5 in Table 7	Multiplier × $2,000,000	Initial Economic Change	Initial Economic Effect	Secondary Economic Effect
Agriculture	.0111	22,200		0	22,200
Industry	.0365	73,000		14,400	58,600
Retail	.2587	517,400		348,600	168,800
Services	.4545	909,000		637,000	272,000
Households	1.3025	2,605,000	2,000,000	19,400	585,600
Total	2.0634	4,126,600	2,000,000	1,019,400	1,107,200

Table 9 Decrease in Local Annual Sales from a $15,000 Decrease in Apricot Sales

Sector	Coefficient from Column 1 in Table 7	Multiplier × $15,000	Initial Economic Change	Initial Economic Effect	Secondary Economic Effect
Agriculture	1.1404	17,106	15,000	1632	474
Industry	.1210	1,815		1294	521
Retail	.2000	3,000		1148	1852
Services	.2758	4,137		1058	3079
Households	.5193	7,790		3772	4018
Total	2.2565	33,848	15,000	8904	9944

The total decrease in sales for the region is $33,848. Of this, $15,000 is the reduction in sales of apricots. There is an additional loss of $8904 of local sales due to lower purchases by the agricultural sector when sales fall by $15,000. Finally, there are secondary economic effects of $9944.

The net effect on local sales of the proposed development is calculated by subtracting losses in sales due to a reduction in apricot sales from the increases in sales resulting from the additional personal income. The total net change in sales for the region in this example is an increase of $4,092,752.

The Size of the Multiplier

The size of the multiplier depends on two major factors. The first is the percentage of the initial dollar that is spent within the region. This, of course, means that the larger the region, the larger the multiplier effect is likely to be; and conversely, the smaller the region, the smaller the multiplier effect from a given dollar change is likely to be.[33] The second major factor is the size of the secondary economic effects produced per unit of the initial economic effect. The same factors bear on this in general as on the initial economic effect. The analyst should then be aware of the fact that if he is utilizing a regional, statewide, or even national study as a base, it is incumbent on him to lower his estimate of the multiplier effect. At the state level a significant portion of inputs will be purchased from industries and enterprises located within the state. By the time one reduces the area to the San Francisco SMSA, the amount of locally bought services would be significantly less. If the region were only Contra Costa County, the proportion of input purchased from the outside would be substantial.

Limitations of Input-Output

Input-output models are based on several important assumptions that are often criticized as much as the technique of using average costing in cost-revenue studies. The most important assumption is that there is a linearity of production functions for each sector. Simply stated, this means that the technical coefficients remain constant. For example, if wages account for 20 percent of the inputs in a particular sector, it is assumed that wages will remain at 20 percent after there has been a change.[34]

A second assumption is that each sector is homogenous in economic character. This means that each economic unit in the sector has the same linear production function or uses the same proportion of input factors (i.e., the technical coefficients are constant). Obviously, this is not true. There will be a range of input combinations within each sector. The more aggregated the sector, the greater is the limitation. Even if the sectors are highly disaggregated, a problem could arise. For example, assume that the analyst is evaluating the introduction of a highly mechanized plant where existing plants are labor intensive. Here the assumption of constant technical coefficients is invalid, and a recalculation is required.

A third assumption is that changes in sales outside the region do not effect the economic flows in the county. Sales to out-of-county locations may have effects in the county, but it is assumed that the effects are small in magnitude.

A final· assumption is that no large structural changes occur in the local economy over several years. This allows the analyst to assume that the estimated multiplier effects adequately reflect the current situation.

The assumption that has been attacked most often is the use of constant coefficients.[35] The critics point to a number of conditions that limit the validity of using constant coefficients. The first is economies of scale which are present in most industries. Second is urbanization economics or external economics which arise when unlike plants all locate in an area. A third is localization economics or external economics which develop when plants of similar industries are built in one place. All these economies would deny the use of a set of constant coefficients reflecting technological relations.[36] Conceivably, if all these types of economies are present, the analyst may underestimate the impact.

Technological advance is also a limiting factor. This is particularly true when the coefficients are derived from transactions of a base year that must reflect the technological structure for that year. For situations where technological advance has been fairly regular, the analyst can extrapolate the trend so as to modify the coefficients in a future year. The problem arises when technological advance is uneven and unpredictable. In this case, the limitation cannot be overcome.

The final problem is changes in prices. Prices shift relative to each other in the real world. Also, in some measure shifting relative prices cause substitution of inputs.

Do the objections raised require the analyst to use input-output models in the same manner as economic base models and their multipliers for mere description of the existing economic structure? Most likely not, as long as the limitations are realized and steps are taken to minimize the objections.[37] The impact process requires the development of economic projections. Projections based on empirical data, guesses, and intuition should provide at least as good results as those developed on guesses and intuition alone.

The use of input-output models for projection is an approximation procedure. The more clearly the analyst can see emerging trends in prices, technology, and economies of scale, the firmer will be the projection. It follows that the accuracy of the projection should increase the closer the projection year is to the base. Therefore, the more current the input-output table, the more useful is the method.

Final Thoughts on Input-Output Models

Like any tool, input-output models have the potential for being misused. Probably the greatest danger is the misapplication of multipliers developed for regions that are not similar to the one under consideration. There is a great temptation to find a set of multipliers from an already existing input-output study and to use them without modification.

If these and other temptations can be avoided, the strengths of this method are many. As long as the user recognizes the weakness discussed, he can provide a much fuller description of the impacts of any project by utilizing it. It is far better to use the tool to investigate the private impacts than to leave them unanalyzed or to use a methodology so imprecise as to possibly provide misleading information.

CONCLUSION

When evaluating the impacts of a proposed project or program, it is essential to include potential impacts on the local economy and on local governmental agencies. However, under no circumstances should the analyst stop at this point. It is essential that the other two categories (environmental and social impacts) listed at the beginning of the chapter also be considered.

The evaluation of the fiscal and economic aspects can be done systematically, using the methods discussed in this chapter. The reader is reminded that each of the methods has shortcomings which must be recognized and admitted. This is particularly true of the cost-revenue study. The sensitivity of the results to the assumptions recommends the use of the two alternative formulations discussed.

The purpose of impact assessment is to provide additional information to the decision process, thus it behooves the analyst to be extremely explicit about the methods used and the assumption made. This holds true whether evaluating the fiscal or faunal impacts of a project. In Chapter 10 an overall framework is discussed as a means of considering all four classes of potential impacts. Although it is essential that the fiscal and economic impacts be considered, they must not be the overriding considerations.

NOTES

1. Alaskan Pipeline Jobs Scarce, Brennan Warns, *New York Times,* Dec. 8, 1973.
2. Oil Pipe Town Girds for Rush of Workers, *New York Times,* p. 22, June 26, 1974, "The population is up 2,000 . . . no housing, no place to put trailers, no place for people to live."

"The city budget has risen from $500,000 in 1971 to $4.25 million next year, and school enrollment in the same period has jumped from 341 to 1,000 in September."

 3. Malott, Patricia R. B., The Oroville Dam Project and Local Impact, unpublished Masters thesis, University of California, Davis, 1967.

 4. Report, Hanford Planning Department, 1966.

 5. Strum, Norman. Comments on Oroville Project, Department of Water Resources, Hearings on Oroville Project, Sept. 25, 1956.

 6. A recent study (City of Davis Cost/Revenue Analysis—Fiscal Year 1971-1972 by Marcia Huddleston for the Davis Planning Department, pp. 2-3, April 1973) allocates police service costs to land uses on the basis of calls to the Police Department: ". . . [A] survey of six months of typical activity was undertaken to determine the type of calls answered by the Department, . . . the rationale was that the distribution of calls throughout the City reflects the relative distribution of time, expertise, and manpower expended by the Department." Calls are weighted by type (e.g., felony, traffic) to develop an "activity function."

 7. Mace, Ruth L., Municipal Cost-Revenue Research in the United States: A Critical Survey of Research to Measure Municipal Costs and Revenues in Relation to Land Uses and Areas: 1933-1960, Institute of Government, University of North Carolina, Chapel Hill, pp. 708 and generally, 1961.

 8. See Ruth L. Mace and Warren J. Wicker, Do Single Family Homes Pay Their Own Way? Washington D.C., Urban Land Institute Research Monograph 15, 1968; L. T. Wallace, George Goldman, Ron H. Tyler, and Joe Hart, A Framework for Analyzing Public Service Costs and Revenues Associated With Land Use Alternatives, University of California Agricultural Extension, June 1973 (mimeographed); H. A. Simon, Fiscal Aspects of Metropolitan Consolidation, Bureau of Public Administration, University of California, Berkeley, 1943, as discussed in Julius Margolis, "On municipal land policy for fiscal gains, Natl. Tax J., IX p. 247, Sept. 1956.

 9. See Dickinson, T., Jeffrey Peters, and John Cupps, The Fiscal Impact of Alternative Land Use in Stanislaus County, Summary Report, Division of Environmental Studies, University of California, Davis, January 1973, and Milpitas Planning Department, 1969-1970 Milpitas Community Comprehensive Land Use Economic Study: Cost-Revenue, Milpitas, California, 1971.

10. See Mace. Note 7, p. 7.

11. See Mace R. and Warren Wicker, Note 8, p. 12.

12. Chambers, John, Do Single Family Homes Still Pay Their Way? in Growth Cost Revenue Studies, Associated Home Builders of the Greater Bay Area, Inc., Berkeley, 1972.

13. See Mace, R. and Warren Wicker, Note 8, pp. 27, 32, 36, 37.

14. See Mace, R. and Warren Wicker, Note 8, pp. 41–42.

15. Education, welfare, and recreation only; health services are left allocated as by Mace and Wicker (according to assessed value).

16. See Mace, R. and Warren Wicker, Note 8, pp. 41–42.

17. See Wallace, L. T., et al., Note 8, p. 5.

18. Cutler, Richard W., Legal and Illegal Methods for Controlling Community Growth on the Urban Fringe, Wisconsin Law Review, Madison, 1961, p. 379; Netzer, Richard, The Economics of the Property Tax, The Brookings Institute, Washington, D.C., 1966.

19. For complete discussion of method of construction of economic base studies see Isard, W. Methods of Regional Analysis, The M.I.T. Press, Cambridge, 1960; Tiebout, Charles M., Exports and Regional Economic Growth, J. Polit. Econ., 64, April, 1956; Andrews, Richard B., Comment re: Criticisms of the Economic Base Theory, J. Am. Inst. Plann., 24, 1958.

20. See Isard, W., Note 19.

21. See Isard, W., Note 19, p. 192.

22. See Andrews, R. B., Note 19, p. 163.

23. Baxter, MacDonald and Smart, Inc., *Socio-economic Impacts of Environmental Policies,* San Francisco, December 1973, p. 34.

24. The discussion in this section is based heavily on the work of Goldman, George, *Explanations and Application of County Input-Output Models,* Cooperative Extension, University of California, Berkeley, I-08, March 1974.

25. Isard, W. and Langford, Thomas W., *Regional Input-Output Study,* The M.I.T. Press, Cambridge, 1971.

26. Goldman, George, L. T. Wallace, and John Mamer, *Sonoma County Economic and Resource Use Study,* Cooperative Extension, University of California, Berkeley, I-0 2 January, 1973.

27. See Isard, W. and T. W. Langford, Note 25.

28. Isard, W., et al., *Ecologic-Economic Analysis for Regional Development,* The Free Press, New York, 1972.

29. See Isard, W. and T. W. Langford, Note 25, pp. 54–80.

30. U.S. Bureau of the Census, Department of Commerce, *Census of Manufacturing: General Statistics for Industry Groups and Industries,* Washington, D.C., 1969.

31. U.S. Department of Commerce, Bureau of Labor Statistics, *Input-Output Structure of the U.S. Economy; 1963,* Washington, D.C., 1969.

32. State of California, Resources Agency, Department of Water Resources, Division of Resources Development, State Wide Input-Output Model: Base Year (1967), Sacramento, California 1973, and Gerald Dean, et al., *Structure and Projections of the Humboldt County Economy: Economic Growth vs. Environmental Quality.* University of California, Giannini Foundation of Agricultural Economics, Research Report Number 318, July, 1973. Isard, W. S. and T. W. Langford, Note 25, Isard, W., et al., Note 28; Goldman, George, various county studies, University of California, Cooperative Extension Service, Berkeley; University of Washington, Graduate School of Business Administration *Input-Output Tables for the Washington Economy,* 1967, Seattle, 1970.

33. See Baxter, MacDonald and Smart, Inc., Note 23.

34. Goldman, G., *Explanations and Applications of County Input-Output Models,* Berkeley Cooperative Extension Service, University of California, I-0 8, March 1974.

35. For a fuller discussion of the limitation of this assumption, see Isard, W., Note 19, pp. 327 and 338–343; and Goldman, G. Note 32, p. 37.

36. A complete discussion of these economics are in Chenery, H., Interdependence of Investment Decisions, in *The Allocation of Economic Resources,* Abramovitz, Moses, Ed., Stanford University Press, Stanford, California, 1959; and Interregional and International Input-Output Analysis, in *Structural Interdependence of the Economy,* Tibar Barna, Ed., Wiley, New York, 1954.

37. See Isard, W., Note 19, p. 341 for suggestions on ways to minimize the objections.

SIX

Social Impacts
of Transportation

R. DANIEL SCHOTT

This chapter deals with individual and social impacts of transporation projects. The concept of social impacts is at this date unclear, as Coop has shown in Chapter 2, both in the letter of the law and in the requirements and practice of impact analysis. The NEPA is extremely vague on aspects of the social environment that are to be considered separately from the economic environment. In the brief history of social, economic, and environmental impact analysis, there has been a very common and popular tendency to include social aspects of analysis as subsidiary aspects of socioeconomic analysis. As we have seen in the chapter in this volume by Coop, this tendency has been resisted by the courts. Several other parts of this book, especially the chapters by Dickenson and Blackmarr and Berns, present specific details of economic theory and analysis methodologies. To avoid duplication and in an attempt to provide an independent line of thought regarding social impact analysis, this chapter excludes principles and factors of social impact analysis whose primary orientation is toward collection and investigation of economic data.

As a further introductory note to this chapter, it should be understood that the principles and methodologies presented are derived from or specially applicable to analysis of the effects of urban transportation systems and projects. There are three reasons for an emphasis on urban effects:

1. The overwhelming majority of political concern and allocation of funds for transportation development is directed toward metropolitan areas;

2. Urban areas provide the broadest range and most frequent occurrence of social impacts; and

3. By simple connotation and appropriate adjustment of data requirements, urban impact methodology can very probably be transferred and applied to rural situations.

DEVELOPING PARAMETERS FOR SOCIAL ANALYSIS

The impetus to the establishment of laws requiring impact analysis has been a concern for preservation or conservation of natural resources. With a good deal of insight, the authors of these laws have seen the necessity of including consideration of economic and social impacts of environmental and technological change on the qualities of life of the human population. Unfortunately, the three-fold interest and attention to environmental, economic, and social conditions has not been accompanied by a parallel understanding of the nature and importance of the factors that constitute these three types of systems. A great deal of popular interest and scientific investigation has been devoted to specifying impacts that occur in the realm of the natural environment. A significant amount of attention has been paid to economics, but in comparison to knowledge of the natural environment, there is a much smaller collection of empirical knowledge about the functions of economic systems. And finally, we come to the area of social analysis. Most of the disciplinary study, primarily in the areas of sociology, psychology, and political science, as McEvoy noted in Chapter 1, has been devoted to examination of topics that are too narrow to be of use in the impact evaluation process. The existing compendium of theory, analysis, and interpretation of data appears to be a relatively weak endeavor when compared with the epistemological basis of natural and even economic science.

OVERVIEW OF THE URBAN TRANSPORTATION PLANNING PROCESS

The impact analyst or reviewer should have a basic understanding of the fundamentals involved in the preparation of plans for transportation development, improvement, change, or expansion. Basically, there are three elements to the planning process: inventory of existing conditions, forecast of travel demand, and determination of need for improvement or change. Selection of techniques to realize the policy determined by these processes depends on several factors. Some of the factors that will determine the specific study design for a planning project include: scale of contemplated project, proficiency and availability of staff, amount of money available for instrumentation and analysis of data, and especially, the mode of transportation under consideration. In practice, for example, transportation planning for systems that require new permanent, fixed road- or railways involves much more complex methodological approaches than planning for transit systems operation on existing roadways.

Operation on Existing Roadways (Planning for Buses)

The technologies of transportation planning are just now beginning to be applied on a large scale in the determination of bus system operations. Most bus systems are laid out according to inductive estimates of highest patronage return. Usually, there is an identification of economic characteristics and probable travel behavior of populations along several possible route corridors. Routes are then selected, and service is scheduled to provide the most attractive service to the estimated highest number of riders. For example, if it is determined that a large number of residents along a potential corridor are blue-collar workers employed in a major industrial section of the town, routes would be drawn to minimize overall travel time; and service schedules would be arranged to provide the greatest frequency of buses in the early morning and late afternoon hours. On the other hand, if the prime potential clientele are largely housewives with single-automobile families, bus routes and schedule frequencies might be selected to maximize convenience of service to shopping facilities during the middle of the day.

Transit operation planning, whether based on rigorous technical analysis or not, is frequently a trial-and-error process. Route and frequency schedules are selected, and service is initiated for a trial period. If patronage does not meet expectations, routes may be changed, schedules may be adjusted, or the service may be terminated and the equipment redirected to trial service in another area. This product marketing approach to bus service has been required in the past by inadequate allocation of public funding for mass transit. Transit planners have been forced to initiate and cancel service primarily on the basis of fare-box cash return. The mid1970s, however, marked by national recognition of the need to conserve energy and a corresponding rise in the possibility of improving the quality of life by reducing dependence on the private automobile, appears to be a turning point for public funding of public transportation. It is inevitable that as more money becomes available for the operation of transit systems, greater emphasis will come to be placed on more technical approaches to the determination of socially beneficial public transportation services. The principles and methodologies described as follows for fixed roadway systems are indicative of the general approach that is likely to characterize all transportation planning in the near future.

Fixed Roadways-System Planning (Expressways, Highways, Freeways, and Railways)

The essential constructs of transportation system planning are the inventory, the estimation of travel demand, and the determination of system needs. The inventory of existing conditions includes: measurement of the system in terms of existing roadway, locations served, and usage of the system. The inventory will also include measurement of population parameters which vary from case to case but usually comprise: population size, income level distributions, residential densities and distributions, and automobile ownership. The inventory phase of the planning process is of the utmost importance to the social impact analyst. A more detailed description of methods and contents of inventory is left for later parts of the chapter.

The third element of the planning process, need determination, is self-evident. The need is the description of a new facility or the size of improvement to an old system that should be undertaken if the existing, inventoried system is to be able to accommodate a travel demand level predicted for a given point of time in the future. Obviously, the meat of transportation planning lies in the second element, travel demand forecasting. Forecasting is a tremendously complex process involving extensive data accumulation and complex statistical and other types of analysis. Whatever degree of complexity may be involved in the mathematical formula and data categories, forecasting is essentially based on the ground plan of economic utility theory—especially the components of demand and supply functions. The demand is the estimated number of trips expected to use a service or system. The magnitude of demand will depend on the level of service offered by the system. Level of service is measured by characteristics such as cost, travel time, accessibility, comfort, and other physical and economic characteristics of the system. As Dietz has shown in Chapter 3, forecasting is inherently inaccurate, but at its best requires a high disaggregation of variables to be of much, if any, value.

Weighting and combination of relevant characteristics of a model system constitutes an estimate of the supply function. As the weights of the constituent components are adjusted for a single mode or between modes, the level of service will vary in a curvilinear relationship to the number of trips that can be provided by the system. The dashed line in Figure 6.1 depicts the supply function. If the cost to the traveler is low, the travel time is fast, and comfort and safety are maximized, only a small number of trips can be provided. If on the other hand cost to the traveler is high, the trip is very slow, and the system has very low standards for comfort and safety, a much larger number of trips can be accommodated.

The demand function in utility theory varies in a manner opposite to the supply function. Demand relationships are represented by the solid line in Figure 6.1. The demand function indicates that people will, as expected, make the greatest number of trips on a system when it is comfortable, cheap, and fast. The underlying principle of transportation planning is that the expense and quality of the system (supply) should be at a high enough level of quality to

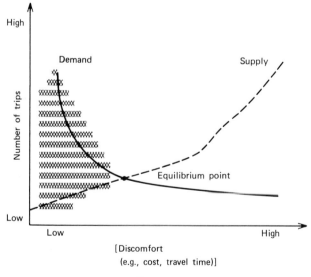

Figure 6.1

attract a large number of users (demand); supply should not, however, increase beyond a point at which incremental (or marginal) increases in facility investment cease to produce an equal or greater return in user demand. Referring again to Figure 6.1, the point at which the supply and demand curves intersect represents equilibrium between net benefit returned and supply investments. The shaded area to the left of this equilibrium point read from left to right indicates that for each additional dollar invested in transportation facilities, the increased demand generated will be at least as great as the demand generated by the previous dollar spent. To the right of the equilibrium point each new trip added to the demand curve will require a larger facility investment than did the previous trip on the curve. These ideas should be reasonably familiar to most of our readers.

In practice, transportation utility is expressed through formulae for estimating travel demand and for describing hypothetical facilities. The demand formulae are mathematical models approximating user behavior. Typically, large amounts of data concerning trip types and the characteristics of travelers are processed by computers with these models. Travel data is in sample form and is obtained from home and roadside interviews. In addition to behavioral data, each working model contains supply information describing the size and type of transportation facilities that could serve specified zones of origin and destination. Data is also hypothesized or supplied from current conditions to represent the nature of attractions in the origin and destination zones.

To develop a travel model, a city or other geographic area is first divided into zones of approximately equal numbers of residents or numbers of commercial establishments' (attractors). Travelers are then sampled to learn their origins, destinations, routes, and frequency of travel. Along with the trip information, the interviewer also learns such things as the traveler's income, family size, age, the number of autos he owns, and on what mode (car, bus, train, foot) he makes various trips. All socioeconomic data is also estimated for the unsampled population to whom sample trip data are assigned. Having collected and estimated resident characteristics and the nature and locations of attractors, trips are mathematically generated and numerically distributed alone major routes between zones.

Obviously, one of the shortcomings of this approach to transportation planning is the endless perpetuation and magnitudinal increase of whatever travel behaviors exist at the time of the planning study. Data are obtained to determine who travels where and how often to which places with what frequency. This long-established planning approach served well during the freeway-boom years following World War II. In recent years, however, the continual expansion of freeway systems and the lack of sophisticated planning in transit services has led to many problems for our nation's cities—most notable among which are pollution, poor land use, and congestion. What follows in this chapter is a presentation of some methods of social impact analysis that may help us to understand better how present and future transportation developments affect our cities. Future results from application of some of these methods may also lead to improvements in current transportation planning policies—improvements that could redirect transportation planning to become a tool for better serving the needs of our communities.

SOCIAL IMPACTS ANALYSIS METHODS

Factors: The first question the analyst must ask is: What constitutes the realm of social impacts? There is no straightforward answer to this question. The best we can do is to draw parameters and cite examples of factors that have been selected for review in case studies. In the first place, social analysis is typi-cally concerned with dynamic social processes extant in a community and with the effects of mobility changes on the system users. Analysis is not concerned with individual impacts on riders; for example, vehicle comfort, sense of identity, self-esteem, and the like are not ordinarily included in social impact analyses, although they may in some cases be essential variables in a particular EIR.

What is or is not a social factor is sometimes a matter of opinion and varies from project to project. In choosing from available alternative factors to review, the analyst is advised to develop his own conceptual framework for categorizing factors. An example of a categorical framework is presented as follows. This proposed framework classifies factors of concern as being of three types.

Physical Displacement

Any transportation facility and its operation are bound to usurp existing land use activities. Freeways present the most visible examples of this type of impact. The construction of a few miles of urban freeway may require the raz-ing of thousands of homes. It may require the removal of factories. It may render parkland unusable. A new freeway may limit access to small businesses to the extent that their survival is impossible. Displacement or dislocation effects represent the most direct impacts of a transportation facility. Many of the other papers in this book elaborate this set of effects in considerable detail.

Disruption Effects

Disruption effects are the influences of a facility on adjacent social activities during the periods of construction and, later, operation. Examples of disruption during construction include attraction of vandalism to supply stocks, temporary severance of utility services and extensive rerouting of pedestrian and vehicle access routes, and the creation of noise, dust, and numerous safety hazards. Following construction and during the life of the facility's operation, some of the disruptions that might be expected from transportation facilities are: termination or limitation of neighborhood continuity' neighborhood division; discontinuity of service areas for fire, police, churches, clubs, schools, and so on; and opportunity for development of conflicting land uses. Disruption effects can be either direct (e.g., removal of homes) or indirect (e.g., encroachment of commercial development into formerly residential areas) results of the facility and the traffic it generates. Disruption effects are different from class and mobility effects, mainly in the fact that the former concern changes in existing circulation, whereas the latter involve changes resulting from new and different opportunities and accessibility.

Mobility Effects

Mobility effects are the longest ranging, most pervasive and least tangible types of impact. Positive or negative, mobility effects include the opportunity for new industry and businesses to locate on sites that were previously inaccessible to shoppers or commodity routes, new residential location opportunities for previously restricted income groups, and new access to social, cultural, recreational, and employment opportunities. Dietz points out the implications of these effects for intraregional migration patterns in his chapter.

Mobility effects, like other effects, may be primary (e.g., a new bus route to an existing employment site), or secondary (e.g., enhanced probability of moderate-income suburban development), or they can be even more indirect. Mobility effects differ, however, by the fact that the secondary effects are frequently more controversial and arouse more concern than the primary mobility effects. For example, a new freeway connecting a large job center with a white, middle-income suburb may make it practical to mass-produce less expensive suburban homes. The availability of lower-priced homes in the suburb will probably attract low-income, minority workers from inner city areas. Primary mobility effects support suburban development and improve travel conditions to the job center. Migration by minority families represents a secondary effect. Finally, a tertiary mobility effect, integration (and any ensuing racial conflict), will likely produce the greatest anxiety and be at the core of all other concerns expressed, especially by the current white suburbanites. As we will see, far less attention has been paid to these relatively long-term mobility effects than to displacement or disruption effects. However, the potential application of census analysis, along with increased citizen concern, hold tremendous promise for this class of effects assuming a prominent role in social impact analysis of transportation developments as they have in the controversy over development of the proposed Century Freeway in Los Angeles.

In practice, not much attention has been given to organizing social impact analyses in any way similar to the conceptual framework just described. Most of the articles that have been written about social impacts of transportation present a "laundry-list" of factors which represent either the author's concerns and knowledge or those of concerned citizens. Although the laundry-list approach is not recommended as a preferred approach to impact analysis, it is the most common and, therefore, is discussed here.

Factor Approach

In a study of probable social impacts of a proposed freeway in the City of Baltimore,[1] researchers used the following format of factors:

1. City-wide social impacts

(a) General population trends (i.e., growth)
(b) Color (ethnic) shift
(c) Age shift

2. Neighborhood impacts

(a) Displacement
(b) Destruction of social facilities (churches, shops, playgrounds)
(c) Migration and resident characteristics changes
(d) Ethnicity

The Baltimore study, from which these factors were extracted, was in part concerned with impacts on established ethnic neighborhoods and in the main with migration patterns of low-income black residents. The factors selected emphasize neighborhood cohesion and racial friction. Although all the factors selected are valid concerns of social impact, the Baltimore study demonstrates the latitude for entry of bias into definitions of social analysis when the researchers begin with an intuitive factor list. Possibly Delphi methods, also described by Dietz, may improve this situation.

At the other extreme are the investigators who have made every possible attempt to remove subjectivity from their studies by trying to cover every conceivable aspect of the social realm, often inserting hundreds of variables and interactions. Although the author is personally familiar with many studies that use the "shotgun" approach, none have attained sufficient rigor and sophistication to merit publication. A tempered attitude toward this approach, however, has found frequent success; and a few have been reported in technical journals. A study by Weiner and Deak[2] demonstrates a method of tempering or refining the range of factors by subjecting them to citizens' evaluations of importance. Weiner and Deak's laundry-list contained the following factors, which could be or were associated with highway and transportation system development:

Aesthetics	Land use
Visual quality of highway	Pattern of land development
Blend highway into background	Number of business firms
Aesthetic value of right-of-way	Amount of open space
Temporary aesthetic effects	Number of housing units
Aesthetic effects of pollution	Number of historic sites
Economics	Health and safety
Number of jobs	Access to emergency facilities
Number of welfare recipients	Effect on national defense
Property values	Health effects of pollution
Temporary economic effects	Personal or group stress
Level of income	Safety on adjacent highways
Political	Social-psychological
Municipal services	Community cohesiveness
Public participation in government	Personal or business contacts
Financial capability of government	Neighborhood stability
Community security	Barrier effects
Satisfaction with government	Community-oriented contacts

Weiner and Deak tempered their list of factors by having citizens assign relative weights to the factors. Thus, although some attention was given to nearly every socioeconomic aspect imaginable, only those factors of greatest community concern entered into final impact assessment scores. Obviously, obtaining adequate data on a set of variables this large and developing a set of empirically derived equations to express their relation and proceed to a simulation is a costly task beyond the capability of most planning agencies and, in any case, of somewhat dubious value.

Finally, many social analyses have concentrated solely on the concept of community or neighborhood cohesiveness. One such study used pedestrian activity as an indication of socialization and cohesion.[3] Another study using the same basic approach employed an indicator of social interaction to estimate neighborhood cohesion.[4] Burkhards's approach is representative of one class of valid approaches to factor identification. It is also illustrative of the tremendous amount of work involved in original identification of social impact analysis factors. At the same time the method has serious weaknesses due to its high degree of aggregation of variables.

Burkhardt began by intuitively selecting component descriptors and behaviors of social interaction. Primary data was collected in Philadelphia on six components. Factor analysis reduced the original six to two or three significant components of interaction levels. Since it would be highly impractical to survey every neighborhood to rate components, Burkhardt looked for extant secondary data that correlated with his primary components. These secondary data, available from the U.S. Census, were then labeled as descriptors of social interaction (partial listing):

Total census tract population
Percent of population 0–14 years old
Percent of population over 60
Persons per household
Persons per residential acre
Percentage of families at current address less than 2 years
Percentage of families who do not own an automobile

The Burkhardt and Kaplan, et al., studies are cited here to underline the fact that it is not uncommon for investigators of social impact to simplify a complex and ill-defined complex of variables into a single aggregated measure of the total range of phenomena that might concern us. Although limited in impact prediction efforts, secondary descriptors of populations (like census data) are invaluable in any impact study. They provide an orderly and fairly valid basis for describing the population to be affected. Among the types of factors for which population indicators are necessary are airport noise, freeway effects on home values, and disruptions of local services. Secondary data are also necessary to compare effects on distinguishable segments of a total area's population. Special segments may be defined by age structure, ethnicity, employment status or economic well-being, and so on. All these factors are covered by Dietz in considerable detail in Chapter 3.

CASE STUDIES

The preceding discussion of factor approaches to social impact analysis demonstrates the research designs most common in current studies. We return, at the end of this chapter, to the needs for (1) integrating social analysis with the planning process and for (2) imposing a superorder of systematic organization to social impact studies. In the meantime, we must acknowledge several facts affecting the demands placed on the impact analyst:

1. A systematic discipline to guide social impact studies does not now exist. Coop's reviews, if nothing else, underline this fact.

2. With or without a superstructure or theory to guide our research designs, we will still be concerned with laundry-list-type factors and with specific methods for analyzing those factors. (We should expect that adoption of an organizing superstructure or framework would result in a more rational approach to the selection of relevant factors from among those now found in lists.)

3. In addition to a lack of a thoroughly scientific (i.e., good theory + good methods) framework for analysis, the laws, regulations, and judicial decisions guiding social impact analysis have provided limited practical advice for the social impact analyst aside from directing that certain features of a litigated issue be considered by an agency.

4. In spite of the absence of clearly-stated disciplinary principles and legal requirements, thousands of privately and publicly-employed individuals are currently engaged in the practice of social impact assessment. To be as charitable as one can while remaining consistent with the facts, most of the material produced thus far is unsatisfactory.

5. Finally, social impact analysis is not an entirely barren field. Many studies have been performed, and a variety of methods of analysis have been demonstrated.

Given this list of real-world exigencies (and the reader may be all too aware of many other demands and uncertainties confronting him), the following descriptions of actual research methods are presented to help fill an immediate need for assistance. For those who are looking for successful methods to replicate, the studies described may provide the starting point for adequate coverage of social aspects of environmental reporting. For those who seek to improve the fledgling science of social impact analysis or who are interested in the potential contributions of social science to the physical planning process, the following is a requisite background for familiarity with the state of the art.

The descriptions provided in the case study reports are not step-by-step instructions for performing studies but are intended to give the reader sufficient information to decide if the methods are appropriate to his needs. The reader is referred to original publications for complete methodological explanations.

BART Residential Impacts

The Bay Area Rapid Transit system (BART) is a fixed rail mass transportation system designed, ultimately, to serve the majority of the urban centers in the San Francisco Bay Area. The study described here was undertaken to assess the impacts of BART and its operation on residential environments surrounding the transit lines and stations. The study[5] is cited for its recency and for its attempt to establish a systematic approach to urban impact analysis. The impact study was systematic in that it delt with social impacts as an ordered set of human responses to environmental change. It was not systematic in the sense of application of a disciplined and ordered set of principles of human organization as proposed in this chapter.* Nonetheless, the BART impact study marks a clear-cut beginning of social impact analysis as a cohesive body of investigation, and it offers some good examples of reliable approaches to specific methodological designs.

The BART impact researchers designed a set of natural controls into their study. Some of these controls can and should be incorporated into other impact studies. The main confusion in any environmental study is the confounding of the relevant variables (e.g., direct effects of BART operation) with other variables that may be expected to change with or without the transportation development (e.g., planned land use changes, population growth, and traffic increase). One control used in the BART study was to match the 27 study sites with two control situations—sites that were essentially similar to the study sites in all respects except that no rapid transit system was present or planned. The intention was to record changes in both the study and control sites with the assumption that changes found only in study sites could be attributed to BART.

This natural observation, control-case method is the most practical means of identifying the effects caused by an independent variable (i.e., BART). The reader should note that this method is an impact identification technique and not an impact prediction tool. Unlike most researchers who are attempting to assess future impacts, Appleyard and Carp were endeavoring to isolate impacts as or after they occurred. The BART impact researchers were performing a muchneeded service to the field of social impact analysis: the identification through an approximate cause-and-effect model of what we can confidently assume to be the probable impacts of transportation improvements. Although the majority of analysts and planners who read this book may never themselves engage in practical research of social impacts, it is essential that anyone who has a responsibility for accurate and knowledgeable preparation of impact reports be aware of the existance and value of studies such as the BART residential impacts project. Very few such studies have been completed and reported, but several are in progress across the country. The interested reader is urged to contact universities and transportation agencies in his area to determine whether similar studies are underway.

Returning to the BART study methodology, we can note two other aspects of the design that might find broad applications in impact analyses. First, great

---

* Although referred to in the past tense, the report cited is ongoing. The BART system began operation of the first trunk line in September 1973. The study is intended to continue beyond total system completion. (1977+).

care has been taken to define the geographic areas of interest. Second, the researchers have devised a thorough program of investigative approaches, rather than settling on a single method of analysis.

In regard to geographic definition, the BART impact study has designated the area of interest as the 2-mile-wide corridor extending out 1 mile on each side of the line. The 1-mile radius was chosen on the belief that as the outer edges of the study area are approached, BART impacts should diminish to the point that other urban variables assume equal or greater influence in effecting change. Thus the entire study area contains an additional and continuous set of experimental (near BART) and control (1 mile from BART) situations.

Within the corridor sites have been further delineated and designated as representative and unique areas. Although the BART study designations refer specifically to so-called transit-environment configurations, the differentiation of normal and unique characteristics of population segments and of their natural and man-made environments is an important ingredient in any impact study. Social impact studies are largely concerned with the equity or distribution of impacts.

The first consideration in assessing equity is to determine whether sites that are unique (when compared to regional norms) are likely to be more directly or intensely impacted than are other sites. The BART study attempted to perform this analysis on a reduced scale by treating the entire corridor as the region with subareas within the corridor representing unique sites. Some further suggestions for treating normal bases and uniqueness are elaborated in the closing discussion to this chapter.

As a final refinement to site definition, the BART study specifies four degrees of impacted units within each impact site: homes, street blocks (or portions), access paths, and local facilities. Homes refers to dwelling units where interviews are conducted. Street blocks are actually portions of blocks defined in standardized sizes to facilitate comparability. Access paths exclusively refers to routes of specified length connecting neighborhoods on opposite sides of the BART tracks. Local facilities include commercial establishments, schools, and libraries.

In regard to methods of analysis, the following approaches and data were incorporated into the overall design. The last, secondary data, provides the most common and easily accessible source for most impact prediction studies. The first four indicate the types of approaches required for impact identification studies:

1. Traffic Data. In the BART study this was limited to street traffic. Other studies might include all forms of motorized and nonmotorized travel in and between sites.

2. Interviews. These are home interviews and were used to obtain information on individual responses to BART-induced environmental changes.

3. Environmental Observations. Analyses were conducted from field observation and of maps and photos of the area.

4. Behavioral Observation. People's outdoor behavior was analyzed for pattern characteristics.

5. Secondary Data. Information about individuals, neighborhoods, and activities were collected from existing sources such as censuses, crime statistics, accident reports, and land value (assessment) records.

The factors for which this complex design was prepared to study were confined to attributes affecting the quality of residential life and purposely excluded concerns such as employment, income, and education. The factors selected for analysis were based on (1) concerns that had been expressed by persons interviewed in previous attitude surveys and (2) undoubtedly, to a degree, the researcher's expertise and interests. (Appleyard is a landscape architect; Carp is a psychologist.) The factors evaluated were

Safety	Territoriality
Convenience	Social Interaction
Comfort	Attractiveness
Privacy	

Perhaps more important than the particular factors chosen for the BART study are the quantitative methods employed for their measurement. The description measurement methods provided in Table 1 are excellent examples of how subjective factors can be translated into numerical terms that may be objective. Readers are urged to refer to this set of descriptions as a guide when developing their own methods for analyzing these or any other social factors.

Washington, D.C.

A before and after study conducted largely between 1958 and 1965 was performed to determine certain socioeconomic impacts of the Capital Beltway.[7] The study is cited here to relate some of the methodologies that were used. The factors heavily emphasize economic aspects of the environment and so are not as useful as they might be in a social impact analysis or identification. As with the BART study, the project was aimed at identifying, rather than predicting, variable effects; but the methodologies are also good examples of useful approaches to prediction for the purpose of impact assessment.

The Capital Beltway is a 64-mile, 4- and 6-lane freeway that encircles the city of Washington, D.C. The researchers defined study sites in the vicinity of the beltway in census tracts and subtracts as well as in city and county tax grids. (Grids or tracts were used for evaluating different factors, depending on the types of data sources needed.) The tax grids were readily available in the

Table 1 Environmental Measures from the BART Study, 1974[a]

Factor	Operational Definition	Measures
Safety traffic	Physical protection from trains, street traffic, and pedestrian hazards	1. Continuity and condition of sidewalks 2. Number of traffic conflict points 3. Presence of speed controls and stop signs 4. Areas of poor traffic visibility
Safety crime	Protection from exposure to crime	Ratings of physical conditions that affect surveillance capabilities
Convenience	Auto, pedestrian, bicycle access to local facilities and to friends and neighbors	Comparison of distance of access paths before and after BART construction
Ambient comfort	BART and traffic noise, fumes, smells, dust, and dirt; air- and ground-borne vibration; glare and shadows	Pollution meter ratings
Privacy	Visability of homes from trains, stations, parking lots	Angle of overlooks, distance from track to home, speed of passing trains
Territoriality	Perceived feelings of control, responsibility, and involvement in local streets and neighborhoods and in their improvement	1. Interview ratings 2. Lack of fences, walls, prohibitive signs 3. Presence of entrances, paths, benches, fountains in public areas
Social interaction	Contact with friends, relatives; involvement in community activities	1. Existence of public meeting places 2. Width of sidewalks, streets; night lighting 3. Distance between, and set-back of, houses (Note: these are features that Appleyard previously determined were indicators of "neighboring" levels. See Appleyard and Lintell.[6] 1971)

217

Table 1   (Continued)

Factor	Operational Definition	Measures
Attractiveness	Aesthetic quality, cleanliness of street blocks, neighborhoods; BART intrusion	Photoanalysis. Ratings from photos of perceived percentages of vegetation, buildings, sky, and of visual intrusion of BART buildings, structures, parking lots; ratings before and after BART of monotomy, clutter, spaciousness

a Prepared from information in Appleyard and Carp, The Bart Residential Impact Study in *Environmental Impact Assessment: Guidelines and Commentary,* edited by Thomas G. Dickert with Katherine R. Domeny (University of California, Berkeley: University Extension Publications, 1974).[5]

form of 61 section maps, each containing a number of grids. Thus tax sections were designated as the study sites, and section maps were selected to define a corridor through which the beltway passed. A similar but less meticulous geographic definition was formed for census zones. (Note that the convenience and suitability of the tax grids and section maps for this study derived from the fact that the study was primarily concerned with tax-assessment data.)

For most of the factors and methods used in the study, data was collected and conclusions drawn for the sections and tracts and for larger comparison areas. The larger comparison areas were the northern Virginia and the Washington metropolitan areas adjacent to the study sites. Data were collected for the following factors:

Population growth and migration
Land values (real estate sales)
Business activity
Traffic
Journey-to-work

In the report of the study traffic and journey-to-work impacts were given brief coverage. The first three subjects (population, land values, and business activity) all involved land use and population distribution effects. The following discussion concentrates on the population effects aspect of the study but is representative of the methods and data sources used in the land value and business activity (site development) evaluations.

Concerning impacts on population, the beltway was found to have had an effect on residential dispersion as measured by new construction in two groups of census tracts: one group inside the circular beltway and the other group outside. Both divisions of tracts were in similar proximity to the beltway. The facility started operation in 1958. Construction data were collected for the two time periods, 1955–1958 and 1958–1963. Inside the beltway 1754 new units per year were constructed in 1955–1958, compared to 1591 per year from 1958–1963. Outside the beltway 2716 new units per year were built in 1955–1958, and this rate increased to 2972 units per year for 1958–1963 after beltway completion. Two reasons were offered for this slowing down of "colonization" in one area compared to a speedup in another. The first reason is simply that the area inside the beltway started in 1955 at a much higher density than the larger area outside the beltway. The outside division was characterized by larger, more vacant land parcels, which were desirable as new home subdivisions. The second necessary reason or condition for growth differential was the increased accessibility of the area outside the beltway.

Although this study was conducted long before demands were placed on impact researchers to estimate growth inducement effects of major developments, it did incorporate some of the key elements needed to make such estimates. There are, at this time, no simple prescriptions for predicting induced growth. And although the researcher is left on his own for a large part of the methodology he employs to predict population growth patterns, the Capital Beltway study does offer some points of departure. Combined with certain demographic projection techniques and land use analyses discussed elsewhere by Berns, Dickenson and Blackmarr, and Dietz, considerable power might eventually be realized through such techniques.

To estimate induced growth resulting from a transportation facility, a background trend of growth for the area concerned must be established. These trends need to be identified in terms of numbers of people, dwelling units, density, and type of structure (single family, 2–6 unit, highrise, etc.). Each of these growth features must be further displayed, preferably on maps, to indicate geographical location of land use and population patterns. Finally, the rates of development for each growth type must be identified for the area as a whole and for each distinctive geographic area. The next step in a growth study is to characterize the area or subareas to be served by the new facility. Characterization should be in the same land use and population terms selected for describing the overall region. The third step requires matching the facility/ study area with comparable areas in the general region. Matching should be on the basis of existing similarity and on similarity between the study area as it is and regional areas as they were before their development. Fourth, locate and quantify attraction zones and features in the general area. These will include shopping and recreational facilities and, most important, employment centers.

The fifth step is to determine travel times (usually displayed by contour lines) between attractions and areas to be served by the new facility. (Traffic studies show that there are definite travel-time/site-selection patterns of development. For example, 75–90 percent of the working population lives within a 30-minute commute of job sites, although, of course, this may not be a strict cause-effect relationship.) The sixth and last step of a growth study requires the assimilation and interpretation of all the data collected in the first five steps to produce a prediction of how current trends and study area suitabilities combine to indicate new, renewed, or revised growth potentials made probable by development of new transportation service.

The preceding outline of a growth inducement study plan can be directly translated into use for predicting commercial, recreational, agricultural, or any other land use development. As Berns points out, the data requirements will differ for various land use types. Although residential and industrial land use estimates will require a knowledge of the availability of urban services (sewer, water, police, fire), predictions of recreational or open space potential may be more interested in unique features of the natural environment. All land use studies would require some analysis of soil and water conditions, but different land use interests would dictate varying degrees of detail required for estimation of development suitabilities. These issues are discussed in detail elsewhere in this book and are not repeated here. However, before leaving the Capital Beltway study, mention should be made of the additional data and methods described in that research project for assessing impacts on land values and economic activities aside from growth effects. Since these subjects are primarily of economic as opposed to social interest, they are not covered in this chapter. The interested reader is referred to Burton and Knapp.[7]

Baltimore

The Baltimore social impact study[1] was selected for exposition in this chapter because it is one of the very few examples of social impact analysis and prediction that incorporates both quantitative data and numerical interpretation over a broad range of social factors. As noted, the Baltimore study differs from the BART and Capital Beltway studies in its attempt to predict and examine probable, future impacts as opposed to monitoring impacts after the fact.

The Baltimore study was a prelocation decision analysis of probable impacts expected to result from construction of Baltimore's portion of the Interstate highway system. The freeway was, at least at the time of the study, the largest public construction program ever undertaken in the city of Baltimore. The conclusions from the study, demonstrating massive potential acceleration of undesirable social and land use trends, ultimately served as a major influence in a decision to reroute the contemplated freeway.

The Baltimore study was undertaken as an attempt to quantify potential negative impacts on neighborhoods through which the proposed route would pass. The factors of interest had been voiced in the form of citizen opposition before the study began. Factors and their trends considered in the study included ones similar to those discussed by Dietz in Chapter 3:

Size of population	Skill levels
Racial composition	Income levels
Age distribution	

Apparent from this list of variables is the fact that the study was most concerned with the almost exclusive use of secondary data. The data were subjected to judgmental scrutiny, and those conclusions which could be substantiated by fact were reported. The Baltimore researcher notes that at the time of the study (1969), social impact analysis was a primitive art. He further states that it was an art greatly in need of improvement and one in which technological advances in social research should make improvement increasingly possible.

The study defined two categories of areas of interest. The first concern was with the city of Baltimore as a whole. The city was selected as a study site (1) to define trends and norms and (2) to assess citywide impacts of the freeway, since it was of such huge dimensions (directly consuming 1000 acres within the city limits). The second category of sites contained individual neighborhoods and communities along segments of the proposed route.

The citywide research initially produced two disconcerting facts: first, over 80 percent of the 3653 housing units to be displaced were inhabited by blacks, most of whom were poor; second, the prefreeway social conditions of Baltimore were shown to be rapidly decaying, and, therefore, highly susceptible to external influences.

In terms of the general stability of the city, census data showed that Baltimore's total population had been declining at a rapidly accelerating rate (averaging 1 percent per year) between 1950 and 1960. The researchers obtained further population estimates from the City Health Department that showed the 1 percent rate accelerated by as much as four times in the succeeding decade of the 1960s. Since one of the Baltimore study areas was the entire city itself, the researchers looked at an even larger site, the greater Baltimore metropolitan area, for comparison. Census data showed that although the city was losing population, the metropolitan area was gaining residents. These demographic trends, of course, have affected many urban centers in the same ways and in the same time frames.

Census information for Baltimore showed that as the total population size was shrinking, two other things were happening to population composition. Using census data and undercount correction data, the researchers determined that the nonwhite, mostly black population increased from 24 percent in 1950 to about 48 percent in 1969. (Undercount is often a significant problem in the census of low-income, minority groups. The U.S. Bureau of the Census provides a variety of formulae for correcting this and other probable errors in tabulated data.) At the same time the proportion of blacks in the suburbs had been decreasing because the migration from the central city had been almost entirely white. The city migration trend is dramatically displayed in Figure 6.2.

The Baltimore researchers pointed out that the color shift was accompanied by marked segregation. Segregation was noted by observation and operationally defined for census data. Segregation was meant to describe any tract in which the population was more than three-fourths white or three-fourths nonwhite. Ninety percent of Baltimore's census tracts were thus found to be segregated.

Exacerbating the color shift and population reductions was the fact that Baltimore was also experiencing a change in age composition. The whites who left the city were mostly young families with high rates of natality. Analysis of birth and death trends showed that the reproductive rate of the city's white population was decreasing to the point of disappearance (see Figure 6.2). In the black population all age groups were increasing in size. For the total population between 1960 and 1966, persons aged 25–64 decreased 43,000, whereas school-age children increased 15,000, and the number of people over 65 grew by 5000. The end result of all these age changes was that the people in brackets most dependent on public services (young and old) were placing increasing demands for support on a taxpaying body (ages 25–64) that was decreasing. The researchers further surmised that since the taxpaying public was also becoming proportionately larger in black residents and that since blacks have less income potential than whites, the tax base was decreasing at a greater-than-arithmetic rate. It is obvious that assessing these types of impacts requires skillful use of demographic techniques and data.

One of the few faults to be found with the Baltimore study was a lack of justification for the underlying and critical assumption that the black population in Baltimore was undereducated, unskilled, of lower income, and with higher unemployment than the whites they were replacing. Although in all probability these features were characteristic of the black population, the study failed to carefully document that assumption and to demonstrate that these disadvantages were indeed indicative of an inevitable downward trend. (Albeit these factors may have been accounted for in original research materials, documentation does not appear in the published report cited in the bibliography. The author's criticism is presented here as a caution to the reader to avoid conclusions that are not evidenced by factual data.)

Having quantitatively outlined the nature of urban trends that most concerned citizens and local decision makers and having set the urban factors in

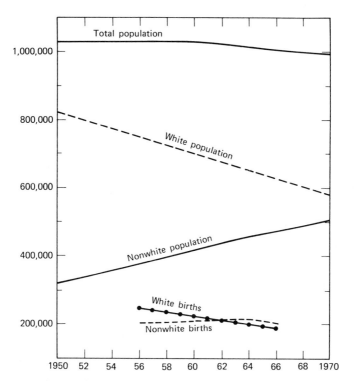

Figure 6.2 Baltimore population shift. (Modified from George W. Grier, Social Impact Analysis of an Urban Freeway System. HRB, *Highway Research Record,* No. 305, 1970, pp. 63–74.

a context of the regional fabric, the researchers turned to specific neighborhood impacts. The neighborhood research concentrated on one community, Rosemont, where special problems were examined.

Rosemont, like most local study sites, was heavily black. Unlike most sites it was not poor, but a consistently middle-class homeowner area. Rosemont was the only study site for which primary or original data were collected in addition to use of available census tabulations. Rosemont had become predominantly black in the mid1950s. Most of the homeowners had resided there for more than 10 years at the time of the study. Sixty percent of the heads of households were over 50 years old. Elderly persons occupied 40 percent of the households and were without automobiles.

The analysis of social impacts in the Rosemont area went beyond the straightforward display and projection of demographic data. It was shown that besides losing 800 households to displacement by the freeway, it would have removed the majority of the neighborhood's shopping facilities. Further, it would have separated most of the remaining households from the three supermarkets where 40 percent of the residents did their grocery shopping. Six churches and a major playground would have been removed. The analysis did not end with this picture of blight effects on Rosemont but went on to indicate implications from the citywide analysis.

Based on well-established and documented migration patterns, the researchers predicted that the Rosemont residents would move to areas that resembled prefreeway Rosemont, thus displacing more whites from within the city limits. Slum and ghetto residents who might settle for conditions in blighted Rosemont would then move in. The researchers presented some backup for this prophecy by showing that anticipation of the freeway had already causd this type of effect: many homeowners had already left under the impending threat of the proposed freeway, and their single family homes had been converted to multifamily rental units.

Reduction Indices: Oakland-Worcester

Scattered attempts have been made over the years to reduce the constellation of urban transportation impacts into one, two, or three representative indices that would summarize the multitude of factors and effects that are liable to occur. The example which follows was intended to serve as a method for deriving impact "scores" to determine relative effects over a number of affected sites. The reduction index approach seems too simplistic to produce results that can provide meaningful input to the planning process. It does, however, demonstrate a way in which discrete data can be mathematically combined to rate social phenomena. The basic mechanics of the study are presented as follows. Those wishing to replicate the approach should obtain the original reports.

This study was a before-and-after freeway examination to identify critical aspects of the community. It was, however, conducted for the express purpose of identifying significant variables that would indicate—in a predictive sense— the degree of negative impact a highway might have on any given urban neighborhood.

What follows is a general description of the Oakland-Worcester project and of the neighborhood index that resulted. The index was actually a composite of four formulae that quantified the pedestrian dependency of neighborhoods. The entire system of formula operation, social characteristics mapping, and interpretation was called the Social Feasibility Model.[3]

The researchers were concerned about five types of community activity, which they operationalized as follows:

Activity	*Operational Concern*
1. Production, consumption, distribution	1. Shopping and work
2. Socialization	2. Schools

3. Social participation
4. Social control
5. Mutual support

3. Churches and clubs
4. Fire and police
5. Community services

By examining before-and-after effects of freeways on these activities (for two neighborhoods each in Oakland and Worcester), the researchers found that the most significant effects were (1) dependence on pedestrian access, (2) vitality of activities prior to construction of the freeway, and (3) degree of physical impact on the neighborhood. With this conclusion in hand, the researchers went on to develop a model for measuring dependency on pedestrian access to viable neighborhood activities.

The model provides a method by which secondary (U.S. Census) data can be used to derive compositional indices of pedestrian dependency; indices include general dependency and dependencies on schools, local shopping, and social institutions. Additional easily acquired data is needed to determine specific attraction locations. Exhaustive instructions for operating the model are contained in a report on the project available from the U.S. Department of Transportation, Federal Highway Administration Washington, D.C. (see full title in chapter bibliography, Kaplan et al[3]). The project report makes excellent reading. It has an abundant display of maps, a description of the researchers' well-conceived research design, and a thorough discussion of the four case studies and reviews of related literature. The model itself, however, is not recommended as a fail-safe, comprehensive approach to impact analysis for two reasons. First, the validation of the indices of pedestrian dependency was based on correlation with information from only 100 direct interviews (25 from each site). Second, although further validation may someday prove this method a useful tool for professional planners who can appreciate its mathematical coherence, it is not acceptable for exposition in environmental impact documents. The indices are indicators (or aggregations) of a broad variety of types of social activities (the five listed previously). Once the researcher removes himself from primary information about those activities by means of a reduction index, there is no way to relate the final score back to differential effects on specific activities like socialization, distribution, or social control. Again, inapplicability to the preparation of impact reports should in no way detract from the model's potential value as a planning tool in early phases of transportation corridor studies.

CONTRIBUTIONS OF SOCIAL ANALYSIS TO THE PLANNING PROCESS

The latter part of this chapter has attempted to present some models and some guidance for the conduct of social impact studies. But the roles of social analysis in transportation planning should not end with the two that have been presented; that is, the identification and the prediction of impacts. Social analysis, of which impact analysis is a subset, can serve as a valuable planning input to prevent some of the negative impacts that are inevitable results in a planning process that considers impacts only after a plan has been prepared.

Demand Models

One important key to the social impact analyst's extent of influence in the planning process will probably lie with the development, extension, and general application of demand models. This model or, more correctly, collection of models constitutes one development in formal systematics that appears to have considerable potential as a planning and forecasting tool. If this prediction itself is valid, the social impact analyst must become familiar with the nature and substance of demand models.

The most practical way of doing this is by acquainting himself with the characteristics of a single model—its data sources and forms, its formulae, and its output. He should find the opportunity to watch how the model is actually used. This may even include assisting in the data collection surveys, which might include home interviews as well as compilation of existing secondary data. Since the actual manipulation of data will probably be done by a computer, it may be difficult for the analyst to participate in that phase, unless he has some programming skills. Nevertheless, he should find someone who can explain what the factors in the algorithms (formulae) represent and how they are combined. He should also participate directly in the process of converting the data into alternative transportation plans. The analyst's role in this, the most important task in the planning process, would depend on his particular skills. His role might be numerical analysis, map preparation, or narrative need and solution analysis.

A second, necessary activity for the analyst interested in learning about demand modeling is a minimum of study. Almost everything didactic that has been written about demand modeling assumes a strong background in engineering, mathematics, economics (utility theory), or computing science. In the field of demand modeling one up-to-date text stands out as being thoroughly comprehendible by the lay reader. This book (especially the first half) is highly recommended as a reference source, even for the social analyst who does not intend to immerse himself in the technical planning process. The book, *Urban Travel Demand Forecasting,* Brand and Manheim, Eds., 1973, is available from the Highway Research Board, 2101 Constitution Avenue, N.W., Washington, D.C. 20418.[8]

Some of the opportunities that *Urban Travel Demand Forecasting* authors perceive for social, analytical improvement of demand modeling and thus the transportation planning process, include:

1. Parameters to estimate the extent to which transportation network configurations should and do serve the ends of (a) special groups (poor, handicapped, elderly); (b) access to opportunities (recreation, new jobs, prospective land uses); (c) air and noise pollution abatement (where some modeling efforts are already being made),

2. Incorporation of more data on specific, individual behavioral influences of alternative transportation developments,

3. Development of better computer graphics to display urban needs/impacts relationships with transportation develompent and

4. More objective simulations of data-based, sociopolitical decision-making processes and criteria.

HEALTH AND SAFETY

Health and safety factors do not fit as neatly into the social impact framework as do topics like community cohesion and residential displacement. Nevertheless, in terms of the history of consideration of the impacts of highways, no other area has been given more attention. Air pollution (actually, a secondary effect of highways) is of prime concern, but vehicle and roadway safety considerations are a close second. These factors differ from the sociological issues by the fact that they have less influence on social organization and economic life-styles but more influence on the physical well-being of individual human beings. The main factors included in the health and safety category of social impacts are, in addition to air pollution: noise, and pedestrian traffic and personal safety. Although each of the health and safety factors does play a highly interactive role with the total social and community system, their exact functions in those roles are difficult to separate from each other. The independent effects of physiosocial factors on the quality of life are, on the other hand, much easier to quantify—though equally hard to evaluate. In the discussions that follow, therefore, only the directly identifiable functions of health and safety factors are discussed.

Noise

Noise is the most readily quantified and best understood of the health and safety impacts of transportation. Noise levels of existing transportation systems and facilities can be measured with a variety of similarly designed audiometers. The measurement instrument is basically a microphone attached to a noise level meter that registers sound levels in increments called decibels (dB). There are several scales of measurements by which sounds are translatd into numerical values. The scale most commonly used in impact analysis (and specified in legislation regarding noise) is the A-scale, most closely approximating human perception or psychoacoustics—decibel measurements are written for the A-scale as dB(A).

Noise readings are always reported as a function of the conditions under which the noise is perceived. Three elements constitute the basis for noise conditions: the noise generation or source, the space through which noise travels, and the receiver (the human ear). Whenever noise levels are typified for generators, the assumptions are made that: (1) the generator is operating normally (2) there are no obstacles in the transmission space and (3) that the receiver is a healthy human ear (i.e., a reliable sound meter). Further, the distance over which the sound travels from its origin to receiver must always be specified.

Some examples of noise generators and their sound levels are presented in Table 2. Note that each 10 dB(A) increase above (or below) 70 dB(A) represents a doubling (or halving) of perceived noisiness.

What kinds of noise impacts should the transportation social analyst consider? To answer this question we should first look briefly at the range of effects noise can have on humans. Loud noise over a long time (jackhammer operation) or intense and sudden noise (a cannon blast) can cause permanent hearing loss. Loud but less intense noise can cause temporary hearing loss. Neither of these types of noise impact are commonly associated with transportation systems. Noise impacts frequently attributable to transportation include varying degrees of social and intrapersonal disruptors. Traffic noise can wake people from sound sleep or render normal conversation impossible. Noise also can have effect even when there is no conscious or visible evidence of impact. Studies have shown that changes occur in brain waves, cardiovascular performance, digestion, and excretion as results of otherwise nonbothersome (i.e., nonconsciously percieved) sound impingement. Although relationships between physical effects and sound intensity/duration have been established among experimental animals for several combinations of sound parameters, little is known about the variety of intensity effects on humans as a consequence of transportation systems. Some effects that can be assumed for transportation systems derive from the facts that sleep level is altered (without waking) at 45–50 dB(A) that conversations are distracted at 40–50 dB(A) and that conversation is made impossible at 70 75 dB(A).

The long-term results of noise are the impacts with which the social analyst must be concerned. If sleep, conversation, and thought are subjected to constant interruption, every other facet of the affected individual's life will suffer. Noise intrusion, even when it is not directly obstructing normal human activity or physical health, is a known cause of stress, discomfort, and frustration. (A noted acoustician from New York City once admitted to the author the possible validity of "outsiders'" stereotyping the natives of Manhattan as unfriendly people. He went on to partially attribute New Yorkers' apparent unfriendliness to an adaptation to living with constant noise. The hypothesis is that people may avoid the frustration of interrupted social contact by avoiding social contact in the first place).

When the analyst sets about predicting noise impacts, he should seek the assistance of expert noise technicians in determining the probable sound levels at various points of future reception. The noise estimates should be displayed on noise contour maps that will reflect the differential intensity levels based on probable type and volume of generation (typically vehicular or rail traffic) as well as obstacles or barriers in the sound path. The contour map and accompanying discussion will provide a thoroughly objective estimate of future conditions but will not describe the impact on potential receivers. The analyst, using his judgment (along with results from his own and others attitudinal noise surveys), must also estimate the probability that transportation noise will disrupt normal activities—and to what extent.

The analyst must also describe the potential receiver of noise. Two types or categories of sound receivers are especially sensitive to outside noise: students and hospital or convalescent patients. Wherever school sites are likely to be subject to noise levels about 40 dB(A), the impact assessment should describe negative affects and propose alternatives or mitigating measures. Other sites that may be negatively impacted by noise intrusion include residences, churches, libraries, and office sites. The analyst should indicate sensitive locations on the contour map and indicate (e.g., by color shadings) relative land use snsitivities to noise. States such as California have enacted legislation prohibiting the operation of schools in high noise areas and have also established maximum standards of noise emissions by vehicles and boats.

Once all alternatives for removing noise (i.e., moving the transportation facility out of hearing range) are exhausted, the impact analyst should assist in developing noise barrier solutions to be incorporated in the facility design. Mitigating measures include: vehicle and equipment silencing and its enforcement; roadbed depression or elevation; and imposition of sound absorbing barriers such as wood or concrete walls or structure containment by the addition of air conditioning and soundproofing. In a survey conducted by McEvoy, noise was found to be the single most obnoxious feature of both the construction and operation of a freeway system.

Air Pollution

For the most part, the measurement and projection of pollution emissions from transportation systems has been left up to air quality technicians. The air pollution sections of impact reports are usually contributed by air quality

Table 2 Sound Levels and Loudness of Illustrative Noises In Indoor and Outdoor Environments[a]

dB(A)	Over All Level (Sound Pressure Level Approx. 0.0002 Microbar)	Community (Outdoor)	Home or Industry (Indoor)	Loudness (Human Judgment of Different Sound Levels)
130	Uncomfortably	Military Jet Aircraft Take-off with After-Burner from Aircraft Carrier at 50 ft. (130)		
120	Loud	Turbo-Fan Aircraft at Take-Off Power at 200 ft. (118)	Oxygen torch (121)	120 dB(A) 32 Times as Loud
110	Very	Jet Flyover at 1000 ft. (103) Boeing 707, DC-8 at 6080 ft. before Landing (106) Bell J-2A Helicopter at 100 ft. (100)	Riveting Machine (110) Rock-N-Roll Band (108–114)	110 dB(A) 16 Times as Loud
100	Loud	Power Mower (96) Boeing 737, DC-9 at 6080 ft. before Landing (97) Motorcycle at 25 ft. (90)	Newspaper Press (97)	100 dB(A) 8 Times as Loud
				90 dB(A) 4 Times as Loud

90	Car Wash at 20 ft. (89)	Food Blender (88)	80 dB(A) 2 Times as Loud
	Prop. Plane Flyover at 1000 ft. (88)	Milling Machine (85)	
	Diesel Truck, 40 MPH at 50 ft. (84)	Garbage Disposal (80)	
	Diesel Train, 45 MPH at 100 ft. (83)		
80 Moderately Loud	High Urban Ambient Sound (80)	TV-Audio, Vacuum Cleaner (70)	dB(A)
	Passenger Car, 65 MPH at 25 ft. (77)		
	Freeway at 50 ft. from Pavement Edge, 10 a.m., (76+ 6)		
70		Cash Register at 10 ft. (65–70)	
		Electric Typewriter at 10 ft. (64)	
		Dishwasher (Rinse) at 10 ft. (60)	
	Air Conditioning Unit at 100 ft. (60)	Conversation (60)	60 dB(A) ½ as Loud
60 Quiet	Large Transformers at 100 ft. (50)		50 dB(A) ¼ as Loud
50	Bird Calls (44)		
40	Lower Limit Urban Ambient Sound (40)		40 dB(A) ⅛ as Loud

a Reprinted, in part, from Branch, Melville C., Jr., Outdoor Noise, Transportation, and City Planning, *Traffic Q.* **25**, No. 2 April 1971, p. 167–188.

experts, without any further manipulation by others responsible for producing the overall report. Indeed, if anyone other than the air experts participates in the smog aspect of the impact analysis, it is usually the natural environmentalists rather than the social analyst. This disciplinary separation of roles is not necessarily appropriate, even though air pollution affects all life forms in the environment and air pollution analysis is a complex process requiring specialized skills. The fact, however, that other disciplines have the lead responsibility for analyzing air pollution effects does not mean that the social analyst can neglect the impacts of this factor. Identification of particularly sensitive segments of the population likely to be affected (e.g., the elderly) for long periods of time is often ignored by air quality analysts whose findings need to be translated into dose rates by type and character of the affected population.

In many cases the air quality and environmental professionals will adequately address some of the social issues of air pollution. When they do not, it is up to the social analyst to appreciate the necessity for addressing those issues and to see to it that all social impacts of air pollution that can be assessed are assessed. The primary function of the social analyst in air pollution evaluation is that of a "quality controller." Infrequently, the social reviewer may himself be called on to describe the social implications of emission projection data.

To begin to understand the social aspects of air pollution it is helpful to look at the federal law that directs air quality control activities. All air pollution studies that are conducted as part of transportation plan impact assessments are performed under the requirements of the 1970 amendments to the National Clean Air Act. The Clean Air Act and related implementing regulations promulgated by the EPA specify the parameters for evaluation, including quality standards to be achieved and specific guidelines for measurement techniques. Although these procedural regulations are too technical to be described in this volume, it is important for the social analyst to know: (1) the concerns expressed in the Clean Air Act (2) the pollutants to be analyzed and (3) the social relevance of air pollution impacts.

The Clean Air Amendments of 1970 require the promulgation of ambient air quality standards. There are two sets of standards: primary and secondary (see Table 3). The primary standards are intended to protect the public health. The secondary standards are designed to protect the public welfare (i.e., effects on soil, water, crops, animals, climate, man-made materials; hazards to transportation; economic values, personal comfort, and well-being). The social impact analyst is concerned with both the primary standards and those concerning economic and personal comfort.

Air pollutants have similar effects, in differing degrees, on all animal species. The effects on man are important to the social analyst in regard to both hazards to the physical health of the population and interference with the normal conduct of human activities. Definite cause-and-effect relationships

Table 3 National Primary and Secondary Ambient Air Quality Standards[a]

Pollutant	Concentration Limit		Averaging Time
	Micrograms per Cubic Meter	Parts per Million	
Carbon monoxide	10,000	9	8 hours[b]
	40,000	35	1 hour[b]
Photochemical oxidants	160	0.08	1 hour[b]
Hydrocarbons (methane free)	160	0.24	3 hours[b]
Nitrogen oxides	100	0.05	1 year
Sulfur oxides	80	0.03	1 year
	365	0.14	24 hours[b]
	(60)	(0.02)	(1 year)
	(260)	(0.1)	(24 hours)[b]
	(1,300)	(0.5)	(3 hours)[b]
Particulate matter	75	—	1 year[b]
	260	—	24 hours[b]
	(60)	—	(1 year)
	(150)	—	(24 hours)[b]

[a] Secondary standards are shown in parentheses; for some pollutants the secondary standards are the same as the primary standards.
[b] Not to be exceeded more than once a year.
SOURCE: Highway Research Board, Highways and Air Quality, *Special Report 141,* Washington D.C., p. 5, 1973.

between pollutants and physical well-being are difficult to extract. Some effects are known; most are topics of continuing controversy. Ozone, a photochemical oxidant, is known to be a primary cause of irritation to mucous membranes of the eyes and respiratory system. Carbon monoxide, by tying up available hemoglobin, reduces the amount of oxygen medium available in the bloodstream. Oxides can form acidic solutions on contact with mucous in the respiratory system, thus exacerbating existing conditions like emphysema. Absorption of lead into the blood stream can cause deterioration of the endocrine and central nervous systems. High smog levels have caused the closing of schools on at least a few days a year in all the country's largest metropolitan areas. Excessive hydrocarbon, monoxide, and particulate levels have been alleged to accelerate heart attacks, strokes, and respiratory diseases of all kinds.

To analyze the possible effects of air pollutants on specific populations, the analyst must have an initial description of pollution levels and their dispersion and a description of the population in the area to be affected by a project. The pollution distribution will normally be prepared by air quality personnel. Standard procedure for air pollution accounting is to report effects on micro- and mesoscales. (We are, of course, concerned with roads.) The microscale includes the immediate corridor surrounding the facility and may extend as far as 1 km downwind from the source. The mesoscale is the area extending from the outer boundaries at which the emission contribution from the planned facility becomes indistinguishable from other source's emissions. Recently, the Clean Air Amendment requirements have required the estimation of the mesoscale's relative contribution to total, regional air quality when the region or air basin is larger than the mesoscale area.

The social analyst should use the established scale measurements and define his subject population as residing in micro- and mesoscale areas. Data should be collected for both areas to describe the population densities and distributions and the levels of outdoor activities (including school attendance). The projected pollution levels should then be contrasted with prefacility levels. If possible, a description of existing effects from air pollution should be included in the analysis. Effects and potential sensitivities that might be enumerated include: number of smog-alert days, incidence of recorded respiratory and cardio-vascular patients, cardiac arrest rates for affected geographical areas, and incidence of critical reliance on extended outdoor activity.

In some cases the analyst may draw his own conclusions about probable health effects. In most cases, given the scientific uncertainty about casual relationships, it will be sufficient to present the pollution and population data as discussed previously, present available facts and expert opinion about hypothesized health effects including projected changes in dose levels, and leave it up to decision makers, the public, and physicians to draw conclusions about the probable extent of physical threat from the projected pollutant levels.

Traffic Safety

Social impacts of pedestrian and vehicle safety features should be reported. As with personal safety, which follows, not a great amount of information is available about impact measurement for traffic safety. Again, the social analyst must rely heavily on the informed judgment of experts (e.g., traffic and design engineers) to estimate the probable threat of accidents related to specific facilities and vehicles.

There are two types of accident rates that must be simultaneously considered in impact reports. First, the analyst should determine an accident rate for the facility or service as a whole, perhaps using analogy and data drawn from similar configurations. Secondly, a separate rate must be calculated as a function of volume of use. The accident or, more felicitously, the safety rates should be expressed in terms of personal liability. Sometimes only fatalities are estimated. More frequently, rates are expressed for fatal injuries and for lesser injuries requiring medical care. Vehicle accident rates are also significant, especially when their number describes the potential level of safety hazard to other vehicles using the same roadway.

As an example of the bimeasure estimation method, the analyst might report that the expectd accident rates for a new commuter rail service are:

	Accident Rates	
	Fatalities	*Injuries*
Per year	12	38
Per passenger mile	.0096	.0304

A third category might also be calculated in terms of passengers, passenger trips, or route miles. The reason for the two kinds of rate measure is that it is important to know the total increase in personal injury that is likely to result from the transportation change as well as to know what the injury rate means in terms of service provided. Giving only a total accident rate may mean, for instance, a de-emphasis of the possibility that the new rail service is not only as safe as alternative facilities but also provides for twice as many passengers. At the same time it is necessary to note the total suffering that might ensue from initiation of the new service. Finally, the statistics of traffic safety do not take time directly into account, relying instead on distance as a surrogate measure of vulnerability. This is an invalid procedure.

The next aspect of accident impacts that needs to be discussed in the analysis is the effect the proposed transportation may have on changing the existing rate. The existing base against which the new service is compared will depend on the modes, routes, and travel volumes involved. The Interstate highway system was highly touted, for example, as a "life saver" and may well in fact have been one. If the new service is a duplication, replacement, or improvement of existing service, the new is contrasted to the old. If the mode and route or destination of service is entirely new, the new is compared to accident rates for similar types of service in the region.

The traffic safety discussion up to this point has concerned primary modal travel on proposed facilities. (The primary mode may be anything from airplanes to bicycles to walking.) There is also another aspect to traffic safety that may not be directly related to travel for which the planned facility is intended. The new transportation system may also affect adjacent and intersecting travel by other modes—primarily pedestrian travel. The analyst must look at three possible intersections between motorized and nonmotorized travel: (1) interruption in existing travel patterns (2) compatibility of shared roadway and (3) probable rerouting of the nonmotorized routes.

If a new route interrupts walk- or bicycle-ways, are there provisions for safe crossing such as signals or grade separations? If the proposed service includes shared routes, are travel and exit access separated and indicated? Finally, if the new route will encourage nonmotorized and/or motorized traffic on or off the proposed facility, is the likelihood of collisions increased? Examples of the last case include new traffic on residential streets to bypass or gain access to the new facility, or pedestrian cross traffic over rail tracks to maintain access to a desired destination. In either of these cases the probability of vehicle-person collision is increased and should be estimated, and mitigation measures should be devised.

Personal Safety

Rape, assault, and theft are the three personal threats clearly associated with transportation facilities and have much to do with their unattractiveness to prospective passengers. Personal safety factors are the most difficult of health and safety impacts to analyze. Insufficient information is available on the relationships between transportation design features and the instance and intensity of criminal acts. One universal feature that appears to be related to high personal threat is the coincidence of darkness and isolation along routes and in terminals, the New York subway system serving as a prime example. Ironically, one form of theft, pick-pocketing, occurs almost exclusively in crowded, well-lighted places.

Although the unknowns of conditions for crime prevent accurate projection of personal threat potential, geographical location is a definable and meaningful parameter of personal safety impact. Similar transportation services in areas with different crime rates display personal safety records representative of the areas in which they are located. Data is available in all parts of the country on local crime rates by type of violation. In urbanized areas these records are publicly reported on a quarterly basis for socially and economically distinctive subareas. The impact analyst can obtain these data from local law enforcement agencies, regional criminal justice planning councils, or from state justice offices. If potential problem areas or situations are suspected, the analyst should obtain interpretive and preventative advice from law enforcement experts and incorporate this information in the EIR. One aspect of personal safety needs to be especially singled out for attention. The analyst will almost always find that crime rates for theft, assault, and rape are highest in economically depressed, densely occupied parts of the city. In addition to incorporating crime prevention measures for transporation in these areas, the analyst must pay special attention to the trade-offs between the probable net crime increase and the opportunities the residents would be forced to forego if the service (in its safest form) is not made available at all. Beyond this, although the presence of police at nodes or in the transit vehicles may lower crime rates to zero, unprotected feeder systems, particularly bus and pedestrian routes, will simply supplant the site of the crimes from one area to another.

SUGGESTIONS FOR THE IMPACT ASSESSMENT PROCESS

This chapter has attempted to give some broad guidance to social impact analysts concerned with transportation. In the course of describing some of the general features, issues, and practices of social impact evaluation, an effort has been made to relay as much practical information on factors and methods as possible without "sinking" the reader in an overabundance of technical detail. The intent of this chapter has been to equip the researcher with an awareness of the first stages of critical expertise that will allow him to carry out further research into the specific factors and techniques she or he chooses or is required to examine. A few summary notes are furnished as follows to help the researcher and the analyst to perform studies that will withstand the scrutiny of reviewers, citizens, and decision makers. Some of the comments are intended to assist in improving primary research; other comments should help improve confidence and accuracy in prediction; all the comments should help to produce presentable and comprehensible analysis.

A. Display all the information that can conceivably be mapped, graphed, or tabulated. Impact reports are meant to convey information and to demonstrate conclusions. Also, if impact analysis components are to be used in the planning process, they must be in a form that is interesting, informative, and easy to understand when presented to groups such as citizen meetings and policy boards. There is a saying making the planning rounds today that carries a serious message in spite of its tongue-in-cheek language: "If you can't map it or count it, skip it." This may seem an impossible rule for social (let alone, natural) sciences as they have historically been viewed; but it is a necessity if social analysis is to find meaningful application in the world of planning and imple-mentation. Even the best of theoretical and logical conclusions will be discarded as unworkable opinions unless they are documented and justified by tangible or quantitative fact that can be understood by the layman. After all, gravitation, after its initial formulation by Newton, remains one of the most complex and controversial fields of physical theory and yet can be "explained" to most people who successfully graduate from high school.

The best display techniques by far are by the medium of the map or graphic displays like film, video tape recordings, or cathode ray tube (computer ter-minal type). Transportation planning, when the work of the computer is done, is performed by graphical technique. Transportation facilities are physical structures that acquire meaning only after they become mapped components of the real world. Of greatest potential utility to the social impact analyst (as Dietz points out in Chapter 3) is the well-developed capability of the computer to produce mapped representation of census characteristics. Computers and their appurtances are now capable of extracting, statistically analyzing, printing, and color coding any combination of available census data in a broad range of scale sizes. An added benefit of computer mapping of census data is that, for all systems-level and many project studies, the census tract (approximately 4000 residents in an urban area) is a convenient and appropriate geographic zone size. Added to this is the fact that census tracts usually duplicate or closely approximate traffic study zone groupings formulated by transportation planners.

In addition to census maps, or as an alternative when facilities or data are not available (computer maps are not cheap), hand-drawn maps add easily recognizable dimensions to impact studies. Features that may be mapped by hand or machine are indicated in the following point.

B. To complement narrative discussions, tabulations, and conclusions, every effort should be made to summarize major points in simple graphs and tables. Tables are often more confusing than verbal descriptions and should be used only when the researcher is certain that they will simplify conveyance of a message. Primary graphs, however, should be used sparingly. Graphs may be pie charts, histograms, line graphs, and so on.

A few rules should be followed: (1) Use no more than two dimensions in a chart. For example, do not try to put three dimensions in one graph by using a cube-shaped design. Also, do not use rates of change as a single factor unless they have been introduced on a separate chart first. For example, if it is desirable to graph births per year by occupational category of head of household, preface that graph with one that simply graphs number of births against calendar years. The majority of the general public (and much of the planning profession) is not accustomed to interpreting multivariate graphs and suffers great confusion when trying to decipher change-rate graphics. Since most social parameters involve trends and rates, this caution should be judiciously observed. (2) Don't put more than two or three types of information in a single graph. For example, if the graph measures magnitude against time for population growth, do not try to show total population, two or three ethnic rates, birth, death, and migration all on one chart. Use two or three separate ones. (3) Use large scales. If the information being relayed requires minute scales to indicate significant changes, the information should probably be transmitted verbally.

C. Each phase should be as nearly completed as possible before going to the next phase. The major phases of the impact study (exclusive of the project description) are three: Describe the setting, determine probable impacts, derive mitigation measures or accept the "no-project" alternative. The first two phases have been elaborated in this chapter; the third is left largely up to the analyst and the physical and financial resources available for mitigation.

Describe the setting in exactly the same terms that will be required for defining impact types and intensities. Start with maps of all the data that are amenable to that medium. The setting should include static current and historic features and graphic-numerical analyses of demonstrable trends and patterns. Features that may be described include, but are not limited to: Density, dwelling types, income, real estate values and appreciation rate, migratory trends, land use patterns, employment types, job center locations, historical monuments, social gathering places, churches, schools, parks, and age shift trends.

The impact analysis phase has been described throughout this chapter. The same display techniques apply to evaluation presentations. The impact assessment phase will assess the transportation impacts on those features that have been chosen to characterize the social environment of the present setting.

D. Decide on a framework that will assist in organizing the study and preparing a good report. Choose a framework that will communicate to the reader of the report that it is a comprehensive approach to impact analysis and one that logically considers the interrelationships of a full range of urban activities. One such framework was proposed earlier in this chapter (i.e., displacement, disruption, mobility effects). Another possible framework of factor categorization was cited in the discussion of the social feasibility reduction index. (See page 000, Activity list.) As mentioned before, there is no common, accepted framework for social impact organization. This is still a ripe area for enterprising theoreticians and reductive empiricists.

E. Identify the temporal nature of impacts as well as their spatial characteristics. Impacts begin to appear at certain times and last for various periods. The accepted classification of initial occurrance is: preconstruction (the period of expectation and apprehension); construction; and short-term and long-term operation. For example, a preconstruction impact might be real estate value changes; a construction impact could be dust pollution or severance of access routes; short-term operational effects might include traffic congestion and business trend changes; and longer-term effects could include land use reorientation, ethnic mix changes, and tax rate changes. The matter of the duration of the effects that are to be considered, regardless of time of their initial occurrance, is left largely to the discretion and judgment of the researcher and his primary sources. Time periods may arbitrarily be defined as: (e.g.,), less than a year, 1–3 years, 3–10 years, and indefinite. Likewise, the assignment of impacts to each duration category may be arbitrary but should represent the analyst's best estimates. Relative durations are important indicators of impact significance and should be estimated with as much precision as possible.

F. Impacts in themselves are neither good nor bad. The analyst's job is to present an objective picture of probable effects. If unbiased in its approach, the citizens and decision makers who read EIRs will be able to draw their own conclusions about how positive, negative, or neutral a given impact should be deemed.

NOTES

1. Grier, George W. Social Impact Analysis of an Urban Freeway System, *Highw. Res. Rec.,* No. 305, pp. 63–79, 1970.

2. Weiner, Paul and Edward J. Deak, Nonuser effects in Highway Planning, *Highw. Res. Rec.,* No. 356, pp. 55–68, 1971.

3. Kaplan, Marshall, Sheldon P. Gans, and Howard M. Kahn, (Universal Engineering Corporation), *Social Characteristics of Neighborhoods as Indicators of the Effects of Highway Improvements,* U.S. Department of Transportation, Fedral Highway Administration, Washington, D.C., 1972. 81 p. (plus 87 pp. appendix).

4. Burkhardt, Jon E., Impact of Highways on Urban Neighborhoods: A Model of Social Change, *Highw. Res. Rec.,* No. 356, pp. 85–94, 1971.

5. Appleyard, Donald and Frances M. Carp, The BART Residential Impact Study: An Empirical Study of Environmental Impact, in *Environmental Impact Assessment: Guidelines and Commentary,* Dickert, T. and Domeny, K. Eds. The Regents of the University of California, Berkeley, pp. 73–88, 1974.

6. Appleyard, Donald and Mark Lintell, Environmental Quality of City Streets: The Residents' Viewpoint, *Highway Research Record,* No. 356, pp. 69–84, 1971.

7. Burton, Robert C. and Frederick D. Knapp, Socio-economic Change in Vicinity of Capital Beltway in Virginia, *Highw. Res. Rec.,* No. 75, pp. 32–47, 1965.

8. Brand, Daniel and Marvin L. Manheim, Eds., *Urban Travel Demand Forecasting,* Highway Research Board, Washington, D.C., 1973, 315p.

SEVEN

Sociocultural Aspects
of the Effects of
Resource Development*

RABEL J. BURDGE

SUE JOHNSON

The desire and requisite skills to broaden our understanding of how people and communities react to planned environmental change is by no means the sole province of the discipline of sociology. The approach presented here combines an anthropological model with sociological and social-psychological concepts and utilizes data from a wide array of sources collected, by and large, for purposes other than the study of social impact.

Unlike economics or political science which are interested only in specialized aspects of human behavior, sociology, anthropology, and psychology have in common their interest in the whole spectrum of human behavior. Their differences are largely those of emphasis and choice of explanatory paradigms. Psychology tends to use the personality of the individual as the locus of its explanation of behavior; anthropology tends to explain variation in human behavior by analyzing variations in culture; and sociology uses the concept of society or social structure as its major explanatory schema[1] (pp. 14–15).

Our interest here is in melding a comparative diachronic model already used by anthropologists to study the social impact of resource development[2,3] to sociological and social-psychological concepts and variables, shown in the past to be related to attitudes and receptivity toward resource development[4,5,6] as well as to quality-of-life measures derived from secondary sources.

The approach here is a practical rather than theoretical one. In seeking to understand the behavior of people and communities affected by resource development, we also seek to predict what the probable impact of development will be. The goal of prediction is, in part, an exercise in applied science. Using a comparative model, we wish to study the course of events in a community where planned environmental change has occurred and to extrapolate from that analysis what is likely to happen in another community where a similar developmental change is contemplated. In other words, we wish to know if given similar predevelopment conditions and similar resource development projects, the social impact of a completed development project in Community A can be generalized to and predictive of what will happen in Community B where development is planned.

Another aspect of the goal of predicting social impact is more humanistic. We want to see if we can discover irreversible and undesirable social effects of resource development before they occur rather than having cause to regret events after they happen. Simply to discover irreversible effects is not enough, however, the implementation of changes to avoid undesirable effects falls outside the province of the social scientist as "scientist." It is the planning agency or agencies that bear the responsibility for intervening in such matters, though social scientists may make recommendations for intervention.

* Early portions of this chapter, the figures, and the tables are similar to the authors' publication titled "Social Impact Statements: A Tentative Approach," published in *Social Impact Assessment,* C. P. Wolf, Editor, Proceedings of the EDRA5. All matter reproduced with permission of the publishers and authors.

Social scientists can also speak to the issues of alternative plans and alternative impacts of these plans using this model. Moreover, if likely social impacts can be assessed, recommendations for mitigating actions on the part of the agencies involved can be made. This is an important part of making a social impact statement—for even reversible but undesirable effects can sometimes be avoided by an aware agency that is motivated to avoid them.

The model and methodology presented here represents the research interests of two sociologists. However, part of the goal is to provide a means of gathering basic data that can be used and generalized to other studies of social impact where it is impossible to collect all the data ideally needed. Moreover, it is hoped that the argument presented here will be persuasive enough that agencies which must provide social impact statements will take the NEPA seriously enough to provide equivalent time and money to those who are doing this work. More support is needed, equivalent to what is currently being done in project planning and even on the ecological side of EISs, if this is to be achieved.

BASIC CONCEPTS

Any kind of natural resource development will bring changes to the community involved whether the development is small, like a new city park or even new equipment for the park, or large scale, such as the construction of a new reservoir or the opening of a new mine. The kinds of social change entailed will naturally vary with the kind and size of a development project as well as the kind of community in which the project resides. To study social change sociologists must switch from their traditional focus on social organization, usually a more structural and static orientation, to a more dynamic and hence more difficult framework: the assessment of the social impact of planned change.

Community is left undefined here because the definition will depend on the area of primary and secondary impact. It may be a neighborhood where a freeway is planned (primary impact) and the city which the freeway is to serve (secondary impact). It may be, and often is in rural areas, the entire county where development is proposed (primary) and possibly neighboring counties too (secondary). When we speak of a dynamic approach to community, part of the meaning is embodied in the past history of a community wherein, as a working, evolving system, lies the capacities for adaptation and change (and outwitting the predictions of social scientists). Also found in the history are certain unique features of the community, factors that will affect capacity for adjusting to planned change. Firey's classic study of land use in central Boston illustrates the importance of such unique factors.[7] What this means in the study of social impact is that both general trends from studying similar developments and the unique features of the community must somehow be balanced in making predictions about social impact. Doing this is an empirical exercise for which no hard rules may be given.

In principle, large-scale planned change which characterizes much natural resource development can have an effect on the entire fabric of a community, on its institutions such as government and schools, and on its size, perhaps, by drawing new people to it or forcing some to move away. Its economic base may grow because of increased potential for industrial development, for example, or the creation of recreation-based revenues. The social interaction patterns of its members may change—for physical reasons if people must relocate because of development or for social reasons if there are dramatic changes in the socioeconomic status of some members who may profit from the development. Its land use practices may change, for example, by turning what was once farmland into a lake with adjoining marinas and vacation homes. In short, the entire matrix of community beliefs, values, attitudes, norms, and practices may be affected.

Unless one spent a lifetime at it, it would be impossible to catalogue and study the true dimensions of social impact; change has a way of creating other changes, much as the proverbial rock thrown in a pond, and the complexity of such changes is beyond the capacity of the sociologist to study. However, there are basic dimensions that can be measured which reflect, albeit imperfectly, fundamental and important characteristics of a community. Studied over time, these same dimensions can give us valid insight as to what are the basic processes of social impact when natural resource development occurs. Faced with a proposal to undertake a natural resource development, the community and the planners and agencies proposing the change can profit from the experience of other communities that have already undergone development and gain a reasonably accurate expectation of how the project will affect their community.

THE COMPARATIVE DIACHRONIC MODEL

One way to capture the dynamic quality of something as far-reaching and complex as social impact is to metaphorically take a series of snapshots over time as things progress and try to fill in what happened in between. This, in essence, is what a diachronic model represents; it is simply the study of the same phenomenon at two different points in time. In this case the time periods are usually before and after development occurs. Naturally, it would be preferable, for a true understanding of the social impact of projects, to live in the community during this time period so we could see changes occurring day by day. This is a practice anthropologists often use to study cultural change.[8]

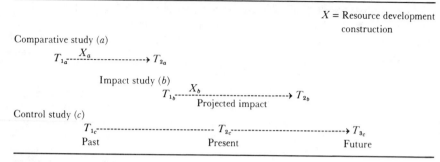

Figure 7.1. Time dimensions of a comparative diachronic study to predict social impact of proposed resource development.

Another way is to use various data sources to attempt what the major events and processes were between the pre- and post-development period and to try to reconstruct the changes that were due to resource development. To do the latter, especially if one is using secondary data sources such as the census or county records, one needs a control community so that changes that probably would have occurred anyway can be isolated from developmental changes. The control community can also help with prediction of what the no-project alternative is likely to be.

The model is comparative in that after studying the social impact of a natural resource development in one community, this community will be compared to a similar community where a similar type of development is proposed, and from that predictions can be made about probable social impact. The model also permits a restudy of the impacted community in the future to assess what the actual impact has been, so that the fit between our predictions and the actual outcome can be seen.

The basic comparative diachronic model is illustrated in Figure 7.1. The major virtue of this model, other than providing an empirical basis for predicting social impact, is that with appropriate data sources (those which can be collected frequently such as land transfer records), it allows for a more dynamic interpretation of events and can provide monitoring of short-term impacts. Moreover, this kind of frequent monitoring provides a continual source of evaluation or check on the direction of predictions made about social impact.

TIME DIMENSION FACTORS INFLUENCING SOCIAL IMPACT

Predevelopment Period

Although the nature and scope of a natural resource development helps define the potential impact of a project, the unfolding of impact in time is an important and somewhat subtle factor as well. Impact actually begins long before actual construction. As soon as people in a community hear that project X is being planned, they begin reacting in various ways. Some will seek more information, whereas others will be apathetic because it seems distant, vague, or unrelated to their lives. Some will seek opportunities by which to profit from the project.

Moreover, there are a host of political considerations depending in part on which kind of group, agency, or governmental office is initiating the project, what kind it is, whether it will require congressional approval or a local referendum. Generally, if the proposed project looks as if it will benefit the community, most local leaders will be in favor of it. This, of course, raises the issue of who will benefit. There are costs, both monetary and personal, associated with almost every form of resource development, and a social impact study should specify who is likely to benefit beyond the community as a whole and who is likely to pay beyond the general taxpayer.

Part of the function of the time dimension is that it allows people to make plans usually to minimize personal costs of the project and to maximize benefits. Drucker's study of the preconstruction period of the Taylorsville reservoir indicates that long before actual construction there was considerable land turnover, mostly on the fringes of a proposed reservoir and park. Much of this land was bought by noncounty residents, and many were from adjoining states.[9] Of course, if there is no recreational component to resource development, this kind of land speculation is unlikely to occur, however, other forms of change in land use are likely to be present. Bern's chapter discusses this process in detail.

If people are going to be relocated to make room for resource development, this opens an entire dimension of impact that is related both to the quality of life of individuals and to the impact of the project on the community as a whole. In his study of the premigration period of residents to be moved for the Taylorsville reservoir, Smith[3] found many to be suffering from "pre-migration stress," that is, they were mourning the loss of their homes and their interactions with friends and relatives before these were actually lost. This is definitely a psychological cost; and this reservoir has been unusually slow getting to the construction phase, thus it was a long-term kind of suffering. As of this date residents have not yet moved, which means they have been knowing about having to move for 10 years or more. This is social impact as surely as actual construction is.

The area of public participation in planning is part of social impact and somewhat problematic and is currently subject to controversy.[10] However, the elements of how communities tend to respond to proposed projects can be delineated in general terms. A study in the Delaware Basin listed four keys to maintaining effective public participation, in this case, for the development of water resources: real problems, concerned citizenry, dynamic leadership, and cooperative agencies.[11] Public participation is crucially important, because an uninformed or misinformed public may fail to act on developmental issues or if ignored, may reject proposals.[12][13] The process of obtaining and maintaining citizen participation is one which often takes a great deal of time in the planning stages.

The community decision-making process typically follows a pattern similar to that described as follows.[14] First, there is awareness on the part of a small group that something is needed. Or it may be that the first initiation of proposed action comes from other than local people, for example, when the state decides it needs a new park in an area. Once awareness of a proposed project or need is present, the second stage is the spreading of awareness to civic groups and the local political structure if these were not the initiators. In the third stage the proposed project or problem is acknowledged by key power holders and the plans legitimated by their participation. This kind of participation tends to minimize opposition from power groups when the proposed project is announced. Diffusion of information to the general public is the fourth stage; here arguments for and against the project are heard. Strong opposition groups may appear and garner enough strength to defeat the proposal or send it back to the "drawing boards." The fifth stage is securing official political approval, sometimes through referendums and bond issues, other times through a show of support and consensus by citizens.

The sixth stage, and one not often carried out systematically, is evaluation of the effects of the project. It is here that a diachronic model makes a very important input to the study of social impact, for it allows for systematic study of a previous project and its impact.

One problem often mentioned in the literature but perhaps understated in its real effects is that altogether too often plans about resource development are created in a vacuum; that is, there is no public participation in the planning period. Rather, the public is confronted with a full-blown plan and asked to accept or reject it. This kind of planning and the concomitant agency view that social impact assessment is a means of bureaucratic compliance with NEPA, means its requirements are seen as pro forma and are treated as such[15] (p. 9).

This kind of strategy cannot help but have a negative social impact, at least in the beginning stages of resource development. This approach may be one reason why so many projects are subject to a good deal of bad publicity at the beginning and lengthy and acrimonious litigation later. This kind of public reaction is expensive in time and money to all concerned. In other words, it appears that the optimal time for public input is at the point where the needs of the community become apparent, right at the birth of the planning to meet those needs.

Wolf[15] distinguishes between "project effects" and "planning effects," and that may be the most succinct way of categorizing the problem discussed previously. The act of planning a project can and often does have significant impact on a community regardless of whether the project ever comes to fruition. Negative reaction to a plan can possibly promote at least temporary community cohesion where none existed before. Similarly, community cooperation in meeting its needs can also enhance its cohesion. It has been noted, not altogether humorously, that "the day may come when a project cannot be justified because it costs more to plan than it does to build"[15] (p. 7).

During Construction of Resource Projects

Optimism about the eventual benefits of a resource development project for the affected community is a fairly widespread perception, as several studies have shown in reservoir construction.[16, 6, 3] This perception of benefits is most often found in urban residents in the affected community or in those likely to benefit directly from development.[17, 3] The general optimism is, however, sometimes sullied by the awareness that during the construction phase there will be a loss in revenues from the land being developed and a strain on services as construction workers move into the community.[2, 16, 18, 19] One community in Oregon so overreacted to perceived economic benefits that they expanded to meet the temporary demands for services and goods of the construction phase and then found themselves without the anticipated economic benefits and straddled with additional costs of the maintenance of these expanded services.[16]

Short-term impact on the community's source of revenue depends on how much land is being taken by the development and if it is an agricultural community, how large a decline in farming will occur as a result of land condemnation. Also important is the rate at which land is acquired by the development agency, because a slow but regular rate of land acquisition allows the community time to slowly adjust its property valuation rates and avoid the decline in revenues.[2] These problems are considered in some depth by Dickinson and Blackmarr in Chapter 5.

Another factor that affects the way a community will be impacted by the construction phase is the size of the community. Stramn[20] found that very large towns or communities and very small ones were usually less affected by the construction phase of resource development. Apparently, large communities just absorb the impact; very small communities sometimes are not saddled with the temporary migration of construction workers who, in this case, tend to commute to work. However, as Peele[19] argues in her study of the social impact of a proposed nuclear power plant in a small isolated town where construction workers must reside for several years during the construction phase, the short-term costs to the local community can be devastating, even though the long-term benefits are surprisingly generous.

After Construction

The example of the Oregon community that overextended to meet demands during the construction phase and for anticipated benefits is just one kind of impact that may occur after construction. Most projects include cost-benefit analyses that specify anticipated benefits in dollar terms for the community for such elements as water quality, flood control, tourism and recreation, and industrial development in the case of reservoir construction. A real question that needs to be answered systematically and empirically is whether these benefits do materialize and to what degree. To our knowledge, there have been very few postconstruction analyses that analyzed the social and economic costs and benefits. Hargrove[21] did a study of 20 reservoirs in Kentucky and Tennessee where industrial development was to be a benefit and found that unless other favorable factors were present and unless water availability fulfilled a need that was lacking, industrial development was not likely to occur at any greater rate than it would have had there been no reservoir. Hargrove[22] found substantial variation in the size and direction of anticipated economic benefits in a number of projects he examined after their completion.

Currently, social impact statements that fit NEPA requirements do not have an evaluative component, that is, there is no follow-up to see if predicted impacts did actually occur. This is a real loss both to researchers and practitioners, because it does not provide a basis for empirical prediction of social or other forms of impact. Most predictions are derived from a study of the community to be impacted and what is in the literature about likely impacts. The model presented here does have a systematic evaluative component built into it for monitoring both long- and short-term impacts. However, it calls for specific kinds of research quite a distance into the future. Moreover, the predictions are derived from a postconstruction study of a similar kind of project.

Projections are at best a tricky business with no guarantee of success. This is why we argue both for postconstruction analysis of projects for purposes of studying specific social impacts and for more general and basic research in the field. The model appears adaptable to both purposes. Acknowledging the tremendous time and money constraints on current practitioners of the social impact assessment art, secondary data, using a comparative model, can provide at least the gross outlines of what is likely to happen. However, as stated earlier, only study of communities that have been impacted and the collection of primary data as well as the collection of primary data about the community about to be impacted can come close to giving us a picture of what is really likely to happen.

Although Gardner[23] does not use a diachronic model in his study of postconstruction impact of reservoir construction, he does compare perceptions about a reservoir that has been in operation since 1959 to a more recently constructed reservoir in a nearby area and to an area that is still living on an uncontrolled river. Gardner found that after the reservoir had been in operation for a while, negative opinions about the operation of the reservoir began to surface, even though the community as a whole had been in favor of its construction.

It appears that many people confuse flood control with the idea of no flooding rather than controlled flooding. Therefore, downstream farmers who began to cultivate floodplain land and those who leased easements from the corps were dismayed to find their land flooded more often and with greater than previous seasonal variation as the operators of the reservoir sought to keep the pool up to recreation-user specifications and to prevent additional flooding in a distant large-river drainage basin. This meant that those who acted on the idea of "flood-proofing" found that instead, there was considerable controlled flooding that interfered with their agricultural activities. Conversely, those living downstream from the newly constructed reservoir were much more optimistic about being flood-proof. One may predict from this a lowering of optimism as seasonal rainfall and runoff varies and controlled flooding becomes more common in their agricultural area.

There has been the predictable buildup downstream of intensive land use on residential, commercial, and institutional properties. However, the build up has been congruent with the peak discharge of the reservoir, and the dam has been quite successful in reducing flood damage in this area. There are beginning to be signs that there may be potential problems upstream as the water table becomes higher on the ground and in the soil. At the time of the study the upstream impact had not been documented; a study of residents' perceptions showed them to be concerned about this impact. In the rest of the study where long-term impact was examined, Gardner found that perceptions of impact were closely related to real impact.

One point that is interesting in Gardner's study is that perceived benefits at the time of the planning phase through the early operation phase are taken to actually be the case. However, as time goes on and weather and operation of the reservoir vary, some of these benefits, particularly agricultural ones, begin to be perceived as costs and seem, indeed, to be costs to the farmers. Many local people feel that if the reservoir were operated differently, some of these costs would disappear. They are particularly incensed at the idea that "their" dam is used to control flooding on another river miles and miles away and that they have to pay the cost of protecting large cities far away from them. Those who are paying the cost feel that they can name the beneficiaries—recreationists, people who own land around the reservoir, and people in the cities downstream, near and far away. They are, in all likelihood, correct. It is unlikely, however, that operation of the reservoir will be changed to suit the farmer's interests at the risk of less flood protection downstream. Clearly, this is a case of conflicting interests and one not easily solved, if solvable at all.

These kinds of findings point to the complex role that time plays in social impact. It may be true that the impact of X project never ends but rather is lost in the current of impacts from projects Z, J, and Q. The order of impacts assessed depends in large part on the methodology used to collect the data, methods of data analysis used, and the time dimension through which discernible impacts are to be traced. Coates[24] traced the impact of such technological advances as automobiles down to sixth-order consequences; however, that seems a little ambitious for a field as immature and undeveloped as is social impact analysis.

APPLICATION OF THE COMMUNITY IMPACT MODEL (AN EXAMPLE OF THE METHOD IN ACTION)

Overview

The work of testing this diachronic model is just beginning, so the methodological details given as follows must be considered as tentative and subject to future change. Figure 7.2 gives general criteria for matching present and proposed development projects. The same criteria, with the exception of a similar resource development project, would hold for selecting control counties. Examples are given from reservoir construction since this is the authors' area of interest.*

Unit of Analysis

The unit of analysis for which data are readily available in rural areas is the county. The county is the geographical and political unit that most generally reflects community definition and identification in rural areas.[9] Since most resource development occurs in rural areas, we are concentrating our attention there. Urban development would require different matching criteria in terms of unit of analysis. Of course, as Schott (Chapter 6) and other authors here point out, impacts occur in all ranges of settings.

In most social impact situations more than one county is affected by resource development, and in these cases all counties of potential impact should be included. Generally speaking, area of impact varies directly with the magnitude of the project. (For the sake of simplicity we refer to a single county,

* The following sections are revised and adapted from Johnson and Burdge.[25]

—County as unit of analysis (rural areas)
—Similar project size and purpose
—Similar geographical and cultural region
—Similar data time frames
—Comparable secondary data sources

Figure 7.2   Key dimensions for matching present and proposed development projects.

acknowledging that in most cases more than one county is involved and that the use of more than one county for comparison purposes makes for better predictions.) A comparison county containing an already completed and operating project is to be selected using the general matching criteria listed as follows. Clusters of control counties (prediction of what would happen without the project) may be selected in a similar manner. This stage sets the scene for the selection of final comparison and control counties along variable-choice lines subsequently discussed.

Time Dimension

Project life may be anywhere from 5 years for a set of wooden swings to 100 years or more for a reservoir. The exercise of future predictions must take project life into account; however, one rarely runs into a social scientist who feels comfortable talking about fairly specific trends more than 10 or 20 years in the future. Realizing that choice of time-frame is somewhat arbitrary and conditioned by type of project, we suggest a 10-year period or more as desirable for studying the comparison county and for making predictions about the impact county.

Much of the data recommended for use in this methodological approach to the study of social impact are gathered at 5- or 10-year intervals and, therefore, provide a reason for choosing at least that long a period. Remembering that even well-collected social science data rapidly lose predictive utility with time, consideration is also given to periodic monitoring of other sources of data that appear more frequently. These data may be used to study the dynamics of impact on such factors as land usage, recreational use, and fluctuations in taxation, as well as checking on the direction of predictions made about the impact county.

The Nature of the Project

Natural resource development projects come in many forms—reservoirs, mines, parks, wild-life sanctuaries, and power plants, among others. The validity of any predictions of social impact rests first with choosing comparative on-going projects similar in as many ways as possible to the one proposed. For example, when choosing an operating reservoir for purposes of comparison, one should look first at the purpose for which it is designed. One intended primarily for flood control and recreation with industrial development, water storage, and quality as secondary benefits would have a different impact than one designed to provide water for irrigation. (However, with reservoir construction this may not be much of a problem in that reservoirs tend to be similar within geographical regions, e.g., all the reservoirs in Kentucky are multipurpose with the exception of one.)

Most public projects have cost-benefit analyses that tell the researcher the size of the proposed project and the hierarchical order of intended benefits. Completed projects selected for comparative purposes should have basically the same hierarchy of associated benefits and be of similar magnitude. The choice will be simple in the case of single-purpose projects, such as national recreation areas or the development of a coal-gasification facility.

Other Matching Criteria: Choice of Variables

In addition to project similarity, there should be locational similarity. Comparable projects should be selected from within the same state where construction is proposed, although nearby states will do if there is cultural and geographical similarity (e.g., proposed reservoirs in mountainous eastern Kentucky would have more in common with operating projects in Appalachian West Virginia or Tennessee than with projects in the western part of Kentucky). Where possible, more than one operating project might be chosen for comparison, especially if the only available comparable projects are dissimilar geographic or cultural areas. The more projects there are for comparison and the greater their degree of similarity with proposed projects, the more reliable will be the results of the social impact study.

Social and demographic characteristics of the counties are also among the general matching criteria. An important consideration about the time dimension is related to this step of the methodology. To compare the predevelopment characteristics of the comparison county with those of the county of proposed development, an adjustment to a 10-year or more difference in time may be required. Since communities change with time, one must look for similarities in patterns of variables rather than fruitlessly search for complete homogeneity. The U.S. Census of Population is published at 10-year intervals and the U.S. Censuses of Agriculture, Business, Recreation, and Industry and Manufacturers at 5-year intervals, and it is to these major and easily available data sources (or their surrogate, the *County and City Data Book*) that one looks for comparative data on counties. Census data is also available on tapes for access through the computer.

We suggest that the following five variables be chosen as final matching criteria. In Table 1 an example is given for locating comparison and control counties in Eastern Kentucky, utilizing secondary data sources. However, for purposes of this section of the paper, we simply list and provide a rationale for the selection of each of the indicators. Most of these measures are available from the *County and City Data Book*. No county is identical to any other; matches on variables descriptive of basic community characteristics will of necessity be approximate.

POPULATION SIZE AND STRUCTURE

In terms of matching criteria, this and area of the county are probably the most fundamental dimensions. Population size is related to ability to absorb impact[26] as is the age/sex structure, particularly the age structure (dependency ratio), because this is linked to the potential productiveness of a population.

AREA OF THE COUNTY

This variable is important from the standpoint of the ability to absorb and adapt to social change. A more relative and more accurate measure of potential magnitude of impact is the size of the project in acres as a percentage of total county size.

PERCENTAGE URBAN

As the population of a county becomes more urban, it becomes more concentrated. A population that is closer together tends to have more community organization and does have different ecological relationships as well as, in general, a more cosmopolitan lifestyle. Social change of any form tends to be more easily accepted by urban persons.

AGRICULTURE (PER CAPITA VALUE OF FARM PRODUCTS SOLD)

In addition to being a famous statistic quoted by administrators, this figure is indicative of the degree to which the county is agricultural versus other uses of rural land. Although not available from the *County and City Data Book*, the amount of minerals produced may be an alternative indicator for nonagricultural counties. Forest products are listed as part of agriculture.

LABOR FORCE PATTERNS

Employment characteristics of the community should be similar, otherwise the force of different economic variables may have a biasing effect on the extrapolation of impact from one situation to another. The occupational categories of the census are particularly important if industrial development is projected in the cost-benefit analysis as an effect of the project or if it is already present in either the comparison or impact county. As an alternative, patterns of retail, manufacturing, and service businesses from the Business Census may also be compared. The percentage of people employed in farming is an important indicator of the relative importance of agriculture in the labor force composition.

SOME CAUTIONS ABOUT USING THE COMPARATIVE MODEL

The real world naturally will not always provide perfect matches with proposed natural resource development. The selection of projects for comparison is the most important step in the process, because claims for validity will be based on similarity and comparability. Therefore, we have recommended using several points of comparison, choosing what we consider fundamental variables to be controlled (as much as possible) in a diachronic model.

A note about the inherent complexity of using the model (especially when juxtaposed with the relative simplicity of describing the model) is in order here.

Table 1 Matching Data on Johnson County and Surrounding Counties as of 1970[a] (Control Counties)

	Johnson	Lawrence	Magoffin	Martin	Morgan
I. a. Population size	17,539	10,726	10,443	9,377	10,019
b. Percent female	50.9	50.5	50.5	49.8	49.8
c. Median age	31.4	31.7	23.9	22.2	29.5
II. Area (square miles)	264	425	303	231	369
III. Percent urban	22.1	0	0	0	26.6
IV. Per capita value of farm[b] products sold (in dollars)	19.78	105.26	37.54	3.63	218.88
V. Percent of persons employed in selected occupations					
a. Farmers and farm managers	.6	5.2	2.2	.4	12.5
b. Professionals and managers	19.7	15.0	16.3	17.7	20.1
c. Clerical, sales, and kindred	16.5	7.0	22.2	10.9	14.2
d. Craftsmen, foremen, and kindred	14.8	20.2	17.7	15.3	12.6

[a] This table was constructed by Tony Crosby.
[b] Farms selling $2500 or more.

Many natural resource development projects are located in or have an effect on more than one county. This means the quantity of data to be collected is somewhat larger than what we have described. It also means that comparability between impact, comparison, and control counties is a more difficult task. It is our recommendation that "best fit" criteria be used, that is, although there may be considerable variation among potential comparison and control counties in terms of matching criteria, if one is to use a comparative model, one selects the best fit of all the possibilities. (Some idea of possible variation in comparison and control and impact counties can be gained from Table 2.)

The attribution of changes due to natural resource development as opposed to changes that would have occurred anyway opens up the issue of causality and the use of causal models. (We only mention that there are great possibilities here, ones we have not, however, examined ourselves.) Enhancement of the model's accuracy in attributing changes due to development comes from the use of control counties selected just as comparison counties but without a development project. This, again, is an exercise in future research of a specific nature. Comparison of rates of change and absolute change in the comparison, impact, and control counties provides the basis for assessing which changes may actually be attributed to resource development.

A distinction between short-term impacts such as loss of the tax base during the construction phase in reservoir development and long-term impacts, such as growth in tourism and second homes should be made. (Table 2 has variables suggested for monitoring short-term impacts.) The time for studying impact begins immediately in the preconstruction phase for baseline data and continues, sporadically, for as many as 10 or 15 years in the future. In addition, data may be utilized from 10 to as much as 30 or more years into the past for comparison counties.

SOURCES OF DATA AND KEY SOCIAL IMPACT VARIABLES

Table 3 lists sources of data that can be used for research into social impact. The data range from decennial censuses to personal interviews. As one moves down the list from category I to category VII, one moves from highly aggregated data about the county to measurements of behavior and attitudes of people. Thus the data become more accurately reflective of what is happening to community residents and their institutions. Also, as one goes down the list to category VI, the data are available in shorter time periods, making possible the monitoring of short-term impacts and the updating of predictions. We feel that all these levels of data need to be collected and analyzed for comparison, impact, and control counties so that we may get a truer picture of which social impacts occur as a direct result of a given project.

Table 2 Basic Matching Data on Johnson and Leslie Counties (Impact and Comparison)

	Year	Johnson	Leslie
I. a. Population	1950	23,846	15,537
	1960	19,748	10,941
	1970	17,539	11,623
b. Percent female	1950	49.7	48.8
	1960	50.4	49.4
	1970	50.9	50.4
c. Median age	1950	22.6	17.5
	1960	25.9	18.0
	1970	31.4	21.6
II. Area (square miles)		264	409
III. Percent urban	1950	18.1	—
	1960	20.4	—
	1970	22.1	—
IV. Per capita value of farm[a] products	1950	22.8	15.9
sold (in dollars)	1960	30.6	10.2
	1970	40.3	6.5
V. Percent of persons employed in selected occupations			
a. Farmers and farm managers	1950	13.6	15.8
	1960	6.1	.4
	1970	.6	.7
b. Professionals and managers	1950	10.9	7.9
	1960	16.5	13.0
	1970	19.7	21.1
c. Clerical, sales and kindred	1950	10.0	5.2
	1960	18.4	7.7
	1970	16.5	11.4
d. Craftsmen, foremen, and kindred	1950	10.4	(.3
	1960	14.5	8.7
	1970	14.8	15.6

[a] Total amount of farm sales for the county.

In the exposition developed as follows about sources of data and what we feel are key variables, we have included tentative hypotheses as a means of illustrating possible directions and types of impact (drawn from reservoir construction research). In a social impact study such hypotheses would derive from the study of the comparison community, past studies of impact, and from any unique features of the impact county that may be important.

Table 3   Sources of Data and Key Impact Variables

I. U.S. Bureau of Census Publications
 A. Census of Population
   1. Area and Population size
   2. Urban population proportion
   3. Labor force composition
   4. Productivity of the population
   5. Extreme incomes
   6. Educational attainment   .
   7. In- and out-migration
 B. Census of housing
   1. Dwelling condition
   2. Household modernity
   3. Owner-occupied homes
 C. Census of agriculture
   1. Value of farm products sold
   2. Average farm size
   3. Agriculture tenure classes
 D. Census of business and industry
   1. Per capita retail sales
   2. Economic complexity
   3. Unemployment rate
   4. Government complexity
II. State records
 A. Marriage rate
 B. Birth rate
 C. Death rate
 D. School attendance records
 E. Public assistance payments
 F. Local educational expenditures
 G. Permits for resource or mineral removal
III. Private records and reports
 A. Per capita disposable income
 B. Median family income
 C. Bank receipts[a]
IV. County and other local records
 A. Improved local highways[a]
 B. Record of deed transfers[a]
 C. Value of real property
 D. Per capita local expenditure for education
 E. Land-use patterns[a]
 F. County relief expenditures
 G. Other measures[a]

Table 3   (Continued)

  V. State and federal agency reports
     A. Cooperative Extension Service
     B. Soil Conservation Service
     C. Farmer's Home Administration
     D. Department of Health, Education, and Welfare
 VI. Archive information
     A. Newspaper reports[a]
     B. Official transcripts of public hearings
     C. Cost-benefit analysis of present and proposed projects
VII. Data from personal interviews
     A. Personal and family background variables
     B. Socioeconomic status
     C. Attachment to place and ancestral ties
     D. Identification with community
     E. Previous occupational and geographic mobility
     F. Attitudes toward and knowledge of resource development and development in general
     G. Quality of individual and family life
     H. Participation in public decision making
     I. Institutional variables

---

[a] Useful variables for monitoring short-term impacts and checking on the direction of predictions made about impact.

Information repeated in this section is essentially a rationale for the variables and data sources listed as Table 2, the master table of variables for the proposed social impact analysis. The attempt in this section is to move from somewhat vague concepts to concrete empirical indicators that can be used and understood by informed and educated lay and professional people interested in this process. This is not a laundry list of social science variables; but rather variables that have been found through investigation to be related to the impacts of natural resource development.

Many of the variables listed under census data have surrogate measures which are available more frequently and which serve the dual purposes of being aids in interpolation of trends between censuses and of being useful for monitoring short-term impacts. These surrogate measures are discussed under categories appropriate to their source.

At a minimum, each of the paragraphs describing the variables includes the following amounts of information. First, the variable label and, if appropriate, its conceptual indicator. Second, information on where the information may be found and, if applicable, how it is constructed. Finally, information on two points: how the information is to be interpreted and how it might change with impact.

U.S. Bureau of Census Publications

Data are reported in census publications generally on a county basis. Certain other forms of information are summarized by municipal place or census tract. Much of the information is available and relatively comparable for decennial periods since 1930. More recent censuses are also available on tape for computer useage. Data on agriculture, business, industry, and manufacturing are collected and reported in 5-year intervals. Special census reports are available for selected areas on an occasional basis. In addition, the monthly survey of the labor market provides important data on nationwide occupational and employment trends. Generally speaking, the more recent the information, the more reliable.

CENSUS OF POPULATION

Information in this section is based on the decennial population census. Interpolation of data from other sources provides estimates during intercensus years. Matching criteria variables are also included in the impact variables.

Area and Population Size

Total population is the most frequently cited and readily available statistic for any political unit. Increases and decreases in population size and some of the most significant indicators of social change, though the reasons why are often complex and intertwined (as Berns points out in his discussion of land use). We would expect most rural counties to lose population as they have in the past. However, if population loss was less than the average or if it actually increased, it may be due in part to resource development. As mentioned earlier, the total area is an indicator of capacity to absorb impact. Changes in population density (persons per square mile) may also be due to development.

Urban Population Proportion

In some areas this would be metropolitan/nonmetropolitan, and this measure is an indicator of the concentration of the population and the general level of community organization. It is also a matching variable. The statistic is readily available and is a further indicator of the degree to which the area can absorb change. Generally, the greater the percentage of urban population the more likely the community is to absorb a resource development, rather than the other way around.[20] An all-rural county faced with large-scale development is usually less equipped to handle development. We would expect that many kinds of resource development would hasten the trend toward urbanization.

Labor Force Composition

These data give us the key components in the county's division of labor and are an indicator of how highly developed the economy is. The percentage employed in farming is an indicator of agricultural dominance. In terms of possible social impact in rural areas of resource development, we would be looking for the addition of new occupational categories, growth in such categories as service and clerical occupations, or changes in the relative importance of the various occupational classifications.

Productivity of the Population

The number of persons 18–64 years old is an indicator that is available every 10 years (and often more frequently if special census data are available) and reflects the percentage of the population that is available for work. Generally speaking, rural areas where resource development occurs would have a high percentage of dependent persons. If resource development brought about general economic development, we would expect to see more people in the productive age range, either through keeping people in the area or through in- or re-migration of people in that age group.

Extreme Incomes

Traditionally, rural areas have been two-class societies: the rich and the poor. A measure of this is the percent of the population having very low incomes (usually below the poverty line) plus the percentage of families having a very high income. Generally, economic development is associated with the emergence of a sizeable middle class. The measure is calculated by adding the top and bottom quartiles of family income for the county. This measure is then compared to a similar figure for the entire state.

Educational Attainment

This is a measure of the average number of years of formal education completed by the population 25 years of age and older. It is reported in the census and is available for farmers every 5 years. Rural people tend to lag behind urban persons in years of education completed. Over a fairly long period of time, resource development and concomitant economic development may have the impact of increasing the general educational level of the population.

In- and Out-Migration

This refers to the number of persons who move into and out of a region in a given period. Generally, in-migration should increase during the construction phase of a development and out-migration should on the average be slowed. Census figures show population changes in a political unit that are due to migration changes, albeit over long time periods.

CENSUS OF HOUSING

The decennial Census of Housing is collected in conjunction with the regular Census of the Population. Information is given on the same political units. Because indicators of housing quality have changed over the last 50 years, comparison of recent data with that of the past is sometimes difficult.

Dwelling Condition

This refers to the percent of the dwelling units in the county that are sound and have all plumbing facilities. Although a particular resource development may take many years to produce an improvement in the quality of housing, generally, if overall economic conditions improve, this will show up as improvement in dwelling conditions.

Household Modernity

This figure for a given county is equal to summing the percentages of the population with home freezers, with air conditioning, with television sets, and with telephones. The measure is calculated using data collected every 10 years. This is a better measure for level of living as opposed to gross income figures and is, in part, indicative of life-style as well.

Owner-Occupied Homes

Communities with a high percentage of home owners are generally stable and, therefore, likely to be resistant to change. We would expect these stable communities would have greater difficulty adjusting to social change due to resource development.

CENSUS OF AGRICULTURE

The Census of Agriculture is collected every 5 years and includes food and fiber in addition to horticulture and floriculture crops.

Value of Farm Products Sold

This figure for the county, the total value of all agricultural products sold, is available from the Agriculture Census, and the interim reports are available from the Crop Reporting Service of the State Departments of Agriculture. In an impacted community the total value of farm products sold is likely to decrease relative to nonimpacted areas if farmland is taken out of production, unless land conversions result in higher dollar yield uses.

Average Farm Size

The number of acres per farm in the county is a readily available statistic from the Census of Agriculture and from the Economic Research Service of the USDA on an interim basis. The average size of each farm in the United States is increasing as persons leave farming and their land is purchased by existing farmers or corporations. We expect that resource development would speed the process of farm consolidation.

Agriculture Tenure Classes

The percentage of farm operators in the county that are, respectively, owners only, owners and renters, and renters only is an indicator of the progressiveness of agricultural practices in the county. In other words, in an impacted county we would expect to see movement from traditional owners only to more owner-renter combinations.

CENSUS OF BUSINESS AND INDUSTRY*

As was the case with agriculture, Censuses of Business and Industry and Manufacturers are available on a 5-year basis with many special censuses conducted in interim periods. The *County and City Data Book* also includes much of the information. Some of the information in this section is not available for all census periods in recent decades. An increase in most of the indica-

---

* A Census of Manufacturers is available for areas where manufacturing is an important component of the economy.

tors in this section would indicate a movement away from a traditional agriculture based economy.

Per Capita Retail Sales

The average per-person dollar sales in the county is available through the Census Bureau and is often available by county from a state department of commerce or the equivalent agency. As development in a particular region increases, we would expect the amount of dollar trade to increase.

Economic Complexity[27]

This refers to the number and kind of industry or business groups having 300 or more employees (male or female) in the county. Although available from the Census Bureau, it may be best to supplement the measure with an inspection of county industrial sites. If natural resource development meets the expressed goal of improving the quality of life of rural people, then the development should attract more business and industrial development.

Unemployment Rate

The number of persons in the county without work who are seeking employment is, generally speaking, higher in most rural areas compared to urban areas. Any change in the unemployment rate may be traced to the development or the secondary impact of increased sales, services, or manufacturing.

Government Complexity

This is the number of federal employees located in the county and is a measure of the federal contribution to the economy of the region. This may be obtained from the population census or the businesses census. It may also be obtained from the county payroll records (if a payroll tax is levied in the county). Any development of any size should bring about a rise in the level of federal and state employment in the county.

State Records

As professional statisticians find more employment in state agencies, the level of record keeping in these agencies improves. However, certain states did not keep birth, death, and marriage records until the late 1930s. Many of the variables in this section are indicative of the vitality and cohesiveness of the community. Many are available on a monthly as well as an annual basis.

MARRIAGE RATE

The number of marriages per 1000 persons in a year is for our purposes a surrogate measure for the number of household formations. Household formations are down in rural areas and up in urban areas, because young people tend to migrate to urban areas prior to or soon after marriage. Any reversal in this trend would represent an improvement in the household formation potential.

BIRTH RATE

The number of live births per 1000 persons is published by each state for the county on a yearly basis. Poor rural areas have traditionally had high fertility rates; movement toward the national norm then would presage growing "modernity" or middle-class values with respect to family size in rural areas.

DEATH RATE

Deaths from all causes per 1000 population, like the birth rate, is published by state agencies every year. Rural areas traditionally have a higher death rate than urban areas because of the large percentage of older persons in these areas. Age-specific death rates are indicative of the general health of the population. The maternal mortality rate is an index of quality of health care in an area.

SCHOOL ATTENDANCE RECORDS

The average daily attendance at school for eligible children is summarized on a school district basis. Rural education levels continue to lag behind urban areas and, in particular, suburban areas where the middle class is located. A percentage increase in school attendance would indicate future higher levels of education and a greater influence by the middle class. School attendance records are, of course, different from increases and decreases in the number of students which are reflective of population changes.

PUBLIC ASSISTANCE PAYMENTS

Total federal and state welfare payments include everything from social security to the food stamp program. These figures are available by county on a monthly and weekly basis. The only problem is that they must be combined into a single index. Total public assistance payments provides an indication of federal and state participation in the economy. It also provides an index, albeit indirect, of the poverty level of the county. Any improvement in the economy coming from development should lessen the amount of public assistance payments.

LOCAL EDUCATIONAL EXPENDITURE

The per-pupil public school expenditures derived from state and federal sources are reported on a school district basis which in most areas is congruent with county lines. However, some within area districts may have to be combined to yield accurate figures. Assuming the quality of education is roughly equal to dollars spent, increases or decreases in the quality of education may be obtained using these figures. An indication of rising standards of education would be the amount of local initiative in seeking state and federal sources. Test scores are also sometimes available in forms that permit comparison between various areas.

PERMITS FOR RESOURCE OR MINERAL REMOVAL

This measure is an important indicator of changing land use when coupled with information on building permits and deed transfers outlined in the fourth section, because it provides an accurate picture of changing land use.

Private Records and Reports

By private we mean nonlocal, state, or federal statistics. Here we include statistics from business, manufacturing, and sales organizations. A problem with the use of these data is that most are summarized on the basis of large aggregates. As such, many may not be reported for rural counties.

PER CAPITA DISPOSABLE INCOME

This measure is calculated on a yearly basis for every county in the United States and is published in *Sales Management*. Since it takes into account such items as state and local taxes, it summarizes the amount of buying power available in each county. It also has the advantage of being available on a yearly basis. As such, any increases or decreases in development activity should bring about changes in per capita disposable income. Researchers should be cautioned in using this information for comparison purposes over too wide a geographical area. Living costs vary tremendously from region to region and between rural and urban areas.

MEDIAN FAMILY INCOME

This statistic is reported by the Department of Commerce as well as by many private business agencies and organizations. It is particularly crucial in measuring inflation rates and monitoring the buying power of the United States public. This figure would be expected to fluctuate depending on the level of economic activity in the county. The only difficulty with this statistic is that it may not be available on all counties every year. Despite these difficulties, the measure has the virtue of being the most frequently cited economic statistic for the family unit.

BANK RECEIPTS

A privately published statistic that reflects the movement of money into and out of county banks, it is a sensitive, quantified indicator of rising and falling economic activity. The State Banking commission or its equivalent publishes these data on at least an annual basis. To obtain figures for a lesser time interval, the individual banks must be consulted. During the land acquisition and construction phase of a reservoir, we would expect increases in banking activity. The degree to which such activity was sustained during the operation phase would be an indicator of the long-term economic impact the reservoir would have on the region.

County and Other Local Records

This phase of the analysis brings us closer to the actual development as we begin the process of monitoring secondary data that may have changed exclusively as a result of the project impacts. Depending on the particular variable under assessment, monthly, weekly, or even daily information may be obtained.

IMPROVED LOCAL HIGHWAYS

The number of miles of county and township highways (other than federal and state) that are improved during a year is available from the county or township road department. This measure is indicative of local building activity as well as the amount of the local budget that is spent on this type of activity. As in all such indicators, the emphasis is on detecting dramatic increases or decreases in local activity. We would expect more road development around areas where development occurs. If the development was massive enough, we would expect very appreciable changes compared with control counties.

RECORD OF DEED TRANSFERS

The county clerk records deed transfers on a daily basis that are reported in the
county newspaper. If no newspaper is available, the information may be
obtained by visiting the court house. Deed transfers may be an early warning
device that development is about to occur or an indicator of speculative activity
associated with some forms of resource development. Deed transfers may occur
prior to the local acquisition phase and then again during the period of second-
home and commercial development. In the case of reservoir development, such
activity has been found to be particularly intense if the proposed facility is near
an urban area.[9]

VALUE OF REAL PROPERTY

The overall value of the property in the county for purposes of assessing real
estate taxes is generally available at the time that yearly taxes are mailed.
Property values are reassessed on a systematic basis, generally every 5 years, or
the value is changed if the property is sold. Suburban areas generally show dramatic rises in real property value in that the turnover is frequent. The same
pattern would be expected for an area under development and exploitation.
However, for most rural counties the trend line will change very little from
year to year.

PER CAPITA LOCAL EXPENDITURE FOR EDUCATION

This is a measure of all local contributions in the form of taxes, tuition, rents,
fines, and gifts to the operation of the public school system. It is interpreted the
same as a similar measure at the state level outlined in the second section. As
suggested previously, the amount of local support for education should increase
with the rising influence of the middle class in the affairs of rural communities.

LAND USE PATTERNS

The changes taking place in the existing use of land within the county may be
measured by an analysis of applications and approvals of building permits. In a
development situation, we would expect land use patterns to change from agriculture to either commercial or residential use. Such information could be
readily obtained if each of the counties under investigation practiced zoning on
a county-wide basis. However, zoning ordinances are generally not in effect for
most rural counties. Land use conversion is a major social indicator and is
further discussed by Berns in Chapter 4.

COUNTY RELIEF EXPENDITURES

The amount of money that is appropriated on a local per capita basis for relief expenditures in the county can be obtained on a local basis by examining the budget of the combined political units in the county. This figure is then divided by the total population of the county. We would expect less per capita welfare payments as economic activity in the county increases. However, this figure may be less on a proportional basis rather than the actual amount.

OTHER MEASURES

Other useful pieces of information can be obtained from knowledgeable local people.[28] For instance, local realtors, mortgage people, and developers can furnish information on preferred housing areas, areas of land speculation, occupancy rates, residential turnover, and changing land use.

A frequently neglected form of impact in resource development with a recreational component is increased traffic congestion and overload on local law enforcement officials.[2] This information can be obtained from the local highway engineer's office and the local county sheriff's office. Police records are useful for locating areas of increasing or decreasing frequencies of kinds of violations. The public health officer is an important source for information on kinds and frequencies of disease and health problems.

These and similar measures can be used in lieu of data from census sources that are collected relatively infrequently and are often not useful, therefore, to practioners writing social impact statements. These data have the virtue of being easily available and localized, that is, pertinent to the impact of resource development at the level at which it occurs.

State and Federal Agency Reports

The Congressional mandate to develop EISs extends, at least, to all federal agencies (see Coop, Chapter 2). Myriad forms of development mean different agencies and organizations will be affected depending on the kind of development. For example, the Army Corps of Engineers deals with reservoir development and river drainage, the National Park Service with recreational expansion, and the U.S. Forest Service with competing demands for forest resources.

Each of the agencies issues periodic reports of its environmental activity. The information contained in agency reports may deal with efforts to expand sewage treatment or, as is the case with the Bureau of Outdoor Recreation, to provide more open space and parkland. Researchers will find records of the interchange of these agencies with the institutions and the people in local communities. A proposed natural resource development could also bring about conflict among various federal and stage agencies.

Researchers must locate agencies that are relevant to the project under consideration. The following is a list of federal agencies that often operate on a county basis. The list is not applicable to all regions of the county, for in the arid and forested west a situation exists where much of the land in the county is owned by either the Forest Service, the Bureau of Land Management, or the railroads.

1. The *Cooperative Extension Service* maintains a county agent and appropriate staff in almost every county in the United States. These persons are increasingly assuming an active role in most forms of community development.

2. The *Soil Conservation Service,* operating through a state and regional staff, is dedicated to helping farmers adopt improved cropping practices and farm conservation practices. The interchange between the Soil Conservation Service agent and the farmer may have much to say about the environmental attitudes of United States farmers.

3. The *Farmers Home Administration* provides long-term, low-interest loans to farmers for the purchase of land and buildings. Rural resource development could bring about a decline in Farmers Home Administration loans while, at the same time, the Federal Housing Administration and the Veterans Administration may be making more loans in the area that is being impacted. The local Rural Electrification Administration (REA) should experience more activity with the opportunity to provide more rural people (nonfarm) with electricity and telephones.

4. Some agencies of the *Department of Health, Education and Welfare* maintain offices at the county or regional level for purposes of administration of the Social Security program. Certain health statistics gathered on a nationwide basis are also collected and channeled through the State Department of Health. The monitoring of data on federal welfare support for the county may be obtained from these agencies.

Archive Information

This refers mainly to newspaper accounts. However, important information is available from public hearings and the agency reports that justify a project. These data need to be collected and summarized by persons trained in content analysis and library research. The idea is to assemble opinions, attitudes, and descriptions of situations in the community that have developed or may develop as a result of the project. Because each source of information is biased in that it represents agency, official, or editorial opinion, it must be introduced as biased information. Other sources such as the transcripts of hearings about a project are located with the agency responsible for the hearings. Archive information is very important in developing social impact statements, for it deals with the actual event under study. It also represents an important transition between the aggregate data discussed previously and data on individuals.

1. *Newspaper Reports* include the events that led to development of the project and editorial opinion about the proposed and completed event. Local news accounts provide only one source of information for, if a local editor or publisher favors a project, he may not print information regarding the opposition. Newspaper accounts also provide a rallying point for local opinions and as such may be used as a reference point for personal interviews with local residents.

2. *Official Transcripts of Public Hearings* provide a composite opinion about a proposed development for those persons who actually attended the public hearing. Except in recent years, few persons other than prodevelopment groups attended the hearings. As such, the hearing provided a ringing endorsement for the proposed project. However, with the advent of EISs, these transcripts should provide important insight regarding opposition and support forces for resource development.

3. *Cost-Benefit Analysis of Present and Proposed Projects* is essentially a justification of a project based on engineering and economic analysis. The benefits (in the case of flood control reservoirs) for such items as migration, improved water supply, flood control, and outdoor recreation should equal the costs of developing and maintaining the project. Since we seldom have post-audit analysis to see if in fact these benefits have resulted, we seldom learn how accurate benefit/cost projections are.

Data From Personal Interviews

To assess the full force of actual and perceived impact of resource development, interviews with leaders in the comparison and impact counties must be conducted. In the comparison community we will have the virtue of hindsight information obtained from leaders who have actually seen the impact of development. This is useful for evaluating what leaders of the impact community say they think will be the impact.

At a level even more reflective of reality, a random sample of residents in the comparison community would foretell how widespread impact is likely to be. The reconstruction of past events due to resource development would be invaluable in assessing the true impact at the personal level. A similar survey conducted in the impact community can give us information on what people think is likely to happen, and a follow-up survey at some future point in time would tell us what the real impact on the population was. Instead of listing specific information sources as was done in the previous six sections, here we list categories of variables that sociologists and other-social scientists are studying in relation to resource development. Although the research effort is still immature, many significant findings have been uncovered.

1. *Personal and family background variables* include such items as age, family life cycle, and residential history. As in most forms of social change, the older, long-term, less viable population experiences more adverse effects from resource development.[6]

2. *Socioeconomic status* here means the composite measure of education, occupation, and income and is calculated for the family head. Although generally, there is an articulated agency goal to help persons in the lower socioeconomic groups benefit by projects, it has usually been the case that they benefit the least by development.

3. *Attachment to place and ancestral ties* refers to the degree to which persons are willing to move from their present place of residence. Two factors appear to be important here, one is the attachment to a particular place and the other is the degree to which the family history is associated with the land. Research has shown that the greater the attachment to place, the more difficulty a person or an individual is likely to have in adjusting to a new location if forced to relocate. Also, these individuals are likely to have more difficulty in general to adopting to social change.

4. *Identification with community* is a dimension similar to attachment to place, with the emphasis being on association with the wider neighborhood, town, or county. Community is undefined in the sense of geographical size. Community ties and esprit de corps could be factors in resisting or encouraging the social change initiated by a reservoir or other major development in a community.

5. *Previous occupational and geographical mobility* refers to the number of changes in occupational classification and changes in location that the respondent has experienced. Research has shown that the upwardly mobile occupational groups and those geographically mobile are more receptive to social change and are more likely to see the benefits of such change. Conversely, persons who experience little occupational mobility or who seldom change residential locations are less likely to perceive and receive the benefits of social change.

6. *Attitudes and knowledge toward resource development and development in general* refers to responses to attitude scales and specific inquiries about the form of development under consideration. These scales provide an indication both of the general attitude and knowledge in the past of the population regarding the development under investigation. Attitude scales are helpful not only to describe the characteristics of those holding positive and negative attitudes

toward the development but also help to describe those people who have no attitudes toward the project. Knowledge of project development reflects a general awareness on the part of the population regarding areas affected, dates, potential benefits or costs, and sponsoring agencies.

7. *Quality of individual and family life* refers to the degree to which the family or the individual have such indicators of the quality of life as good housing, a good job, adequate diet, adequate educational opportunity, and good health. These dimensions are important because most federal developments have the expressed goal of improving the quality of life of the population that they affect. Although standard measures of all these dimensions have not been developed, it is generally agreed that these elements constitute an adequate quality of life definition. Some social scientists may add to this the dimensions of opportunity for individual self-expression.

8. *Participation in public decision making* refers to the degree to which the individual and the community were able to participate in any decisions that may effect their future. Although specific social science methodology has yet to be developed to assess public participation, it is assumed that each individual or family should have something to say about their future and that no outside agency or group has the right to impose unilateral change.

9. *Institutional variables*

Those with a sociostructural orientation are probably dismayed at this point by the notable lack of emphasis on community institutions—law enforcement, local government, transportation, health and sanitation, religion, even family stability. Objective data may sometimes be gathered from personnel files for turnover and growth in local government employees or from school files inspected for parental characteristics. However, most of the data on institutions and their role in and reaction to natural resource development can be gained through personal interviews with officials in the institution. A novel, unobtrusive measure along these lines is given by Burch[28]—that garbagemen be interviewed as to rates of change in volume and distribution of kinds of waste materials. A rationale for these kinds of measures is found in Webb, et al.[29]

The local Chamber of Commerce is a valuable source of information concerning major institutions, services, recreational opportunities, and industries in the community. From this one may proceed to interview functionaries of the major institutions. At a more local level impacts on such features of community life as home-owned grocery and retail stores may be delineated by interviews with those concerned.

Much can be gained through simple observation of the community and how it functions. What is to be observed and for what reasons is a research decision contingent on the kind and size of the community and the kind of natural resource development under study. (See Gold[30] for an example of ethnographic techniques.)

SUMMARY AND CONCLUSIONS

In this chapter we have concentrated our attention on how a social impact study could be done. The model presented here has the virtues of providing for basic research in the field of natural resource development, and we hope that it may be of some use to current practitioners in the field.

By outlining a relatively utopian schema, we have endeavored to provoke our peers into thinking in more dynamic, comparative, and holistic terms about natural resource development (see Figure 7-3). We feel the community profiles that appear in many EISs are considerably lacking in perspective. The current state of the art is ofttimes analogous to looking at a snapshot of a family and trying to reconstruct its history, present status, and future.

There is a large body of relevant literature we have not drawn on, except implicitly. Studies of phenomena as diverse as the development and demise of railroad transportation[31] and dissonance reduction in water managers[32] or, more accurately, the fields of sociology, anthropology, geography, political science, economics, ecology, and psychology—all have theories, findings, and methodologies that have relevance to the study of research development.

We have purposefully limited ourselves to citing studies of water resource development in part because it is our field of research and in part because we feel much from this field can be generalized to other forms of rural development.

As we see it the major drawback to the model is that it calls for specific research at some future point in time. However, there are artful compromises that can be made with the model. An example is the reconstruction of past events (through analyzing secondary data sources) in time the dynamics of previous social change if we are called in during the construction phase of a project to predict its impact. Or we can stay with data sources that exist solely in the community of impact if we are sufficiently armed with previous, relevant studies to provide the comparative dimension.

The limitations of our discipline to meet immediate community needs are quite severe if we approach this complex phenomena in the simplistic way many community and agency decision makers would wish. As Warner[33] (p. 197) says:*

The sociologist cannot at this time provide either *an* empirical description or *a* theory of the social world that is operationally meaningful for either policymaking or empirical research.*

He qualifies this by noting that we can "give many empirical descriptions and many theories of the various aspects of the social world."

* Quoted by permission of the author.

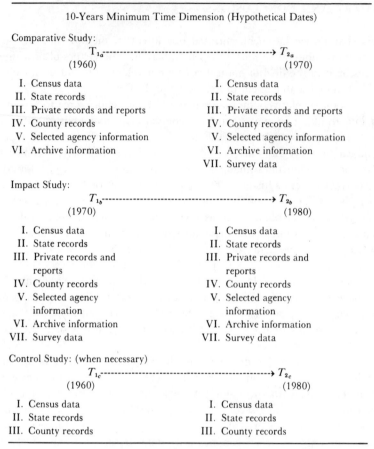

Figure 7.3 Schematic outline of the relationship of key information sources to observed and predicted impact.

In our discussion we have attempted to move beyond enumerating the hundreds of social variables that have some potential bearing on the study of social impact to try to isolate what we feel are major variables which, if studied, monitored, and interpreted, will yield a fairly accurate view of the dynamics of social impact. Researchers' choice of crucial variables will naturally differ from those enumerated here but probably not entirely.

Our desire, if time and space permitted, would be to discourse further on the linkages between the variables and why they are presented as "packages," to use Warner's term, that is, as "representative categories depicting a cross section of societal variables"[33] (p. 175). This endeavor, however, awaits in the future with more research, after which the variables are likely to change.

NOTES

1. Rose, Jerry D., *Introduction to Sociology* (second ed.), Rand McNally, Chicago, 1974.

2. Drucker, Phillip, J. E. Clark, and L. D. Smith, *Sociocultural Impact of Reservoirs on Local Government Institutions,* Research Report No. 65, Kentucky Water Resources Research Institute, University of Kentucky, Lexington, 1973.

3. Smith, Charles R., *Anticipation of Change, A Socioeconomic Description of a Kentucky County Before Reservoir Construction,* Water Resources Research Institute, University of Kentucky, Lexington, 1970.

4. Burdge, Rabel J. and Richard Ludtke, Social Separation Among Displaced Rural Families: The Case of Flood Control Reservoirs in William R. Burch, Jr. et al., Eds., *Social Behavior, Natural Resources and the Environment,* Harper and Row, New York, 1972.

5. Johnson, Sue, Recent Sociological Contributions to Water Resources Management and Development in L. Douglas James, Ed., *Man and Water,* University Press of Kentucky, Lexington, 1974.

6. Burdge, Rabel J. and K. Sue Johnson, *Social Costs and Benefits of Water Resource Construction,* Research Report No. 64, Kentucky Water Resources Research Institute, University of Kentucky, Lexington, 1973.

7. Firey, Walter, *Land Use in Central Boston,* Harvard University Press, Cambridge, 1947.

8. Nodel, S. F., *The Foundation of Social Anthropology,* The Free Press, Glencoe, Illinois, 1951.

9. Drucker, Phillip, *Impact of a Proposed Reservoir on Local Land Values,* Research Report No. 51, Kentucky Water Resources Institute, University of Kentucky, Lexington, 1972.

10. Potter, Harry R., Social Aspects of Recycling Municipal Waste Water on Land, Workshop on Research Needs Related to Recycling Urban Waste Water on Land, Chicago, March 1974.

11. Felton, Paul M., Citizen Action in Water—Asset or Liability? Phillip Cohen and Martha Francisco, Eds., *Proceedings of the Fourth American Water Resources Conference,* American Water Resources Association, Urbana, Illinois, 1968.

12. Connor, Desmond M. and Keith T. Bradley, Public Participation in the St. John River Basin, Preprint, Conference Proceedings of the American Society of Civil Engineers, Washington, D.C., 1972.

13. Burdge, Rabel J., Comments on Sociology and Water Resource Management, unpublished manuscript, Department of Sociology, University of Kentucky, Lexington, 1970.

14. Rogers, Everett M. and Rabel J. Burdge, *Social Change in Rural Societies* Appleton-Century-Crofts, New York, 1972.

15. Wolf, Charles P., Social Impact Assessment: The State of the Art, Conference Proceedings of the Social Impact Assessment Workshop in *Environmental Design Research Association* V, Milwaukee, Wisconsin, 1974.

16. Smith, Courtland L., Thomas C. Hogg, and Michael J. Reagan, Economic Development: Panacea or Perplexity in Rural Areas, *Rural Sociol.* **36** 2, 173–186, June 1971.

17. Andrews, Wade C. and Dennis C. Geersten, *The Function of Social Behavior in Water Resource Development,* Research Report No. 1, Institute for Social Science Research on Natural Resources and Center for Water Resources Research, Utah State University, Logan, 1970.

18. Hogg, Thomas C., Social and Cultural Impacts of Water Development in *People and Water,* Emery N. Castle, Ed. Oregon State University Water Resource Research Institute, Corvallis, 1968.

19. Peele, Elizabeth, Social Impacts of a Remote Coastal Nuclear Power Plant: A Case Study of the Mendocino Proposal, Oak Ridge National Laboratory, Oak Ridge, Tennessee, 1974.

20. Stramn, Gilbert G., Water Development and Society in *Sociological Aspects of Water Resources Research,* Report No. 1, Wade H. Andrews, Ed., Social Science Institute Series, Utah State University, Logan, 1968.

21. Hargrove, Michael B., *Economic Development of Areas Contiguous to Multi-Purpose Reservoirs: The Kentucky-Tennessee Experience,* Kentucky Water Resources Institute, University of Kentucky, Lexington, 1971.

22. Hargrove, *Ibid.*

23. Gardner, James S. and Nancy B. Hurtquist, *The Human Ecological Impact of Structural Flood Control on the Iowa River, Iowa,* Completion Report, Iowa State Water Resources Research Institute, Ames, 1973.

24. Coates, J. F., Technology Assessment: The Benefits . . . the Costs . . . the Consequences, *The Futurist* 5, 6, pp. 225–31, December 1971.

25. Johnson, Sue and Rabel J. Burdge, A Methodology for Using Diachronic Studies to Predict the Social Impact of Resource Development, Paper presented at the Annual Meetings of the Rural Sociological Society, Montreal, Canada, August 1974.

26. Bates, Clyde T., *The Effects of a Large Reservoir on Local Government Revenue and Expenditure,* Research Report No. 23, Kentucky Water Resources Institute, University of Kentucky, Lexington, 1970.

27. Munson, Byron E., *Changing Community Dimensions,* Ohio State University, Journal of Administrative Science, pp. 7–15, Columbus, 1968.

28. Burch, William R. Jr., Classroom handout for course in Sociology of Natural Resources, Yale University, New Haven, 1974.

29. Webb, Eugene I., et al., *Unobtrusive Measures: Nonreactive Research in the Social Sciences,* Rand McNally, Chicago, 1968.

30. Gold, Raymond L., Social Impacts of Strip Mining and Other Industrializations of Coal Resources, Paper given at a workshop on Social Impact Assessment, Environmental Design Research Association V, Milwaukee, Wisconsin, May 1974.

31. Cottrell, W. F., Death by Dieselization: A Case Study in the Reaction to Technological Change, *Am. Sociol. Rev.* 16 pp. 358–365, June 1951.

32. Bauman, Duane D., Potential for Policy Change in the Recreational Use of Domestic Water Supply Reservoirs in *Proceedings of the Fourth American Water Resources Conference,* Phillip Cohen and Martha Francisco, Eds., American Water Resources Association, Urbana, Illinois, 1968.

33. Warner, W. Keith, Some Problems in Measuring the Social Consequences of Large-Scale Development Projects in *The Social Well-Being and Quality of Life Dimension in Water Resources Planning and Development,* Wade H. Andrews, et al., Eds., Conference of the University Council on Water Resources, Utah State University, Logan, 1973.

EIGHT

The Organization of
Social Impact Information
for Evaluation by
Decision Makers and Citizens

ROBERT A. JOHNSTON

This chapter explores various ways of portraying social impact data to fulfill NEPA's mandate for detailed statements of environmental impact which give appropriate consideration to unquantified values using a systematic interdisciplinary approach.[1] We also focus our attention on the mandate to convey impact information in a form easily understood by the public.[2]

To understand NEPA we must sketch the historical facts underlying it and the probable directions in which future planning system changes will occur. NEPA is part of a large-scale movement toward open planning, planning with more public participation, more impact information, a broader consideration of alternative plans, and more mitigation of adverse impacts through intelligent foresight.

Since impact reporting is part of a larger planning process, the NEPA mandate cannot be fulfilled simply by tacking an EIS phase onto the end of the planning sequence. Information will not be adequate if it is developed after the plan is formulated. Only on-going data collection, as part of the agency planning system, can generate the detailed baseline information required to estimate net impacts. Public participation, necessary for estimating impacts on interest groups and for technical assistance in determining local environmental states and defining political issues, will not be effective in a post-hoc situation: people do not like to participate in bogus analyses of already chosen projects. Finally, agencies cannot make a pretense of generating a broad array of reasonable alternatives in the EIS context where the proposal is well defined and several "straw man" alternatives are developed as the EIS is being done. Broad consideration of alternatives, as required by most courts, can only take place as part of the planning process of the agency, not as an afterthought in the EIS phase. For environmental impact assessment to be meaningful, agencies will have to redesign their planning systems to allow for: early designation of a wide range of alternatives, evaluation of the impacts of these alternatives, redesign of alternatives to improve impacts, and final evaluation of these second-round alternatives.

The intent of NEPA is to open planning to the scrutiny of the public and other agencies. For impact reporting to be meaningful in the role of reducing environmental and social damage, it must occur in a way that stimulates agencies to modify their plans substantially, if necessary, to reduce adverse impacts. The structures of agency planning systems need to be considered then in an analysis of data portrayal, because data portrayal is the link between technical research and citizen participation and between technical research and impact mitigation. Whereas many of our recommendations in this chapter require changes in agency planning processes, we focus our attention on actual data portrayal techniques.

Issues in Social Impact Portrayal

POLITICAL RELEVANCE

The conversion of more or less objective impact data into politically useful information requires a certain amount of data interpretation and/or reduction by the impact report writer. Data must be conceptualized into categories through the use of some sort of mental model. Most of these models are implicit and not explained by EIS writers. It is important to emphasize that it is the portrayal of impact information that is the focus of this analysis. Not nearly enough attention has been devoted to the question of how to categorize and display impact information: portrayal is one of the weakest links in the process of reporting impacts to decision makers and citizens, even though other problems such as data quality are severe as well.

By focusing our attention on summary information accounts in an EIS, we are forced to consider the information set as a whole, to see if the information is understandable to the public and balanced in detail among alternatives or among classes of impacts (such as social, economic, environmental). Indeed, the EIS writer can best begin organizing his ideas of how to conduct the research by thinking about the general format for the data first, then conducting a synoptic research scan, and then elaborating the portrayal categories and finishing the research. The report's narrative or body should be organized to follow the logic of the summary portrayal, so that after reading the narrative, the summary account page brings to mind all the impacts previously discussed. In this way the reader will be helped to comprehend all the important impacts at one time and can review the value trade-offs among alternatives.

DATA ACCURACY

In dealing with social impacts, many intangible variables will have to be given conceptual form. It is important to be very careful to not overrepresent the agreement on the concept itself or the measures used to indicate the impacts on the conceptualized value. Concept and data "hardness" should be specified as clearly as possible in the report. Data sources, of course, must always be accurately referenced. A major problem with plan evaluation and impact portrayal schemes is that they often overrepresent the hardness of their data by pseudoquantification. A related problem that we also are concerned with is the question of methods to use for "scaling" or ranking data according to the degree of impact.

MITIGATION

A major failing of agency planning under NEPA has been that mitigative actions have not been systematically identified. The purpose of the act is not to produce files of unutilized information, nor is it to employ planning consultants such as the author. Rather, NEPA was intended to lessen environmental damage through revised planning procedures and mitigation. Few EISs go about identifying mitigative actions in any coherent, comprehensive fashion. To summarize, social impact portrayal should: •

1. Utilize politically relevant impact categories that allow for citizen understanding of the impacts of alternative plans on their values for the purposes of negotiating with the agency,

2. Represent social data accurately, especially when ranking and performing tradeoff analysis, and

3. Link adverse social, economic, and natural environmental impacts to mitigative actions where possible.

POLITICALLY RELEVANT IMPACT CATEGORIES

Social impact portrayal must be discussed as part of total impact portrayal for two reasons. First, social impacts tend to be played down in EISs and, therefore, all impacts need to be structured in a way that places social impact information on an equal basis with other information. Second, trade-off identification between social values and other values cannot take place unless all impacts are organized in a coherent fashion. In this section, then, we consider methods for portraying all impacts.

There are three principles of importance in designing a portrayal framework for representing total impacts:

1. Impacts should be grouped in a way that allows trade-off analysis to occur. High-level categories must be devised that aggregate impact topics in a coherent way, politically and scientifically. These categories must be mutually exclusive to avoid double counting and to reveal trade-offs clearly.

2. Impacts should be broken down by incidence. Effects on various human populations and interest groups should be estimated if these groups are to enter into decision making in an informed fashion.

3. Impact reporting should be issue oriented. That is, research should be done in more detail in those topical areas where political concern is high and better information is needed. We now discuss these three principles in turn.

Mutual Exclusivity of Impact Categories

A method for categorizing impacts that is both scientifically and politically useful is by the major headings of economic, environmental, and social. These categories allow for reasonable separation of analytical tools and assumptions along academic disciplinary lines and also lump impacts together into conceptual categories that roughly correspond to major contemporary political interests: economic development interests, environmental preservation interests, and social welfare interests. One attribute of this breakdown that is of use in politically relevant analysis is that the direction of impacts in each category will tend to be coherent. That is, in the aggregate economic impacts from a dam, for example, will generally be positive, environmental effects negative, and social effects positive from the perspective of certain interest groups and the opposite from that of other groups. The impacts of a health program will generally be viewed as economically neutral or negative, environmentally neutral, and socially positive by many interest groups. The effects of a water quality control program will generally be seen as economically negative, environmentally positive, and socially positive. There will always be subcategories of effects that are estimated to occur in the opposite direction from most of the subcategories of effects in each of the three major categories; however, this system of data organization allows for a relatively meaningful aggregation of impact data for summary presentation.

The U.S. Water Resources Council (WRC) adopted a similar system in 1973. The two objectives of water development are stated to be national economic development and environmental quality. Impacts are also to be estimated on two categories of (presumably) unintended effects, regional development and social well-being. Elsewhere, I have criticized this system as being somewhat politically misleading.[3] Recreational impacts are included in the definition of environmental, allowing the padding of this category with positive effects, presumably to have the total category appear positive in a summary analysis. The provision of recreation is, of course, an economic impact in terms of dollar expenditures and personal incomings and a social impact in terms of the psychic and social effects it has on people. For the environmental account to be politically relevant it should be redefined as "natural environmental quality." Other problems with the WRC accounts are that they allow for great overlap of economic and social benefits by not clearly defining subcategories.

There appears to be convergence toward the use of these first-level social, economic, and environmental categories. For example, the EPA uses these three concepts.[4] These three terms can be defined in a mutually exclusive fashion, allowing trade-offs among categories to be seen and avoiding double counting of impacts. Exclusivity requires that environmental be written natural environmental and exclude human uses. The rationale for this exclusion of man from the environment is that it is important in project, program, and policy analysis to be able to distinguish major sets of impacts from each other. For many governmental actions, if the economic effects are positive, the effects on natural systems will be generally negative. To muddle the environmental category with human impacts would result in a reduction in the level of negative impacts in this first-level category, obscuring the trade-offs between economic benefits and environmental costs of development.[5]

Exclusivity also requires that social be defined as excluding gross monetary effects normally associated with economic development. It should include psychic and social impacts, however. In this way the impacts of developmental programs that increase national or regional aggregate economic worth but decrease income equality or solitude, for example, can be seen clearly. The point here is that one wants to be able to see if groups of project impacts are moving in different directions, if social is improving and economic is worsening, or economic is improving, social is improving, and environmental is worsening. See Table 1 for a sample listing of impact types grouped in this way.

The conceptual exclusivity of these three categories is also useful in maximizing their political relevance. Many major political battles of the sixties and early seventies have been over the trade-offs between aggregate economic values and social (distribution, quality of life) values and between aggregate economic values and natural environmental values. A recent conflict is that between natural environmental values and social (distribution) values. It is important to define these first-level account categories in a fashion that highlights and informs these conflicts and enhances the quality of the political bargaining process. Many interest groups can be expected to support one category pri-

Table 1 Politically Useful Impact Categories

Social	Economic	Natural Environmental
Aesthetics	Basic employment	Air quality
Belonging/respect	Congestion	Climate
Civil rights	Efficiency	Energy use
Community cohesion	Growth	Erosion
Desired growth rate	Incomes	Fauna
Displacement	Land values	Flora
Economic opportunity	Nonbasic employment	Natural amenities
Employment status	Service expenditures	Natural hazards
Food quality	Tax revenues	Noise
Health		Nonrenewable resources
Historic/archaeologic		Renewable resources
Housing quality		Smell
Integration		Water quality/quantity
Land tenure		
Level of services		
(school, transport, recreation, shopping . . .)		
Noise		
Personal development		
Political access		
Safety/security		
Spiritual experience		

marily in these battles. Rather than just increasing the political divisiveness in American society, politically relevant account categories would help weaker groups bargain (with better data) and help all groups see the issues clearly. Discussing and deciding issues on their merits (projected impacts based on best possible data) helps to bring about understanding among groups and facilitates consensus formation.

Intangible values will lie chiefly within the social category and, thereby, through comparison receive an equal aggregated portrayal with the economic and the environmental data. The intangible values in life will receive greater attention if they are concentrated into one account grouping. Most economic impacts will be quantified monetary and most environmental impacts will be quantified nonmonetary. This general alignment of major impact categories with types of measures available will help highlight one of the major value issues of contemporary Western society: the need to reassert the importance of nonmaterial values and, more broadly, the need to expand our reliance on sensual and ethical forms of experience and knowledge.[6]

Calculation of Incidence of Impacts; Examples from Planning

A role of impact information in government that is closely related to measuring overall welfare achievement and program effectiveness is the role of measuring the distribution of welfare among citizens. The principle of equal opportunity for all is inherent in democratic theory. Increasingly in this country since the 1920s, we have realized that the large scale of public and private organizations required for (narrowly defined) efficiency, the speculative nature of our entrepreneurial economy, and the speed of technological change all have subjected great numbers of people to temporary or permanent unemployment. This realization has created an awareness of the disadvantaged one-third of our population that has not benefitted relatively from the economic progress of the twentieth century. Increasingly, impact information serves the purpose of assessing the impacts of programs on various disadvantaged groups who, as such social-technical events such as air pollution emerge, begin to include the economically advantaged as well.

American society is composed of many conflicting interests. The distribution of welfare outcomes, both costs and benefits, is a major concern of theorists, applied researchers, agency planners, decision makers, and these publics themselves. Increasingly, information systems must not only show project impacts on disadvantaged groups, but also on all relevant economic, social, and political groups affected by the proposed actions.

Bromley, Schmid, and Lord in 1971 recommended that broad information display accounts be used in water resources planning.[7] They state that secondary impacts and intangibles are important in water resources decisions and that "meaningful impact assessments are only possible when tied to specific groups of individuals, and to specific regions" (p. 28). They reject the current WRC approach of portraying information by objectives, because objectives are not agreed upon early in project politics and the false imposition of a priori objectives does not enhance discussion by interest groups. They argue that impacts must be exhaustively displayed by groups.

In 1960 Lichfield formulated his "planning balance sheet" which portrays impacts on groups in a rigorous fashion for the first time.[8] An urban economist, Lichfield views urban planning as a supra-investment activity: As a result of city plans, government agencies invest money in public works developments. Therefore, city planning requires a welfare test to assist in decision making. According to Lichfield, urban planning is more complex than government infrastructure investment, requiring intuition in the design of complex alternatives, consideration of many intangibles, and the enforcement of laws requiring public and private agents to internalize indirect costs of their activities.

A city plan is used to illustrate his planning balance sheet. The city plan is a set of goals and objectives and a land use map indicating future government investments. A cost-benefit analysis describes the costs and benefits of fulfilling the city plan and their incidence on various "sectors [users] of the community." The analysis can be of net impacts (future with plan minus future without plan) or of gross impacts (future with plan minus present) (p. 276. This is a current definitional problem in impact reporting under NEPA.). Generally, a 20- to 25-year time horizon will be used. Direct and indirect costs and benefits are included, as are one-time and annual, and tangible and intangible.

Lichfield briefly enunciates his concern for incidence of impacts by stating that effects should be spelled out in social accounts by the major groupings of producers and consumers (p. 277). Producers can be disaggregated into three groups: town development agencies, landowners, and municipal government. Consumers may be broken into those buying services individually (residents, businesses, and industries) and those buying services collectively (e.g., consumers of parks and roads) (p. 278).

The planning balance sheet as applied to a city plan was reported by Lichfield in 1969.[9] This study is especially useful in this discussion, because it analyzes several sketch plans for the expansion of Peterborough, England. Sketch plans of a medium-sized city present two problems for the analyst. First, the range of social, economic, and environmental attributes is great and second, the specificity of the impact estimates will be low, since the plans are preliminary. This situation is very similar to large-scale public works project proposals in the United States where impact reporters are asked to identify impacts with almost no solid research on which to derive their estimates for a wide range of effects.

The town of Peterborough was designated in a regional plan to double its size from 80,000 to roughly 160,000 in the year 2000. Five hypothetical plans were outlined involving different arrangements of new villages, streets, town centers, and industrial areas. Residential, industrial, commercial, and open-space acreages were very similar in the five plans. The sectors of the community were designated as "producers/operators" and "consumers" of the urban development. These two groups were then broken down into sectors, according to the operations performed. Then costs and benefits were estimated. The analysis was rapidly done and is quite judgemental. It had to be related to the physical/spatial plans so that the conclusions could be implemented in physical modifications of the best alternative or alternatives. The sectors were disaggregated as follows:

Producers/Operators	Consumers
1.0 The Development Agency	2.0 The Public
	2.2 In central areas and secondary centers
	2.2.1 New occupiers
	2.2.2 Users of central area facilities
	2.2.3 Stopping traffic
	2.2.4 Pedestrians
	2.4 In principal residential areas
	2.4.1 New occupiers
	2.6 In principal industrial areas
	2.6.1 New occupiers
	2.6.2 Working public
	2.8 In principal open space and recreation areas
	2.8.1 Users of regional open space
	2.8.2 Users of country facilities
	2.10 On principal communication system
	2.10.1 Vehicle users
	2.10.2 Public transport
	2.10.3 Pedestrians
	2.12 Town as a whole
3.0 Current Landowners	4.0 Current Occupiers
3.1 Displaced	4.2 Displaced
3.2 Not displaced	4.4 Not displaced
5.0 Local Authorities	6.0 Ratepayers [taxpayers]

SOURCE.   adapted from Note 9, p. 130, with several subcategories of 2.10.1 omitted. The numbers are identifiers.

Note that this portrayal allows the comparison of costs and benefits accruing to producers and consumers of employment, housing, shopping, recreation, and transportation.

Next, "instrumental objectives" were defined for each sector "being the requirements in respect to operations they wish to perform against which people within the sectors would judge the quality of the expanded town" (p. 132). For example, the instrumental objective for the development agency is minimum net cost of land acquisition, main services, building construction, site engineering, and returns.[10] Sample instrumental objectives for new occupiers in central areas and secondary centers are overall benefit, location, suitability of structure for occupation, and general environment. Several specific measures are given for each of these instrumental objectives. For example, suitability of the structure for occupation is measured by amount of space, arrangement of the space, and provision for specialized requirements.

Schaenman and Muller present a simpler framework for displaying impacts on clientele groups in an urban setting. They select groups by: physical proximity to the project, business relationship to project, political jurisdiction, social/demographic class, and other interests.[11] See Table 2 for an illustrative impact display by groups.

As another example of interest group identification, Bromley, Schmid, and Lord,[12] in their study of water resources project evaluation, designate producer groups of: project farmers, nonproject farmers, agricultural suppliers, agricultural processors, recreation services, and business and industry. Consumer groups are: warm water fishermen, cold water fishermen, bird hunters, big game hunters, power boat users, white water boaters, and hikers. This example provides groups very different from those used in Lichfield's urban analysis.

These three examples should make it clear that analysis of incidence requires a detailed understanding of the social and economic systems that are being modified to identify relevant groups. Portrayal of impacts by major political objectives (social, economic, environmental) will serve to aid in understanding the overall effects of projects on major societal values and on agency objectives; impacts also need to be broken out by incidence on population groups as we have illustrated if meaningful political participation is to occur and if project design is to be modified to mitigate adverse impacts.

Issue Orientation in Impact Analysis

Presumably, analysis of impact incidence will help in orienting project analyses toward political issues. As impact evaluation is carried out, however, certain

Table 2 Impacts on interest groups. From *Measuring Impacts of Land Development*; copyright © 1974 by the Urban Institute. Used by permission

Hypothetical Proposal: 20-story office building with shopping plaza replacing tenement housing

		IMPACT ON CLIENTELE GROUPS[2]			COMPLIANCE WITH COMPREHENSIVE PLANS
		A. Local Jurisdiction (50,000 people)	B. Immediate Neighborhood (500 people)	C. Low-Income Families in the Jurisdiction (5,000 people)	
IMPACT AREA	MEASURE[1]				
Local Economy	(1) Change in net fiscal flow	+ $200,000 to $300,000	N/A[3]	N/A	N/A
	(4) Net number of new jobs	+200 to 300 jobs	+10 to 20 jobs	+50 to 70 jobs	Yes
Aesthetics	(15) Number of people whose views will be blocked	300 to 400 people	250 to 300 people	250 to 300 people	N/A
	(16) Percent people (in random survey) finding development attractive	75% (of sample)	40% (of sample)	N/A	Partly Yes, Partly No. (General opinion is in compliance, local opinion is not.)

Air Pollution	(7) Number of additional people expected to be exposed to x p.p.m. for over y hours more than z times a year	+4000 to 8000 people	+ 300 to 500 people	N/A	No
Local Transportation	(37) Change in average auto travel time to reach destination x in neighborhood	+3 to 5 min.	+3 to 5 min.	N/A	No
Housing Stock	(42) Change in number of housing	-50 substandard units	-50 substandard units	-50 substandard units	Partly Yes (removal of substandard housing) Partly No (accommodations for displaced families)
Neighborhood Stability	(48) Number of residents displaced	150	150	130	Yes

1. Numbers in parentheses refer to measures in Exhibit 1.

2. See Chapter IV for a discussion of clientele group interests. These are illustrative of only a few clientele groups; others would also be pertinent. Note that some of the same people may be in groups A, B, and C.

3. An estimate of whether the remaining families in the neighborhood will pay more or less property taxes due to changes in property value might be given here.

Reprinted by permission from *Measuring Impacts of Land Development*, Philip S. Schaenman and Thomas Muller, 1974, Washington, D.C.: The Urban Institute.

classes of impacts will show themselves to be controversial. These impacts will then have to be analyzed in more detail.

Again, Lichfield's work provides us with a good example of focusing impact research on those variables of concern in the political process.[13] He re-analyzes the data used by the Roskill Commission to evaluate potential sites for the Third London Airport. In Lichfield's secondary analysis several issues are revealed that were covered up by the benefit-cost data as presented in the commission's reports. For example, the farthest site from London is shown to be the most expensive in terms of travel costs but will displace fewer people than the other alternatives. Since this is the largest value trade-off among alternatives, Lichfield investigated the travel cost calculations in greater depth and shows that most of these costs are passed on in transfers from businesses to customers and that the final incidence of these costs is very low. No sector is badly hurt, a politically relevant finding.

Another revealing analysis is the recalculation of all costs and benefits on a per-household basis, rather than evaluating the aggregated national data. This analysis ranked the sites very differently from the commission's study, primarily because of the heavy cost burden placed on a relatively small number of displaced households in the alternatives that were in built-up areas. The whole point of these two exercises is to show that when one item in an analysis is the crucial one because of its large absolute size, it should be analyzed very carefully. This is a management efficiency principle: Spend your money researching impacts of political importance.

For agencies to do issue-oriented analyses, at least two rounds of planning and analysis must occur to allow the impacts identified in the first round to have an effect politically. Then a second round of research would investigate the areas of concern where data was important scientifically or politically. Performing issue-oriented analysis and determining incidence of impacts both require that planning be done in a cyclical fashion so that impact reporting can be refined after an initial impact study. We return to this point later.

Now to summarize, we have impacts portrayed by objectives (social, economic, environmental) and by groups. The next step in impact analysis is to identify trade-offs among alternative plans. Each alternative will produce a different mix of benefits and costs falling on the objectives and the groups. A major problem in project evaluation is that some values will be monetary, some will be quantified nonmonetary, and some will be qualitative. Methods are needed for portraying data so that values are accurately described and overall evaluation is not biased toward quantified values.

ACCURATE DATA REPRESENTATION

When analysts are faced with alternatives that have value attributes measured on different dimensions, they generally try to aggregate data into fewer categories through the use of various techniques. Complex decisions cannot be made into mechanical (technical) ones, however. Staff can only hope to reduce the data to an understandable level of complexity without obscuring important distinctions. There is great disagreement on the degree to which data should be reduced by the use of technical decision rules.

We now examine two ranking and weighting schemes that have been recently suggested as methods for comparing social values with economic and environmental values in decision making. These are single dimensionality techniques (they reduce all values to 1 unit of measure), and they represent a current thrust in multiobjective evaluation research.

Inaccurate Data Representation through Pseudoquantification

Sonnen in 1970 developed an additive weighting methodology for including nonmonetary attribute values in the evaluation of water resources projects.[14] The procedure determines nonmonetary project values by multiplying monetary project outputs (determined through typical economic methods) by coefficients. The suggested coefficients are listed in a series of tables by nine major economic benefit categories: flood control, fuel and mineral mining, irrigation, navigation, power generation, recreation, land development, timber harvesting, and water supply. Each of these categories is broken down into several subfactors, such as number of people served, and subcoefficients are assigned according to the attribute level of each subfactor. For example, in flood control 10^3 people served annually get a subcoefficient of 0.0, 10^3–10^4 people 0.1, 10^4–10^5 people get 0.2, 10^5–10^6 0.3, and 10^6 people 0.4. Subcoefficients are determined similarly for other aspects of flood control, such as scope of protected landowner's influence. Each subfactor has corresponding subcoefficients ranging from 0.0–0.4. When all subcoefficients have been assigned for flood control, they are added, giving a coefficient totalling between 0.0 and 1.0 for some factors, 0.0 and 1.2 for others, 0.0 and 2.5 for others, and so on. Recreation is broken out into the separate factors, all totalling a potential of 23.0. After coefficients have been determined for the nine categories, monetary benefits in each category are multiplied by the coefficient in that category and the result is a monetary equivalent of nonmonetary benefits. These are then entered into the economic analysis.

The Sonnen approach is conceptually weak. It relies on a series of questionable assumptions concerning public values and is based on the novel logic that nonmonetary benefits of water projects are proportionate to the monetary benefits, prima facia. Other criticisms are that the social and economic costs of projects are ignored in the accounts and benefits are double-counted through the use of conceptually overlapping categories. No theoretical or empirical basis is provided for assigning the category or subcategory weights.

Whitman et al. in 1971 produced another additive weighting scheme for the

Bureau of Reclamation (BOR).[15] This environmental evaluation system assigned 1000 environmental quality units to the total environment. Four subcategories were specified and maximum units assigned: ecology (315), environmental pollution (321), aesthetics (159), and human interest (205). A total of 17 subcategories are identified and units attached. There are 66 parameters identified for the 17 subcategories with units assigned. The measures for the parameters are poorly described. Therefore, an evaluation is not reliably replicable. The report states the need for further research to determine value functions for the 66 parameters and to determine more reliable weights through interviewing of bureau personnel, experts, and politicians. The interviews would involve a stepwise pair comparison technique.

The Whitman approach ignores a variety of problems. Why would one set of weights apply to all BOR projects, ones in deserts and ones in swamps? Why aggregate values into one environmental value when it will still need to be evaluated against social and economic values? This system is fraught with interpretive problems such as how to account for positively cumulative effects or cancelling effects of changes induced by a project. The analytical framework is highly reductionist.

Before discussing our recommendations for accurate data portrayal/decision analysis methods, let us summarize the problems associated with deterministic approaches to data evaluation such as those we have reviewed. There are two general problems of evaluation: First, the inability of individuals to state their value preferences in an independent and comprehensive fashion befuddles analysts. Even if someone could tell you their value preferences in a sufficiently exhaustive and mutually exclusive fashion at one point in time, their preferences would change over time. Certainly, their values would vary according to each concrete decision situation.

The second difficulty with rigorous evaluation of public projects is that some social aggregate must be constructed mathematically. As Arrow has shown, it is logically meaningless to assert a statistical happiness (utility) function for three persons, much less a whole society.[16]

Another fundamental problem is the difficulty encountered in the measurement of attribute values and in determining the relationships among different attributes in a decision model. A water resources task force recently concluded that the quantification of attributes and multiattribute relationships would be an endless task, with the possibility of establishing some relationships being "extremely doubtful."[17]

An example of the perennial problems facing the comprehensive decision modelers is the additive weighting problem. When different attribute values are summed, often certain very low values get averaged out and are not observed in the later stages of the analysis. Sometimes these low values are critical. Therefore, the evaluation scheme must be modified to "flag" values going below specified amounts. Multiplicative weighting takes care of this problem, because low values lower the aggregate value, but much greater care must be taken in establishing the weights.

Another thorny conceptual problem general to evaluation schemes is the problem of encompassing enough values. Generally, you can determine which project to select, but you never know if any of the alternatives is good enough, according to some higher-level criterion or opportunity cost. An increasing body of discussion in the economics literature has criticized benefit-cost analysis as technically inadequate for multiobjective project evaluation and seriously questions its use for anything more than a contributing study in a broader evaluation program. Other economists have questioned the validity of using benefit-cost techniques at all in politically important and socially complex decisions.

Weaknesses of Benefit-Cost Analysis

Mishan undercuts the value of benefit-cost analysis in his review of the much-criticized Third London Airport Study of 1970, perhaps the most exhaustive civilian benefit-cost study ever undertaken in the world.[18] He questions the usefulness of economic techniques, because they are so inevitably biased toward the display and analysis of market effects (monetary values). This inherent characteristic of economic analysis seriously biases not only the kinds of benefits and costs considered, but also their summation, since benefits are generally monetary and costs are often intangible. Mishan finds greatest fault with the inability of benefit-cost analysis techniques to deal effectively with the issue of quality of life not only in balanced consideration of intangibles, but also in considering the equity effects of projects—the politically important information concerning which interest groups receive the benefits or costs.[19]

Self, a professor of public administration, also responding to the Roskill Commission's benefit-cost analysis, states in stronger language that the inadequacy of benefit-cost procedures must be realized to counteract "the existing tendency to convert genuine political and social issues into bogus technical ones."[20] He scores the commission's figures as arbitrary and unintelligible to the average citizen or even educated persons. Self calls for political judgments debated in the public arena in a planning context, which he defines as "a coordinated framework of policy considerations. . . ."(p. 10).

Hamill states the problem with economic evaluation methods in broader terms.[21] He argues that economic theory, with its reliance on mistaken (or at best, arbitrary) assumptions about human behavior and quantification, is not as useful in resources evaluation as is decision theory such as found in management science. Decision theory, he says, was based on the operations of organizations with multiple goals, not on the profit maximization concept, irrelevant to resource management. Hamill also argues that economics techniques are difficult to comprehend if not intentionally obscure and are, therefore, inimical to public participation.

Citing earlier work by Cyert, Simon, and Trow, he states that economic models ignore: (1) the need to search for alternatives (the design process), (2) the need to search for consequences (impacts), (3) the need for multi-attribute decision criteria involving many intangibles, and often (4) the need to define the problems themselves.[22] He goes on to say that the theoretical approach used by economists often limits their work to a descriptive formalism. Resource managers need analysis systems that work every time, flexible systems that account for particular values involved in each decision. Another failing of economics is the lack of concern for information costs and for the psychological processes of information assimilation and transmission engaged in by decision makers. Hamill urges resource managers to drop their reliance on economics and to use the empirically derived techniques of administration science, known as planning.

We now examine an innovative recent development in information portrayal where these concepts of planning have been applied to produce accurate balanced data about project effects. Our concern is with methods by which value comparisons can be made without overrepresenting the accuracy of the data or biasing against intangibles.

Accurate Data Portrayal by Lichfield

We again use Lichfield's work, this time as an example of accurate data portrayal, because it is the most detailed one found in commonly available journals. Regarding measurement of impacts, Lichfield states that it is "not strictly necessary in a city planning cost-benefit analysis." Their precise description with an indication of incidence would of itself help decision making, for it would give a framework within which all relevant arguments for and against a planning proposal could be organized.[23] Effects should be measured as well as possible, however, to allow precise description, comparison with standards or the degree of the problem, and accurate comparison of costs with benefits. When the first analysis is done, all available data is used, monetary, quantitative nonmonetary, and qualitative. If a qualitative item emerges as an important factor, more research will then be done. This is a mixed scanning management approach, one that minimizes information costs.

The costs and benefits are arranged in double entry and a summary account is derived that offsets monetary costs against monetary benefits and sums any quantifiable nonmonetary costs and benefits that are in the same units. This summarization does not aggregate impacts falling on consumer and producer groups. These are left in the final summary accounts as the major categories.

The choice of city plan is determined by the cost-benefit information and within the constraints of higher level government decisions made by legislative bodies and by courts of law. Two considerations are important in evaluating the planning balance sheet information: first, the total costs and benefits in terms of efficiency, and second, the distribution of the effects in terms of the government's principles of equity. Complex value judgments will be necessary, since benefit-cost ratios will rarely be possible, given the intangibles.

Lichfield extends his theory in several later articles, but we follow only those concerned with city planning, since these are complex multiattribute decisions which test his methodology best. In 1968 he differentiates his planning balance sheet from economic analysis per se.[24] He starts with a critique of economic theory and practice. Economic theory, according to Lichfield, is weak on handling the economics of space, although recent work by urban and regional geographers is filling the gap. Economics has only recently begun major theory work on the analysis of the public sector. The chief failing of economic theory and practice is its inability to analyze performance relating to social objectives, such as income distribution, for example. His next criticism was discussed earlier in this chapter, the problem of interpersonal comparisons of utility. Lichfield states that "after decades of heart searching and controversy" welfare economists have failed to "reach conclusions on objective measurements of interpersonal comparisons of utility and, therefore, whether people would be better off or worse off by changes proposed in a plan" (p. 10). Finally, economists have been unable to develop rules for political choice because of the noneconomic values involved. For these reasons, he urges that town planners use economic techniques with care in a broader framework.

This framework should be one "which brings out to the decisionmakers the features with which they, as opposed to the professionals, must be concerned in their choices" (p. 13). This evaluation scheme should help the community understand what resources it will be giving up to get what values, what kind of life, for which sectors in the community. These decisions should be "open and defensible" (p. 19).

An example of the notation used by Lichfield for impacts that can only be ordinally ranked (greater than, or lesser than) is found in the Peterborough Plan, reviewed previously for its handling of incidence of impacts.[25] The handling of effects where no quantitative data was available in the Peterborough Plan evaluation was done by using letters: Capital Ms for capital monetary costs, lower case ms for annual monetary costs and benefits, ts for time costs and benefits, ps for physical effects, and is for intangibles. Signs $(+, -)$ denote directions of change (benefit or cost). Relative magnitudes are indicated in crude ordinal ranking fashion by the use of additional signs. M is less than $M+$ is less than $M++$, and so on, up to four signs; similarly for ms, ts, ps, and is. Subscripts were used to identify each item. This ordinal scaling of nonquantified impacts proves to be very useful in his example analyses. Often, only a few data are important enough to require further research.

Lichfield, in his more recent works, allows for placing weights on sectors of the community. Benefits and costs are then multiplied by these weights. Although this procedure may be possible in England with its greater faith in social planning and political leadership, it would not be wise in most political situations in this country. The setting of the intergroup weights would absorb all the political activity in major decisions, perhaps causing stalemating. The principle of making these weights explicit is valid. Each decision maker, however, has to decide these weights individually. There is no reason to believe that the weights would be similar among deciders.

In summary then, we conclude that many intangible impacts cannot be given quantitative values through the use of coefficients or shadow pricing or any other techniques in a scientifically valid way. Impacts should be left in a matrix, with only the monetary ones summed at the bottom. Decision makers will have to read the report and examine the disaggregated data set and decide on the value trade-offs themselves in choosing a "best" alternative.

Once a project or plan is chosen, we want to assume that its implementation will include all necessary measures for mitigating adverse impacts. Ways of relating negative effects to mitigative actions are needed.

LINKING ADVERSE IMPACTS TO MITIGATIVE ACTIONS

NEPA indirectly requires the discussion of mitigative actions in sections 101(B)(3),(5), and (6). The CEQ guidelines require consideration of project alternatives and design modifications that reduce or avoid adverse impacts, finding their authority in NEPA section 102(2)(C)(iii) which requires detailed consideration of alternatives to the proposed action.[26]

The U.S. District Court in Sierra Club v. Froehlke stated that courts may require further agency consideration of mitigation when efforts were not made or were "half-hearted."[27] The court held that "genuine efforts" had not been made by the Army Corps of Engineers to "mitigate any of the major impacts" resulting from the proposed Wallisville Dam, and for this and many other reasons enjoined the dam and all others in the Trinity River Basin (Texas) pending the preparation of a sufficiently detailed EIS on the Wallisville Dam and for all other major dams in the Trinity River Basin, which documents must be reviewed by Congress, the CEQ, and relevant federal agencies (sec. J., Summary and Holding). The Army Corps' current EIS guidelines state that "the feasibility and cost of eliminating or minimizing adverse effects" will be given "full consideration" when effects are significant. Adverse effects can also be compensated for with "counterbalancing" measures.[28]

CEQA requires that mitigation measures be included in EIRs.[29] Whereas this addition is beneficial in terms of the informational usefulness of the California Act, there is no requirement in the act or the state CEQA guidelines for ensuring that the mitigative actions in fact take place. Experience to date indicates that NEPA and CEQA statements have lacked consideration of mitigative actions.[30]

Even if mitigative actions were fully described in impact reports, there are generally no mechanisms for ensuring that they are undertaken, a point discussed earlier by Coop. Since agencies adopt their own impact reports, they can ignore many of the mitigative actions described in the reports when the project is undertaken. Agencies that fund projects such as the FHWA and agencies that permit projects such as the Forest Service does with timber leases often make the funding or permission conditioned upon the performance of the specified mitigative actions. Agencies that undertake their own projects directly, such as the Army Corps, however, can ignore the mitigative actions described in their EISs if they so desire. The EPA and CEQ do not enforce mitigation. One court has stated that this view, that mitigations should be "inextricably linked" to projects, has merit.[31]

If NEPA is to protect the environment, EISs must identify mitigative actions and legal techniques of assuring that the mitigative actions occur. Projects must be approved on the condition that mitigations actually occur. The need for effectuating plans for environmental protection was stated by Heyman and Twiss in 1971.[32] This issue is ignored in the various legal and technical reviews of NEPA.[33] Let us, then, examine the recent development of techniques for linking adverse impacts to mitigative actions and mitigative actions to legal effectuation mechanisms. Whereas our examples are concerned with natural environmental impacts, the most developed field in impact reporting, the techniques are transferable to the analysis of social impacts.

The first widely popularized impact matrix was developed by McHarg in 1969.[34] This matrix relied on earlier work done by landscape architects and planners and less directly on more remote work done by economists and mathematicians. The McHarg matrix, Figure 8.1, relates land use categories to land use categories to show intercompatibility of adjacent land uses, relates natural determinants to land use categories to show the development capability of various environments, and relates land use categories to consequences to show the impacts of land uses. This matrix uses four levels of severity in its ratings, using symbols (the visual method). McHarg's matrix is useful for its compression of so much information onto one page. It includes a land use conflicts matrix, a development site competition matrix, and an environmental impact matrix all in one. Mitigative actions to reduce adverse consequences are not included in the matrix; however, McHarg's approach can be adapted, as we will see subsequently.

Category			Urban	Suburban residential	Industrial	Institutional	shaft-mined coal	active opencast coal	abandoned coal spoil
Consequences	Soil erosion		▶	▶	□	◁	□	▶	□
	Floor and drought control		▶	▶	▶	◁	○	□	◁
	Stream sedimentation		▶	▶	□	◁	□	▶	◁
	Water pollution		▶	□	▶	◁	□	▶	◁
	Air pollution		▶	◁	▶	○	○	○	○
Natural determinants	Climate	temperature extremes	▶	□	□	□	○	○	○
		fog susceptibility	□	□	◁	□	○	○	○
	Water supply dependability		○	○	○	◁	○	○	▶
	Aquifer recharge areas		▶	□	▶	◁	▶	▶	▶
	Soils	silts							
		loams							
		sands							
		gravels							
	Vehicular accessibility		○	◁	○	◁	○	○	▶
	Slope	over 25%	▶	□	▶	□	◁	□	▶
		15-25%	□	◁	▶	◁	○	○	◁
		0-5%	◁	○	□	○	◁	○	○
			○	○	○	○	□	□	○
Intercompatibility of land uses	Water management	watershed management							
		reservoir							
	Recreation	driving for pleasure							
		cultural recreation							
		general recreation							
		wilderness							
		freshwater oriented							
		saltwater oriented							
	Forestry	hardwood							
		uneven-stand softwood							
		even-stand softwood							
	Agriculture	livestock							
		arable							
		row crops							
	Vacation settlement								
	Quarrying	sand and gravel							
		stone and limestone							
	Mining	abandoned coal spoil							○
		active opencast coal						○	
		shaft-mined coal					○		
	Institutional					○	▶	▶	◁
	Industrial				○	▶	○	○	○
	Suburban residential			○	▶	○	▶	▶	□
	Urban		○	◁	○	□	▶	▶	▶

Quarrying — stone and limestone; sand and gravel
Vacation settlement
Agriculture — row crops; arable; livestock
Forestry — even-stand softwood; uneven-stand softwood; hardwood
Recreation — saltwater oriented; freshwater oriented; wilderness; general recreation; cultural recreation; driving for pleasure
Water management — reservoir; watershed management

▶	Incompatible
□	Low compatibility
△	Medium compatibility
○	Full compatibility

▶	Bad
□	Poor
△	Fair
○	Good

Figure 8.1 From *Design With Nature*, copyright © 1969 by Ian McHarg. Used by permission of Doubleday & Company, Inc.

301

Leopold et al. in 1971 produced a widely copied environmental impact matrix.[35] This matrix, partially reproduced in Figure 8.2 places existing characteristics and conditions of the environment on the left edge and proposed actions which may cause environmental impact along the top. Starting with the first action and running down its column, the impact reporter places a slash in each box where an impact is possible on the corresponding component of the environment. This checkoff is done for all actions and all components of the environment. Numbers from −10 to +10 (no zero) are placed in the upper left corner of each box to indicate the (objective) magnitude (scale, degree) of the impact and in the lower right corner to indicate the (subjective) importance (in the ecosystem) of the impact. A narrative report accompanies the matrix, describing the impacts in detail. The matrix serves as a checklist of causes and effects to help arrive at a complete identification of impacts. No mitigative actions are identified in the matrix, although the authors discuss the usefulness of this summary portrayal method in identifying the most significant impacts in need of mitigation (pp. 12–13).

The following three reports are all derived from the work of Robert Twiss at the University of California at Berkeley. In 1971 Corwin wrote a paper giving an excellent critique of NEPA procedures in use by agencies.[36] She recommended that mitigative actions be stated as requirements in the EIR and accompanied by criteria specifying levels of required mitigation and a monitoring program to ensure that the criteria were met (p. 11).

Twiss and Streatfield in 1971 integrated these concepts, identification of mitigative actions and identification of requirements to ensure that the mitigative actions are undertaken, into the matrix impact identification process, thus increasing the ability of impact reporters to systematically identify mitigative actions and effectuation requirements.[37] Two matrices are used. The first, Figure 8.3, relates types of developments to common actions on the environment, allowing impact reporters to deduce categories of operationally useful environmental alterations from land use types. Their second matrix, Figure 8.4, relates these common actions on the environment to environmental variables in the manner of the Leopold et al. matrix. In addition to identifying environmental impacts, however, the Twiss-Streatfield matrix allows the identification of potential control mechanisms, and types of monitoring to ensure mitigation of adverse impacts (pp. 39–40). The matrix does not identify mitigative actions per se, but they can be inferred from the control mechanisms.

Sorenson in 1971 elaborated the concept of systematic description of mitigation and control mechanisms.[38] His matrix relates land uses to immediate effects to short-term effects to long-term effects to corrective actions and control mechanisms. The portrayal framework, Figure 8.5, does not, however, allow for multicausal analysis of cumulatively caused short-term effects, long-term effects, corrective actions, or control mechanisms. These events are all identified in a linear fashion from the immediate effects list.

We suggest a portrayal format, schematically shown in Figure 8.6, that allows the stepped identification of uses, immediate actions, short-term effects, medium-term effects, and long-term effects. Multiple interrelations are also identified for the documentation of impacts, the identification of corrective or preventive actions for sets of impacts, the identification of required controls for sets of mitigative actions, and the identification of monitoring processes for sets of impacts to determine if mitigation is adequate. Whereas the use of stepped matrices reduces immediate public understandability, they are very useful as staff devices to ensure the systematic consideration of multicausal impacts and responses.[39] Whereas the examples we have examined confine their interests to natural processes, the methods will work just as well for identifying actions to mitigate adverse economic and social impacts.

For the portrayal of mitigative actions, required controls, and monitoring processes to have any effect in protecting the environment, agencies must adopt plans that include: long-term monitoring procedures and funds for this monitoring activity; provision for performance bonds to be posted by construction contractors to ensure that mitigative actions will be taken during construction; and performance conditions on the construction, operation, and maintenance of the project which allow intervention and cessation of activities by the agency in charge or by higher authorities, such as the courts (through citizen or agency suits).

There are many precedents for this type of conditional project approval. The Forest Service typically leases lands for timber production conditioned by long lists of performance requirements. They typically monitor logging operations to ensure that the contract conditions are met. State air quality and water quality control districts throughout the United States permit activities that can potentially pollute, conditioned on their meeting certain emission (effluent) requirements and conditioned on the maintenance of certain ambient environmental quality levels. The lack of concern for requiring mitigative actions in project approvals is the weakest aspect of current agency procedure under NEPA in this author's opinion.

CONCLUSIONS

We have suggested several methods whereby social impact data can be related to other impact data in ways that will increase its political relevance and its accuracy. We have also recommended a technique to aid in identifying actions needed to mitigate adverse social, economic, or environmental impacts. Clearly,

INSTRUCTIONS

1- Identify all actions (located across the top of the matrix) that are part of the proposed project.

2- Under each of the proposed actions, place a slash at the intersection with each item on the side of the matrix if an impact is possible.

3- Having completed the matrix, in the upper left-hand corner of each box with a slash, place a number from 1 to 10 which indicates the MAGNITUDE of the possible impact; 10 represents the greatest magnitude of impact and 1, the least, (no zeroes). Before each number place a + if the impact would be beneficial. In the lower right-hand corner of the box place a number from 1 to 10 which indicates the IMPORTANCE of the possible impact (e. g. regional vs. local); 10 represents the greatest importance and 1, the least (no zeroes).

4- The text which accompanies the matrix should be a discussion of the significant impacts, those columns and rows marked with large numbers of boxes marked and individual boxes with the larger numbers.

SAMPLE MATRIX

	a	b	c	d	e
a	2\1	8\8		3\3	9\5
b	7\2	8\1		9\1	1\7

A. MODIFICATION OF REGIME

a. Exotic flora or fauna introduction
b. Biological controls
c. Modification of habitat
d. Alteration of ground cover
e. Alteration of ground water hydrology
f. Alteration of drainage
g. River control and flow modification
h. Canalization
i. Irrigation
j. Weather modification
k. Burning
l. Surface or paving
m. Noise and vibration

B. LAND TRANSFORMATION AND CONSTRUCTION

a. Urbanization
b. Industrial sites and buildings
c. Airports
d. Highways and bridges
e. Roads and trails
f. Railroads
g. Cables and lifts
h. Transmission lines, pipelines and corridors
i. Barriers including fencing
j. Channel dredging and straightening
k. Channel revetments
l. Canals
m. Dams and impoundments
n. Piers, seawalls, marinas, and sea terminals
o. Offshore structures
p. Recreational structures
q. Blasting and drilling
r. Cut and fill
s. Tunnels and underground structures

Figure 8.2 Leopold et al. impact matrix. U.S. Department of the Interior, Geological Survey (portion)

DIRECT ACTION

COMMON ACTIONS ON THE ENVIRONMENT

TYPE OF DEVELOPMENTS	Excavation, cutting	Earthmoving, filling	Paving	Building	Tiling, drainage improvement	Irrigation	Fertilization	Landscape planting	Fencing	Timber clearing, cutting	Chemical waste products	Biological waste products	Burning	Stream blockage	Stream channel straightening
Intensive (High density)	●	●	●	●	●	●	●	●	●	●	●	●			●
Medium density housing	●	●	●	●	●	●	●	●	●	●	●	●			
Low density housing	●	●	●	●	●	●	●	●	●	●	●	●			
Playgrounds	●	●	●	●	●	●	●	●	●	●		●			

Regional parks

Golf courses

Fishing

Commercial recreation
& tourism & resorts

Roads

Commercial timber

Grazing

Mining

Figure 8.3 Common development actions

Figure 8.4 — Effects on the environment

	ENVIRONMENTAL VARIABLES	Excavating (large scale)	Filling, Moving (large scale)	Paving	Building	Drainage improvements	Irrigating	Fertilizing	Landscaping (large scale)	Fencing	Timber clearing, harvesting	Chemical waste	Biological waste	Burning (slash, forest fire)	Grazing, mowing	Mining (sand/gravel)	Stream blocking	Stream channel improvement
GEOLOGY	landslide potential	●	●		●	●					●			●		●		
	settling, compacting loose material		●		●	●	●											
	deposition of sediment	●	●	●							●			●	●	●	●	●
	deposition of alluvium	●	●								●			●	●			
	reaction to seismic shock		●															
HYDROLOGY	total available water						●											
	timing, period or duration of flow		●	●	●	●	●				●			●	●			●
	high water level		●	●	●	●					●			●			●	●
	flood peak frequency		●	●	●	●					●			●				
	stream blockage (vegetation, damming)		●			●			●	●	●			●				
	suspended sediment	●	●		●						●			●		●	●	
	bedload	●	●								●			●		●	●	
	force, speed of flow			●	●	●					●			●			●	●
	runoff rate	●	●	●	●	●					●			●	●			
	water temperature		●				●				●			●			●	●
	chemical content (residue, salts)					●	●	●			●	●	●	●				
	clarity	●	●	●	●			●			●	●	●			●		
	pathogenic organisms							●				●	●	●				
	ground water flow, level	●	●	●	●	●	●				●			●				
SOIL	depth	●	●	●	●				●							●		
	consistency, density, compaction	●	●	●	●	●					●				●			
	fertility	●	●	●	●			●	●			●	●	●	●			
	water holding capacity	●	●	●	●	●	●											
	erosion hazard	●	●	●	●				●		●			●	●			
	permeability	●	●	●	●						●							
	shrink-swell behavior	●	●	●	●													
	corrosivity	●	●	●	●									●				
	reaction (pH, acidity/alkalinity)	●	●	●	●	●	●	●						●				
	soil-forming micro-organisms	●	●	●	●							●	●	●	●			
VEGETATION	type of plants	●	●	●	●	●	●	●	●		●			●	●		●	●
	amount of vegetation (biomass, fuel)	●	●	●	●	●	●	●	●		●			●	●		●	●
	plant community succession	●	●	●	●	●	●	●	●	●	●			●			●	●
	evapo-transpiration rate	●	●	●	●	●	●	●	●		●			●	●		●	●
	soil holding properties	●	●	●	●	●	●	●	●		●			●	●			
	plant pathology	●	●	●	●	●	●	●	●		●		●	●				
	food or cover properties	●	●	●	●	●	●	●	●		●			●	●		●	●
CLIMATE	temperature		●	●	●				●		●			●				
	humidity		●	●	●	●	●		●		●			●		●		
	wind speed		●	●	●				●		●			●				
	wind direction				●				●		●							
	precipitation and fog drip								●		●			●				
	fog cover, summer type																	
	fog cover, winter type		●		●	●											●	●
	insolation				●	●			●		●			●	●			
WILDLIFE	types of fish and wildlife	●	●	●	●		●	●	●		●	●		●	●	●	●	●
	number of fish and wildlife	●	●	●	●		●	●	●		●	●		●	●	●	●	●
	food-chain system	●	●	●	●	●	●	●			●	●		●	●	●	●	●
	behavior (predator/prey, home range)	●	●	●	●				●		●			●	●	●	●	●
	disease	●	●	●	●		●					●	●	●			●	●
VISUAL	form	●	●	●	●				●	●	●			●	●	●	●	●
	texture	●	●	●	●				●	●	●			●	●	●	●	●
	color (hue)	●	●	●	●				●		●			●	●	●	●	●
	color (brilliance)	●	●	●	●				●					●	●	●	●	●
	reflective property	●	●	●	●				●	●	●			●	●	●	●	●

Figure 8.4 Effects on the environment

TYPES OF MONITORING	POTENTIAL CONTROL MECHANISMS
engineering-geology-maps and reports detailed site studies	grading permits zoning hazard areas public acquisition geologic reports
stream gauging flood-plains mapping well drilling logs well production records	well permits grading permits impoundment permits watershed plans fish & game & health codes flood control legislation water quality legislation
agricultural soil surveys site surveys farm and ranch conservation plans post-fire rehabilitation	grading permits planting plans soil stabilization requirements soil report review
detailed maps range carrying capacity studies landscape analysis brush conversion plans timber management plans	state forest practice rules fire control codes landscape architecture review boards recommended plant lists logging plan review
detailed topoclimate studies air pollution monitoring weather records	air pollution codes development plan review highway location density zoning
wildlife census wildlife management plans	state fish and game codes firearm ordinances refuge development
seen-area mapping scenic classification detailed landscape analysis	scenic easements architectural review boards open-space acquisition

Figure 8.4 (Continued)

many of these methods require agency planning to expand to include a greater number of impact considerations.

Broader Planning Concern Needed

Agencies need to account for all impacts of proposed projects: social, economic, and environmental. Direct participation of potentially affected parties is necessary to identify many impacts, especially social ones. Many impacts, especially growth-inducing impacts, will have to be estimated over large areas and long periods of time.

Whereas economic effects may be more or less accurately represented by the present value method, social and natural impacts cannot. These noneconomic changes must be simply estimated for arbitrary time periods, such as: during construction, 0–10 years after completion, 11–30 years, 30–100 years, 100–500 years. This is similar to how nonmonetary impacts are currently described in EISs where "lives saved annually" are totalled for a 30-year period or "437 acres of open space preserved" is stated as a one-time benefit. Portraying the incidence of impacts on groups may also require that impacts be examined in space and time.

The need for planning and plan evaluation to take place in a regional context has been pointed out by Lichfield in his re-analysis of the Roskill Commission's data used in its evaluation of potential sites for the Third London Airport.[40] He criticized the commission for: failing to deal with the incidence of impacts, not including many important intangibles in their analysis, not indicating the need for broader studies such as a national airports plan and a national seaports plan, and not considering the airport proposals in the broader context of regional planning for southeast England. He argues that the planning balance sheet is a useful tool for dealing with incidence, intangibles, and contextual policy issues.

Lichfield criticized the omission of certain intangibles in the analysis, such as open space, wildlife, and secondary employment in the associated urban development. Especially lacking in the commission's very expensive study were considerations of mass transit linkage potentials and British seaport development possibilities, both of great importance. Lichfield argues that the analysis of such a massive undertaking is meaningless without a regional transportation plan. The commission was merely going to "recommend a site to cater for a growth of traffic at existing airports serving the London area" (p. 170, quoting from Hansard, Parliamentary Debates—House of Commons, Vol. 765, No. 121, Monday, May 20, 1968). This approach ignored the potentials for rerouting certain kinds of traffic to the several other airports already existing in the metropolitan area. In addition, the commission never considered whether any of the alternative sites were economically feasible at all.

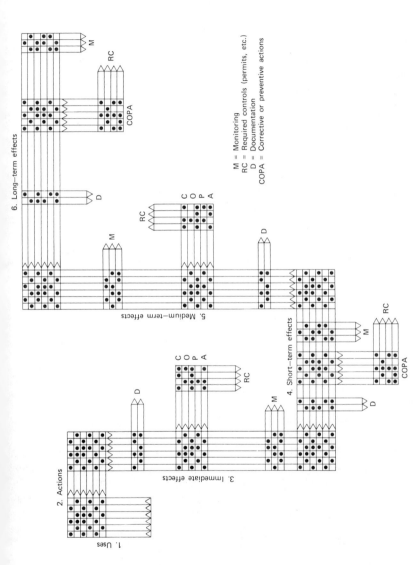

Figure 8.6 Matrix for identifying environmental impacts and controls to mitigate impacts. This matrix is derived from the R. Twiss and J. Sorenson versions (University of California, Berkeley, Department of Landscape Architecture). The evaluation phase follows this identification phase, where we identify changes by direction and magnitude. A new page is required for each alternative project (mix of uses and actions). Uses, actions, effects, and their interactions are numbered at intersections or along lines to reference accompanying discussions of the interactions and effects. All effect predictions are documented. All potentially negative effects have corrective and/or preventive actions specified to mitigate through controls which are also specified, linking impact identification to development and use controls in a nonarbitrary way

M = Monitoring
RC = Required controls (permits, etc.)
D = Documentation
COPA = Corrective or preventive actions

311

Lichfield contends that project evaluation cannot be performed meaningfully unless it is done in a planning context. The problems of narrow mandate and narrow benefit-cost analysis are evident from this example. His criticisms of the Roskill Commission apply to most major public works decisions made in the United States. Since the planning balance sheet is the best developed methodology striking close to our preferences for a flexible, open-ended, issues-oriented evaluation framework, we have reviewed its principles and application in some detail. This is essentially the approach recommended by the author and the senior editor in a report to the California Department of Water Resources in 1972.[41]

The Role of the Planner

The planner needs to provide accurate data, estimating impacts on all systems of concern politically or scientifically. The data should be in a framework so that trade-offs among values can be seen and understood by laypersons. This means that potential costs (negative impacts) must be researched with as much gusto as benefits are studied and that the incidence of impacts on groups must be spelled out. It is unlikely that personnel of the proponent agency will be allowed to conduct this kind of research, designed to bring out conflicts. Therefore, EISs should be prepared either by private groups or independent regulatory agencies not subject to direct lead agency influence. The latter would be the desirable solution to the problem of objectivity.

Whereas we propose that impacts be investigated in a flexible fashion with attention focused on those effects specific to the project and of most concern politically, we caution against a completely unstructured format. Agencies should utilize a broad outline of impact categories for all projects to allow citizen groups to master the techniques of analysis and to become experts in critiqueing the EISs. Likewise, the methods for calculating impacts in major categories should be standardized, insofar as is practical.

Groups may always come forth with additional impacts not identified by the agency and argue their importance. However, the use of one overall framework for analysis and portrayal of impacts will reduce political struggles over the rules of the game and focus attention on the project. Over a period of time groups will succeed in getting new categories of impacts added to the required list. The agency should formulate and publish detailed rules for estimating impacts in each category so that arguments can be specific. If agencies could change their EIS format and estimation methods with each new project, interest groups would never be able to contend with the agency on a technical basis. Continuity of analysis over time will benefit smaller advocacy groups with limited resources.

The planner, then, should provide a standard "menu" of information about projects plus additional information appropriate to the nature of the specific project plus information desired by participating interest groups. The issues that arise as the project analysis unfolds determine the additional research to be done to add new categories of data or to get more detailed estimates of certain subcategories of impacts.

The approach suggested here is a rough one for executives in administrative agencies to accept. High officials want to weather out all storms during their appointments and then retire or move up. Conflict reduction is the number one unwritten rule for bureaucrats. Planning to overtly resolve conflicts will have to be forced on most agencies by higher authorities, such as the courts, the legislature, and the executive. NEPA and many other statutes in the last few years have explicitly opened planning to public scrutiny. We can expect the trend to continue with the burden of proof shifting more and more to agencies to show why they should be able to undertake or permit projects that are environmentally or socially damaging. The costs of closed planning are high expenses for legal battles, long delays on projects, and reduced appropriations over the long run.

The planning processes of agencies must also be modified in the way that tasks are ordered. Planning with extensive input from the public requires that the traditional linear approach with only one project evaluation step be replaced by the cyclical model where plans are recycled after the first evaluation brings out the issues. Goals are reformulated, new alternatives are designed, criteria are set forth, and alternatives are reevaluated. This approach has been recommended by Boyce, Day, and McDonald, and by Manheim for transportation planning, and by Burke Heaney, and Pyatt for water resources planning.[42] If planning is performed in this way, public participation can have a significant effect on plans.

NOTES

1. P. L. 91-190, 42 U.S.C. 4321 et seq., Sec. 102.

2. Federal Register, Vol. 38, no. 147, Sec. 1500.8(B), Wed., Aug. 1, 1973.

3. Coy, J. G., R. A. Johnston, and P. J. Richerson, A Critique of Water Resources Council's Proposed Principles and Standards for the Planning of Water and Related Land Resources in C. R. Goldman, J. McEvoy, and P. J. Richerson, Eds., *Environmental Quality and Water Development,* W. H. Freeman, San Francisco, 1973.

4. U.S. Environmental Protection Agency, Quality of Life Indicators, p. 69, December, 1972.

5. Senate Document 97 (the previous water project evaluation policy) defined the natural preservation objective as being "apart from use."

6. See Erik H. Erickson, *Ghandi's Truth: On the Origins of Militant Nonviolence,* W. W.

Norton, New York, pp. 251—252, 1969, quoted in Richard S. Bolan, Generalist with a Speciality—Still Valid? Educating the Urban Planner: An Expert on Experts in *Planning 1971,* American Society of Planning Officials, Chicago, p. 373, 1972.

7. Bromley, D. W., A. A. Schmid, and W. B. Lord, Public Water Resource Project Planning and Evaluation: Impacts, Incidence and Institutions, Working Paper No. 1, Center for Resource Policy Studies and Programs, School of Natural Resources, University of Wisconsin, Madison, 1971.

8. Lichfield, Nathaniel, Cost-Benefit Analysis in City Planning, *J. Am. Inst. Plann.* **26**, 4, pp. 273-279, November 1960.

9. Lichfield, Nathaniel, Cost Benefit Analysis in Urban Expansion: A Case Study—Peterborough, *Reg. Stud. 3* pp. 123-155, 1969.

10. English towns are often expanded by public development agencies.

11. Schaenman, Philip S. and Thomas Muller, *Measuring Impacts of Land Development,* The Urban Institute, Washington, D.C., p. 30, 1974.

12. See Bromley, Schmid, and Lord, Note 7, pp. 36-38.

13. Lichfield, Nathaniel, Cost Benefit Analysis in Planning: A Critique of the Roskill Commission, *Reg. Stud.* **5,** pp. 157-183, 1971.

14. Sonnen, M. B., Wild Rivers: Methods for Evaluation, Water Resources Engineers, Inc., Walnut Creek, California, 1970; prepared for the U.S. Department of Interior, Office of Water Resources Research.

15. Whitman, I. L., et al., Final Report on Design of an Environmental Evaluation System, Battelle Columbus Laboratories, Columbus, Ohio, 1971.

16. Arrow, K. J., *Social Choice and Individual Values,* Wiley, New York, 1951. For a discussion of this and other commensuration problems, see Peter Richerson and Robert Johnston, Environmental Values and Water Quality Planning, Paper of the Technical Council on Water Resources Planning and Management, *J. Hydraulics Div., ASCE,* **101,** HY2, Proc. Paper 11136, pp. 259-276, February 1975.

17. Water Resources Centers of the Thirteen Western States, Technical Committee, Water Resources Planning and Social Goals: Conceptualization Toward a New Methodology, Utah Water Research Laboratory, Pub. PRWG-94-1, Logan, pp. 17 and 46, September 1, 1971.

18. Mishan, E. J., What is Wrong with Roskill?, *J. Transp. Econ. Policy,* pp. 221-234, September 1970.

19. For another similar argument from a planner, see M. Hill, A Goals Achievement Matrix tor Evaluating Alternative Plans, *J. Am. Inst. Plann.* **34,** 1, pp. 19-29, January 1968.

20. Self, Peter, Nonsense on Stilts: The Futility of Roskill, *New Soc.,* pp. 8-11, July 2, 1970. Quote from p. 8.

21. Hamill, Louis, The Process of Making Good Decisions about the Use of the Environment of Man, *Nat. Resour. J.* **8,** pp. 279-301, April 1968.

22. See R. Cyert, H. Simon, and D. Trow, Observations of a Business Decision, *J. Bus.,* p. 237 ff., 1956.

23. See Lichfield, Note 8, p. 277, 1960.

24. Lichfield, Nathaniel, Economics in Town Planning, *Town Plann. Rev.* **39,** 1, pp. 5-20, April 1968. Two earlier articles are Cost-Benefit Analysis in Plan Evaluation, *Town Plann. Rev.* **35,** 160, 1964; and Cost-Benefit Analysis in Town Planning: A Case Study-Swanley, *Urban Stud. 3,* 215, 1966. For other economists' critiques of benefit-cost, see Leonard Merewitz and Stephen Sosnick, *The Budget's New Clothes,* Markham, Chicago, 1971. For a lawyer's view

with reference to NEPA and NEPA cases, see Edward D. Burmeister, Cost-Benefit Analysis and the National Environmental Policy Act of 1969, *Stanford Law Rev.* **24**, pp. 1092–1116, June, 1972.

25. See Lichfield, Note 9, 1969.

26. In the 1973 guidelines, the requirement is found at CFR, Title 40, Chapter 5, Part 1500.8 (A) (4), (5), and (8), *Fed. Reg.* Vol. 38, No. 147, Part II, p. 20554, August 1, 1973. Similar requirements are found in the earlier guidelines.

27. ERC 1066 (sec. E. 1. of the Memorandum and Order by J. Bue, February 16, 1973). An earlier holding on lack of consideration of mitigation grounds is Natural Resources Defense Council, Inc. v. Morton, 458 F. 2d 827, 830, and 838 (3 ERC 1558).

28. U.S. Army Corps of Engineers, Engineering Regulation ER 1105-2-105, pp. 2, A-4, and A-5, Dec. 15, 1972.

29. California Resources Code, Division 13, sec. 21100 (C).

30. The author has been involved in several lawsuits involving NEPA and CEQA statements. In 1975, the state CEQA guidelines were amended to urge the adoption of mitigative actions, even if more costly, and to require a "statement of overriding concern" to give causes for not mitigating each and every adverse impact. (Cal. Admin. Code, Sec. 15088).

31. Environmental Defense Fund, Inc. v. Froehlke, 8th Circuit, Civil No. 72-1427 (4 ERC 1829).

32. Heyman, Ira M. and Robert H. Twiss, Environmental Management of the Public Lands, *Ecol. Law Q.,* **1,** 1971.

33. See, for example, Frederick R. Anderson, *NEPA in the Courts,* Johns Hopkins Press, Baltimore, Maryland, 1973; and Robert B. Ditton, and Thomas Goodale, *Environmental Impact Analysis: Philosophy and Methods,* University of Wisconsin Sea Grant Program, Madison, 1972.

34. McHarg, Ian, *Design with Nature,* Natural History Press, Garden City, New Jersey, p. 144, 1969.

35. Leopold, Luna B., F. E. Clarke, B. B. Hanshaw, and J. R. Balsley, A Procedure for Evaluating Environmental Impact, Geological Survey Circular 645, U.S. Geological Survey, Washington, D.C., 1971.

36. Corwin, Ruthann, Some Preliminary Suggestions for Evaluating Environmental Impact Statements—A Checklist, unpublished paper for Landscape Architecture 209, University of California, Berkeley, Spring, 1971.

37. Twiss, Robert H. and David Streatfield, *Nicasio: Hidden Valley in Transition,* Marin County Planning Department, San Rafael, California, 1971? (no date). Cooperatively undertaken with the Department of Landscape Architecture, University of California, Berkeley and the Pacific Southwest Forest and Range Experiment Station, U.S. Department of Agriculture, Berkeley, California.

38. Sorenson, Jens C., A Framework for Identification and Control of Resource Degradation and Conflict in the Multiple Use of the Coastal Zone, Masters thesis, Department of Landscape Architecture, University of California, Berkeley, June 1971.

39. For an example of the use of time-stepped impact matrices, see California Polytechnic College, Pomona, Laboratory for Experimental Design, *The Coastal Lagoons of San Diego County,* Department of Landscape Architecture, June 1971. For a review of impact matrix techniques, see Sorenson, Note 38. For a review of resource evaluation methods, see Carl Steinitz, et al., A Comparative Study of Resource Analysis Methods, Department of Landscape Architecture, Harvard University, Cambridge, Massachusetts, 1969. The most useful comparative analysis is

Reinhardt et al., A Critique of Water and Related Land Resources Planning, California Department of Water Resources, Sacramento, 1972, in which the author participated. See especially p. III-4 of this study in which a summary comparison of nine planning and impact analysis methods is made.

40. See Lichfield, Note 13, 1971.

41. Reinhardt, Note 39, 1972. For a brilliant essay on the need for broadening agency mandates, see Joseph L. Sax, The Unhappy Truth about NEPA, Okla. Law Rev. **26,** pp. 239–248. 1973.

42. Boyce, D. E., D. Day, and C. McDonald, *Metropolitan Plan Making,* Regional Science Institute, Monograph Series, Number Four, G.P.O. 8776, Philadelphia, Pennsylvania, 1970; Manheim, Marvin L., et al., *Community Values in Highway Location and Design: A Procedural Guide,* Urban Systems Laboratory, Massachusetts Institute of Technology, Report No. 71-4, Cambridge, 1971; Burke, R., J. P. Heaney, and E. E. Pyatt, Water Resources and Social Choices, *Water Resour. Bull.* **9,** 3, pp. 433–444, June 1973.

INDEX